Doctor's Orders: Go Fishing

Dean Shrock, Ph.D.

First Publishers Group, Ltd.
State College, Pennsylvania 16801 USA

Doctor's Orders: Go Fishing

Acknowledgments:

excerpts from *SAVED BY THE LIGHT* by Dannion Brinkley,
copyright © 1994 by Dannion Brinkley, Introduction Copyright © 1994
by Raymond Moody, reprinted by permission of Villard Books,
a Division of Random House, Inc.

excerpts from *DR. DEAN ORNISH'S PROGRAM FOR REVERSING HEART DISEASE*
by Dean Ornish, M.D., Copyright © 1990 by Dean Ornish, M.D.,
Reprinted by permission of Random House, Inc.

First Printing, September, 2000

Printed in the United States

ISBN No. 0-9704254-0-6

Table of Contents

Foreword 3
Acknowledgments 5
Chapter 1 - In the Beginning 7
    Evidence of the Power of the Mind to Heal...................................... 10
Chapter 2 - The Will to Live 15
    When You're Busy Doing What You Like, You Tend to Forget Your
        Aches and Pains 16
    If Your Doctor Didn't Tell You to Do It, Does That Mean
        It's Not Important?.. 17
    Does Going Fishing Mean I'm Selfish? 18
    You Need to Feel Listened to and Cared For 21
    Doctor's Orders: Have Fun 1x Daily.. 22
Chapter 3 - Your Beliefs Are Potentially As Powerful As Any Medical Treatment 25
    Varieties of Alternative Treatments.. 26
    How Emotions Affect Your Health 27
    The Power of Prayer and Faith 29
    What about "False Hope"?.. 31
    The Body Will Do What You Tell It 33
    Hypnosis... 35
    You Can Increase Your Odds 36
Chapter 4 - Relaxation and Imagery Techniques...................................... 41
    When You're Relaxed Your Body Works More Effectively............. 42
    Meditation and Mindfulness 45
    Guided Imagery Is Mental Rehearsal 49
    Suggestions for Using Guided Imagery... 52
Chapter 5 - Explanations for the Effectiveness of Guided Imagery 59
    Biofeedback Is Essentially Guided Imagery.................................... 63
    Trigger Mechanisms 67
Chapter 6 - Simple Recommendations for Nutrition and Physical Exercise 71
    Nutrition – You'll Feel Better... 71
    Physical Exercise – Use It or Lose It.. 76
Chapter 7 - Stress and Stress Management.. 79
    Learning to Roll with the Punches and to Keep Perspective 81
    Stress Can Kill You 82
    How Stress Contributes to Chronic Disease 84
    The Most Stressful Thing You Can Do or Have Done to You 85
    Some Additional Things You Can Do to Defuse the Stressful
        Effects of Criticism 91
Chapter 8 - Some Big Questions and Answers.. 95
    Did I Cause My Illness? 95
    What Will Bring Me the Greatest Peace of Mind? 100
    Be Gentle with Yourself and Each Other 101
    Don't Let the Bastards Wear You Down... 101
    It's Normal to Question Your Faith or Spirituality........................ 102
    Ask How You Can Help, Then Listen.. 105
    Am I a Burden to Others?... 106
    The Four D's to Problem Solving... 107

Chapter 9 - Self-Esteem: How Do You Feel about Yourself? 111
   You Think You're No Good and Unloved.....................................114
   You Only Feel Good about Yourself When You're Pleasing Others 117
   It Gets Even Worse...118
   How to Reparent Yourself...123
   Celebrate Your Uniqueness...124
Chapter 10 - Who Are You?...127
   You Are Not Just Your Physical Body 128
   What about the Spiritual Part of You? 129
   We Are One with God..130
   Does Love Matter? 131
   Why Suffering? 136
   Does Life Serve a Purpose? – The Role of Love and Compassion.................139
Chapter 11 - Intuition and Creativity 143
   How Do We Determine Truth? 143
   Intuition Is a Fact of Life..146
   My Personal Experience with Intuition.....................................149
Chapter 12 - Uses of Intuition in Medicine...159
   Your Inner Guide or Advisor 160
   A Scientific Explanation of Intuition 171
   A Personal Experiment 173
Chapter 13 - Creating a Personal Health Plan.......................................175
   Interests..176
   Needs 176
   Values 177
   Feelings...178
   Writing Your Own Prescription 178
   Social Support 179
   Nutrition..179
   Play 179
   Life Purpose...180
   Imagery and Meditation 180
   Exercise 181
Afterword 183
Appendix..187
Index 209

Foreword

Dr. Dean Shrock is a bright, kind, and precise man. He thinks deeply about things before he speaks, and when he speaks it is with clarity and focus. He's a serious man, but has a twinkle in his eye and a grand sense of humor. All of these qualities are evident in the book you are about to read: a book that contains everything from a moving human story and a simple way to de-stress your life, to details about his research which shows that mind/body influences can affect the progression of cancer. That's a lot to include in a book, but *Doctor's Orders: Go Fishing* manages to cover all this ground in a way that holds our attention throughout.

Dr. Shrock, like me and millions of others, was taken with the work of Carl Simonton, M.D., the radiation oncologist, who, with his wife Stephanie, reported in the early 70's that he was seeing unusual cases of cancer regression with a psychological approach utilizing guided imagery techniques. The Simontons' work created a furor within the conventional cancer world, followed by a 25-year debate over whether or not their findings were real. It took all this time, and Dean Shrock, to conduct a study to test these methods. Dr. Shrock's research with breast and prostate cancer patients was reported last year, and clearly indicates that a Simonton-like program really does have cancer-fighting effects. While there need to be many more such investigations, his research, along with the Spiegel study at Stanford and the Fawzy study at UCLA, now represent the vanguard of research that show us just what people can do with mind/body/spirit approaches to cancer.

Interestingly, this book isn't about cancer, but about life. Dr. Shrock draws from his work with cancer patients to teach us lessons about living in good health and spirits. The lessons he teaches us are about creating pauses in our busy lives, slowing down and enjoying the things that are most valuable and precious to us. We may say that we've heard these things before, but it is useful to hear them again and again until we "get it," and this book instructs us in a kind, informative and entertaining way. As with all self-help books, the valuable lessons contained only work if you act on them. That's one of the best things about this particular book: It gives you such simple and enjoyable choices to act on that it is very likely you will translate them into action.

The study of mind/body effects in cancer is one that has taught us a lot about mind/body effects in general. Too often we pay attention to things like relaxation, time for ourselves, time for our loved ones, and time to "smell the roses" only when a life-threatening illness has developed. Why must this be the case? In Chinese medicine there is a saying, "Treating people once illness has manifested is like beginning to dig a well when you are already dying of thirst." While we have treatments the ancient Chinese never dreamed of, there is still much wisdom in this statement and point of view. Do we need to wait till disaster strikes to assess our lives and the way we live? What if we decided to live our values while we were healthy? To treat ourselves with respect before the prospect of death and dying finally grabs our attention?

I remember being invited to speak to one of Dr. Dean Ornish's early groups. Dr. Ornish showed us that people could reverse advanced heart disease through diet change, physical exercise, stress reduction, and improved communication. As I sat with the group members, all men at that time, and all with serious heart disease, I was taken with the level of communication and respect in the group. By the end of the meeting I found myself wondering, "Do I have to get heart disease to get into a group like this?"

In my medical practice, I sometimes stand back in amazement when I realize that so many of the good people I treat have gone through multiple medications, chemotherapies, radiation therapy, and repeated surgeries, and are then, and only then, desperate enough to try relaxation and guided imagery as a way to help themselves. I'm not saying that mind/body techniques are substitutes for these sometimes life-saving interventions, but I do wonder how much of the serious disease we see would be manifest if these things were a regular part of our lives from childhood on, if we were used to taking time to punctuate our busy days with rest, relaxation, enjoyment, and contemplation. Whether it would or not is almost a moot point, however, because of the positive effects it can have on your life in virtually any circumstance.

The lessons Dr. Shrock teaches us are worthwhile in themselves. That they also have health benefits that may positively influence diseases as difficult as cancer is a welcome side effect. We can't live only to avoid death, because we will all ultimately lose that battle. Instead, let us live to love, to increase our wisdom, and to enjoy life while we are here. This is what I take away from this book, and I am very grateful for the reminders.

Martin L. Rossman, M.D.
Mill Valley, California

Acknowledgments

This book is dedicated to Ken McCaulley, my great friend and mentor, who taught me most of what's in *Doctor's Orders: Go Fishing*. There is a metaphysical saying, "When the student is ready, the teacher appears." God surely sent me Ken McCaulley. I am indebted especially to his patience and love, and for reconnecting me with the spiritual side of life and health.

I extend my gratitude, also, to my mother, Mrs. Jean Shrock, who has always believed in me. Thank you for your constant love and support.

While it is important to me to acknowledge Ken McCaulley and my mother, this book is truly the labor of love of my wife, Shelly Shrock. Shelly has been intimately involved with the contents of this book for nine years, starting with her participation in the "Taking Control of Your Health" classes in 1991, when her first husband was dying of cancer. She has heard me teach these classes hundreds of times. And to her everlasting credit, she typed and retyped every page of this book more times than she cares to remember. I certainly express my gratitude for Shelly's patience, wisdom, and love given to me and this project. I love you.

It pleases me greatly, additionally, to acknowledge the friendship and guidance of Sherry Hogan. Sherry and I had met only one time, years ago when her fiancé was hospitalized and dying of cancer. Years later she phoned seeking further help for a friend, and "saved my life" by offering her skills as a writer every step of the way, from assisting me with the writing of my book proposal to the last draft of the manuscript. Sherry is proof that angels really do exist.

I need to acknowledge another good friend, Mary Lou McNichol, a writer and health education instructor at Penn State University, for her excellent, thorough, and helpful editing in the later stages of this book.

I must also express my gratitude to Dr. Carl Simonton for his pioneering work in the field of psychosocial cancer care, and the time and support given to me as an intern and throughout the research of "Taking Control of Your Health." Carl was a significant contributor to the study published in *Alternative Therapies in Health and Medicine* confirming his early research that patients who make changes in their lives which are more compatible with who they are, and that take them in the direction of greatest joy, can affect their survival with cancer.

I certainly want to thank Dr. Ray Palmer, the co-author of the above research, and his research assistant, Bonnie Taylor, for their having rescued the study that Carl and I had originally planned. Angels even come in the form of epidemiologists and statisticians.

I wish to thank also Dr. Douglas Colkitt, Dr. Jerry Derdel, and Dr. Dave Moylan, who supported me and referred their patients to me as medical directors of the primary cancer departments and centers where I taught and researched "Taking Control of Your Health." Without their interest and support of psychological support services, this program and research would not have been possible.

I want to thank, additionally, the tumor registrars at Centre Community Hospital in State College, PA; Lewistown Hospital, in Lewistown, PA; and The Good Samaritan Hospital in Pottsville, PA for their concerted efforts in generating the data necessary to conduct this research.

It is essential that I also acknowledge the patients and families who came for radiation treatment to these cancer centers who were open to our encouragement to complement their medical care with a psychooncology program. I truly am indebted to you for allowing me to participate in your care at such an important time in your lives.

When I was admitted to the doctoral program in counseling psychology at the University of Akron, I vowed to acknowledge publicly my appreciation for the opportunity to study and demonstrate the effectiveness of mental imagery techniques. My special thanks go to the University of Akron, the Counseling Psychology Department, and Dr. Jack Cochran, my academic and dissertation advisor and friend. I also want to thank Dr. Izzy Newman for his assistance with the research design for the study that Carl Simonton and I had initially conceived.

Bette Midler sang, "You've got to have friends." One of my very best and most trusted friends is the publisher of this book, Ray Caravan. I have known Ray from the very beginning of my working with the physician management group where I developed and taught "Taking Control of Your Health." Ray has been my "touchstone" throughout my work with these cancer centers. Ray proposed to be my "agent" for this book years ago. As things developed, he has become so much more for me, and I truly look forward to a life-long professional and personal relationship.

I am fortunate also to have valued friends within my family. My brother-in-law, Roger Vilsack, has an emmy award-winning advertising agency, Vilsack Productions in Arlington, Virginia. Thanks, Roger, for years of support in my varied professional life, and for designing the cover and taking the photo for the book jacket.

Similarly, I want to thank my sister- and brother-in-law, Denise and Don Ronalter, for their help with computer-related questions and for reviewing early manuscripts of the book. Your wonderfully wild sense of humor has been very therapeutic and just what the doctor ordered.

There are so many more people who have been instrumental in my work and life, but it would be unwieldy to attempt to acknowledge all of them here. I extend a great, big thank you to all of you.

1

In the Beginning

It was an accident. I really didn't mean, not consciously, to work with cancer, or to be a psychologist either, for that matter. Actually, I began my college education studying engineering. But I soon realized that I had chosen that field for the wrong reasons, and decided to become a school guidance counselor. This led me to study psychology, and I graduated from Cleveland State University in 1968 with a bachelor's degree in psychology.

But I had borrowed heavily to pay for my schooling, and I was tired of being penniless. I knew I couldn't find much work in my field with only a bachelor's degree, so I began to train as a buyer for a major department store in Cleveland, Ohio. This lasted about a year and a half, when I left and opened a small store, selling mostly blue jeans, across from Cleveland State. It was relatively successful and I opened another store the next year. None of this really accounts for my work with cancer, I suppose, except that I developed a business sense and experience at being self-employed.

Another very significant event occurred, however, while I was in undergraduate school. I developed hay fever symptoms during my first final exams in 1963. For years I tried any number of medications, but with little or no relief. I was told, "You'll have to live with it." That was probably the wrong or right thing to say, depending on how you look at it. "Wrong," in that I could not accept that I would just have to live with it. And "right," because now I was motivated to look beyond conventional medicine.

At first I investigated nutrition. This was a very big step for me then. Over the next two years I was a vegetarian, a fruitarian, ate only raw foods, took supplements, fasted, etc. While these regimens did not lead to a reduction in my hay fever symptoms, I learned a fair amount about nutrition and that it certainly could help, but it was not a cure for my hay fever.

Soon after that I met a man named Ken McCaulley and enrolled in his self-help course called HELP (the letters stood for Human Expansion to

Liberate Potential). This was my first introduction to the techniques of guided imagery and self-hypnosis, and began my in-depth rethinking about almost everything. I left the store, began to study privately with Ken, soon became his business partner, and started to teach his program which we now called PROBE (the idea was to *probe* or develop your inner- or sub-conscious mind). Ken was a genuine seeker-of-truth, and my working with him changed my life completely.

Not only did Ken and I begin to work together, but we would walk and talk for hours about many things, mostly it seemed about a spiritual side of life. Ken had been an ordained Presbyterian minister as part of his life path, but he was largely self-taught in many ways, especially from his years of daily meditation. He also had a master's degree in psychology and a doctorate in some kind of divinity studies. We soon became best friends.

It was somewhat difficult for me at first to accept Ken's strong beliefs in the power of the mind to heal. He would tell me of his own experiences and others he had worked with. But I remained skeptical until I realized that after using guided imagery to attempt to heal my hay fever, the next year I had no symptoms. This was no small event for me. I had suffered for 15 years. Now I began to study the power of this technique very seriously, but, I have to admit, I initially was attempting to prove it couldn't work. It was too good to be true and actually offensive to my way of thinking at that time. I used to call it "Walt Disney": All you have to do is wish upon a star and your dreams come true. But the more I studied, the more evidence I found supporting the power of the mind to heal.

Then one day Ken encouraged me to use guided imagery (I'll explain this in depth in Chapter 4) to heal my knee which I had injured playing soccer for Cleveland State 12 years earlier. I tore cartilage and ligaments in my right knee during a soccer game in 1966. I returned home to Pittsburgh and had Dr. Albert Ferguson, an orthopedic specialist for the Pittsburgh Steelers, examine my knee. He told me I could try to rehabilitate it, but that I would need surgery. I really didn't want the surgery, so I tried rehab, but I remember Dr. Ferguson telling me that I would need surgery within 10 years.

As it turned out, I needed it in 12 years. My knee hurt considerably and I was becoming much less mobile. But now I had known Ken McCaulley for a year, and he suggested that I try guided imagery instead of the surgery. You don't really want to know what I said in response to this outrageous proposal that guided imagery could heal my knee and that I wouldn't then need the surgery. But he had a way of challenging me, and said that I could try the imagery for one week, and that if it didn't work I could still have the surgery. And I had the recent successful experience with my hay fever to help motivate me.

Together we developed an imagery script, which I practiced several times each day. My knee really hurt and I didn't like it. Maybe that was a particular strength of mine: I was determined to make this work if it could, because I didn't like feeling bad (or being "out of control," but that's for a later story). Within two days I had no pain! And within one week I had complete use of my leg again! And 20-some years later, I have never had surgery on my knee, and I've learned to downhill ski since.

Make no mistake, I have many physician friends who disbelieve this story. Mostly they're certain my knee was misdiagnosed. I'm as certain as I can be that Dr. Ferguson did not misdiagnose my knee, and what I do know is that after one week of disciplined use of guided imagery my knee was back to normal functioning without any pain. This got my attention. And, again, the more I studied trying to determine what really had healed my allergy and knee, the more convinced I became that this technique of guided imagery or self-hypnosis was the reason.

At some point in 1978 I also used this technique to gain weight without increasing my waistline and also to stop smoking. I hope these claims don't sound exaggerated, because I was not easily convinced then, but I trust that relating these experiences helps you understand my reason early on for pursuing this work.

Eventually Ken encouraged me to apply for graduate school. I had finished my undergraduate degree in psychology 13 years before, and I never thought to return to school. It became the most stressful time in my life. I was a good student, but I had to work very hard. Fortunately I was admitted into the University of Akron's Counseling Psychology doctoral program and my dissertation committee allowed me to research guided imagery with the admonition, "as long as you support it well." My dissertation was titled, *Relaxation, Guided Imagery, and Wellness.* I graduated in 1986. That year I interned with Dr. Izzy Newman at the University of Akron developing a research proposal for the Cleveland Clinic to test guided imagery with their cancer patients. The following year I interned as a staff psychologist in a rehab hospital in State College, Pennsylvania. Dr. Sally Baker, the Director of Psychology in this hospital, had a special interest in biofeedback and pain management, so I was fortunate, again, now to be working with someone who valued guided imagery as a therapeutic tool, and I would gain additional important experience.

That same year, June 1987, I took continuing education time and money and participated as an intern at the Simonton Cancer Center. There I met and was greatly impressed with Dr. O. Carl Simonton and his program for cancer patients. I was especially pleased to have this opportunity to work with someone of Dr. Simonton's background and his special interest in guided imagery. Actually, while the media and press generally cite Dr. Simonton and imagery in the same breath, his program is far more than teaching people to imagine their immune systems gobbling up cancer cells. It is so much more about making major changes in your life that are more compatible with who you really are and that will take you in the direction of greatest joy. It was in this first week of meeting one another that Carl and I agreed we would work together to research his program.

Evidence of the Power of the Mind to Heal

Following my internship at the Simonton Cancer Center, my hospital asked me to write a protocol for a cancer program. They were willing to let me implement Dr. Simonton's approach as part of this proposed protocol. I phoned Carl very excited about this possibility, and I went back to the Simonton Cancer Center for another internship in November 1987 to prepare for what seemed then like an overwhelming responsibility to teach and test this program.

Dr. Simonton was especially supportive and told me just to present the basic ideas of the program, and "Bring your own enthusiasm to it." He knew that I had been teaching the PROBE program for 10 years, and I had the recent graduate school background to be able to support the ideas scientifically when I could. Unfortunately, the hospital where I had been asked to develop this oncology protocol never followed through with the program, but two radiation oncologists in State College who were going to refer their cancer patients to me to test the Simonton model asked me to develop a program for them. It turned out that they were involved with a physician management group and a number of cancer centers primarily in Pennsylvania.

With my experience and training with the PROBE program, I made sure I incorporated the basic ideas of the Simonton program, which were very similar, and I began teaching this approach weekly to cancer centers within the physician management group, Oncology Services, throughout Pennsylvania in 1988. While teaching the program went relatively well, the research did not. It was very difficult to get all of the data we originally set out to obtain from patients to see whether or not this psychosocial intervention could affect immune function and quality of life variables. My responsibilities as Director of Psychological Support Services for these cancer centers made it additionally difficult to manage the data collection.

Within a few years, the project essentially fell apart, but I always thought I could test and demonstrate the effectiveness of this program. Then in 1996 I met Dr. Ray Palmer, an epidemiologist in the Biobehavioral Health Department at Penn State University. He was genuinely interested in the content of the program and proposed a way we could measure its effectiveness. Although it required me to collect a considerable amount of additional data, we began to compare patients who had been through the program at least four years with matched controls from the same hospitals. We asked tumor registrars in the three cancer centers/hospitals where the program had been offered most extensively to find patients who had the same type and stage of cancer to compare to the cancer patients in our program. They were also matched on age, date of diagnosis, age at diagnosis, gender, and types of medical treatment. We found two or three very close matches for 50 patients who had stage 1 breast and prostate cancer. There were not enough patients with other than stage 1 breast or prostate cancer to analyze statistically and include in the study. In the final analysis, 21 stage 1 breast cancer women and 29 stage 1 prostate cancer men were compared to 74 and 65 matched patients. The details of the study were published in May 1999 in the journal, *Alternative Therapies In Health and Medicine*. The results were that the intervention group lived significantly longer than did their matched-controls. At four to seven years follow-up (median = 4.2 years), none of the breast cancer patients in the intervention group died, while 12% of the control group died. Twice as many of the matched-control prostate cancer patients died compared to the intervention group, 28% vs. 14%.

This supported Dr. Simonton's earlier research where he and his then-wife, Stephanie, found that patients going through their program with advanced breast, bowel, and lung cancer lived twice as long as a matched control population based on national norms. They published their findings in *The Medical Journal of Australia* in 1981, and wrote an excellent and very popular book, *Getting Well Again*, explaining their program in detail in 1978. However the Simonton's approach was not well accepted in this country. At that time, and even at this time, medicine and medical journals in the United States are not particularly open to therapies, especially with cancer, which are other than "medical."

In 1977 Dr. Larry LeShan, one of the true pioneers in investigating and practicing psychotherapy with cancer patients, published a book: *You Can Fight For Your Life: Emotional Factors in the Treatment of Cancer*. He reported in a number of studies that cancer patients had feelings of hopelessness far greater than patients without cancer. His strong message to counter these feelings and to affect the course of their disease was to find their own unique song to sing, that is, to develop "a will to live." Again this message largely fell on deaf ears within the medical community. While LeShan's and the Simontons' programs were not well received within the American medical community, at least they had attempted to research their claims.

Then along came Dr. Bernie Siegel, a cancer surgeon, who wrote a book, *Love, Medicine and Miracles*. It became the most widely read book on psychosocial cancer care, promoting the role of "the will to live," the power of the mind, and the fact that people can work to heal themselves. Only at this point Dr. Siegel had not researched his program, "Exceptional Cancer Patients," and was traveling extensively touting his techniques and clinical experience.

Larry LeShan and Carl Simonton had created quite a stir within the medical community, but Bernie Siegel seemed to be the straw that broke the camel's back. Now even the American Cancer Society was calling these programs "unproven" and "quackery," and, at best, they were giving people false hope. There was very little research done in this field at this time, and none was considered methodologically strong enough to even begin to make the claims of LeShan, Simonton, or Siegel. Enough was enough.

Dr. David Spiegel, a psychiatrist at Stanford University, applied for a grant to research and demonstrate once and for all that no psychological factor could affect survival with cancer. Interestingly, Dr. Simonton applied for this same grant to attempt to prove psychosocial factors do affect the progression of cancer. He was not funded, but Dr. Spiegel, attempting to refute these claims, was funded.

The Spiegel study involved a one-year weekly supportive group therapy where 50 women with advanced breast cancer were encouraged to live as fully as possible. These women were compared to 36 randomized controls. Survival time was almost twice as long for the women who attended the supportive-expressive group therapy. Dr. Spiegel and his colleagues believed that this type of psychosocial intervention could affect the quality of life of cancer patients, but they were stunned when their well-designed study in fact concluded that it nearly doubled their life expectancy.

If any "medical" treatment had been researched to demonstrate it could increase survival this well, it would have been front-page headlines in every major newspaper. As it was, this study was published in 1989 in what is generally regarded as one of the world's foremost medical journals, *The Lancet*. This very prestigious medical journal thought well enough of the quality of this research that they considered it worthy of publication, when it normally rejects nine out of 10 of all submitted research manuscripts. With the publication of Spiegel's research, the possibility that psychosocial factors could affect cancer survival became a legitimate research question. The National Institutes of Mental Health is currently funding Dr. Spiegel to replicate his study.

Then in 1990, Dr. Fawzy Fawzy, a psychiatrist at UCLA, evaluated the effects on immune function of a psychoeducational group intervention with 35 patients with malignant melanoma. These patients were compared to 26 randomized controls. At a six-week and six-month follow-up the intervention patients showed a significant improvement especially with number and activity of natural killer cells. Because these were early stage cancer patients, no consideration was given to whether or not this six-week program would affect their survival. With appropriate medical treatment these patients should have a normal life expectancy. But what Dr. Fawzy found as he followed these patients was that at five to six years later for control patients, there was a trend for recurrence of their cancer (13/34) and greater rate of death (10/34) than for the treatment group (7/34 and 3/34, respectively). Dr. Fawzy concluded that "Psychiatric interventions that enhance effective coping and reduce affective distress appear to have beneficial results on survival…" Both of Dr. Fawzy's studies were published in the highly regarded medical journal, *The Archives of General Psychiatry*.

The good news is that these well-designed studies strongly supported the role of psychosocial factors affecting survival with early and late stage cancer. The bad news is that these are the only high quality studies published to date. Within science a single study on any intervention cannot be accepted as proof of its efficacy. It must be replicated. While these interventions are being researched further, the sad part is that so little attention is being given to these results. Not only do very few programs like Spiegel's and Fawzy's exist for cancer patients to potentially benefit from, but also very little research still is being conducted investigating these psychosocial approaches.

Other research, though less strong methodologically, has been published suggesting cancer progression can be affected by psychological factors such as a "fighting spirit" vs. stoic acceptance and feelings of hopelessness and helplessness. An excellent popular book documenting the role of psychosocial factors affecting cancer is Lydia Temoshok's and Henry Dreher's book, *The Type C Connection: The Behavioral Links to Cancer and Your Health.* Dr. Temoshok is one of the world's leading and most respected researchers in the field of psychoneuroimmunology (the study of how emotions interact with immune function). And Henry Dreher is one of the most prolific and respected medical writers in the field of mind-body medicine.

All the while I was working with Ken McCaulley and Carl Simonton, I found these other research findings and books especially stimulating, and they further motivated me to advance my understanding of psychosocial cancer care. The following chapters will begin to detail the information and insights I gained and taught in a program I now call "Taking Control of Your Health."

2

The Will to Live

I often begin lecturing by saying that when I speak I will support as much as I can with scientific research. But I also state, at the same time, I need to tell you that science and research are limited. Science says only that which is objectively measurable is valid or true. If something hasn't been tested and supported with research, scientists say that it is unproven and, therefore, of questionable merit.

Scientists often claim when something has not been researched that it is "quackery," fraudulent, sham, or some other unflattering label that suggests only science and research know and can claim what's true. Consider the logic or reasonableness of the position that only that which is objectively measurable is true.

It is well known that one's thoughts and feelings can change blood pressure, heart and oxygen consumption rate, blood sugar and hormone levels, and a large number of other physical variables. Thus, feeling happy or sad, relaxed or tense, or any change in feelings can directly affect and change one's physical functioning. However, one's thoughts and feelings are not easily objectively measurable. In fact we're prone to believe that thoughts and feelings are nothing. So how can thoughts and feelings which are "nothing" affect your body which is clearly perceived as something physical and solid?

The logic, I believe, is clear and simple: Nothing can't cause something. The problem here is with the idea that something has to be objectively measurable before it's true. Rather than saying that thoughts and feelings are nothing and can have no impact on something physical, it seems more reasonable to say that we do not have instrumentation to date that enables us to measure one's thoughts and feelings or other mental activity in an objective manner with which science is comfortable. It's not that thoughts and feelings don't exist and don't have the ability to affect other physical matter. This is a primary controversy for scientists when trying to explain (or explain away) any mind-body interaction.

When You're Busy Doing What You Like, You Tend to Forget Your Aches and Pains

Another way to understand the reasonableness of a mind-body interaction is with the common adage: "When you're busy doing what you like to do, you tend to forget your aches and pains." I find this consistently true. People report that when they're engaged in some meaningful activity that they tend to feel better at least for the time they're doing something they enjoy.

I have a dear friend who often can't walk across a room without getting out of breath and having to sit down to rest. But when a special mushroom grows on his acres of land, he walks for hours searching for these mushrooms and digging them up – without any of the heart and respiratory problems he would normally have.

The most common example of this kind of mind-body interaction that I gave in my seminars was of deer hunting. I was born in, and spent the last 11 years teaching my program in, Central Pennsylvania. In much of Pennsylvania, public schools are closed the first day of buck and doe season. This is not normal behavior! But it does in fact show the extreme value placed on deer hunting.

Let's say that we have an avid deer hunter who unfortunately is sick - so sick he or she can't even get out of the house or even out of bed. Come the first day of buck season, where will our deer hunter be? My consistent response from native Central Pennsylvanians is, "In the woods." There's no way, essentially, you're going to keep a true deer hunter out of the woods in deer season.

Now let's say that our sick deer hunter gets a buck. Do you think our deer hunter is going to feel better or worse for having gone hunting? Again, the overwhelming response is, "Better." And to add further validation for the benefit of doing what you love to do, do you think our deer hunter will be nicer to live with when he or she gets home after getting that buck? Everybody wins when you "go fishing." Understand that "going fishing" is a generic way of saying: doing that which brings you joy, meaning, passion – an enthusiasm for life.

Of course, "going fishing" for you might not mean deer hunting, and it may not literally mean fishing at all. What is it that you love to do, that makes your life meaningful and in some way gives you a "will to live?"

If Your Doctor Didn't Tell You to Do It, Does That Mean It's Not Important?

This brings up another point. My frequent experience in working with cancer patients, in particular, is that they say, "If my doctor didn't tell me to do it, it's not important." And so with cancer, physicians are going to promote surgery, chemotherapy, and radiation as primary treatments, but they aren't as likely to emphasize other treatments in your care.

Now I need to say something very important: Everything I am recommending in this book is meant to complement your medical treatment, not replace it. I hope to make a strong case for the benefit of medical treatment AND an equally strong case for additional things you can do to affect your health and longevity. There is much you can do yourself to increase your odds.

So – back to my point about a "will to live." Do you think that a strong "will to live" makes a difference in your health? The definite response I've gotten over the years is that most people by far believe that their will to live affects their health. Do you think that nutrition and physical exercise make a difference in your health? Most people, again, believe that these are important. What about stress and stress management? Do you think that these affect your health? Of course. But the probability is that your physician has little expertise in any of these.

This is not meant as a criticism of physicians. It makes sense, ethically and legally, that they would only tell you about things which are their expertise. Can you spell "malpractice"? (Just kidding.) Sincerely, if your doctor has not studied these subjects, or is not familiar with the research in these areas, how can he or she feel comfortable promoting them? The great probability is that your physician has not studied in depth these major components of what tend to be called "wellness": nutrition, physical exercise, and stress management. While most medical schools today offer courses in these areas (this is a very recent phenomenon), most are offered as electives, which means that medical students do not have to take them.

If medical schools choose not to require their students to learn about wellness approaches, then why should we expect their graduates (our physicians) to promote their benefits? It would seem prudent, however, for specialists in these areas to be part of one's health care, using the best of medicine and other approaches, including the role of the mind to affect one's health and healing. So if your doctor doesn't tell you to do something, it doesn't mean it isn't important or beneficial. It more likely points out the limitation of your doctor's expertise. Would you expect a psychologist or nutritionist to explain or practice surgery? Then why would you expect a surgeon to explain or practice other than his or her specialty? In fact, if you have a question about nutrition, exercise, or stress management why would you go to your doctor? And, I'm sure you know that there is considerable compelling research supporting the role of these wellness variables in affecting your health and well-being.

Actually, I believe that most physicians believe that nutrition, exercise, and stress management are important and can affect your health status, but research regarding "the will to live" is almost nonexistent. One of the most respected physicians in the field of mind-body medicine today is Dr. Larry Dossey. He is the author of several best-selling books. In his book, *Meaning and Medicine*, he reported eloquently on the importance of meaning in one's life and how it can have a positive or deadly effect on the body. When people feel helpless and hopeless (the opposite of feeling their lives have purpose, value, and meaning) this directly affects their physical health. This is documented well, also, in Norman Cousins' book, *Head First: The Biology of Hope*, a very readable book supported with years of research at UCLA's medical school.

Unfortunately, a common experience for people diagnosed with cancer, in particular, is that they feel helpless and hopeless. Except for the disease AIDS, there is probably nothing that scares people more than being told, "You have cancer." You imagine the worst. For most people, cancer is equivalent to death. Of course today, with proper medical treatment, if cancer is diagnosed and treated in an early stage, one can expect a favorable outcome. And I believe we in the healthcare profession can do more to offset people's fears and feelings of hopelessness and helplessness, and the potential impact of these feelings on their physical health.

Not only can we educate people about how hope, joy, meaning, and other psychosocial factors can affect their health and longevity, but we can help also by explaining more of the biological facts of cancer. Cancer cells are weak cells biologically. Most oncologists I've worked with believe that we all have cancer cells in our bodies all of the time, and when the immune system, in particular, is working properly, it automatically identifies, destroys or neutralizes any foreign substance, including cancer cells. This suggests that your body has been fighting cancer very effectively all of your life. This is a quite different understanding than the more common belief that if you get cancer your body is not strong enough to fight it. Treatments like surgery, chemotherapy, and radiation are only doing what your body's natural defense mechanisms like your immune system should be doing all of the time. Do you want to have to rely on this medical technology the rest of your life? A key in your treatment then would include psychosocial and wellness approaches that would boost your immune system.

Does Going Fishing Mean I'm Selfish?

But however much common sense and research exist suggesting that a strong "will to live" really can affect your health, a very practical problem arises if people truly take time to think about what gives their lives the most joy, meaning, and enthusiasm. There's a strong tendency for people to think that this is selfish. Somehow we've come to believe that doing for others is much more appropriate than creating a balance between taking care of ourselves (that's the selfish part) and taking care of others. It's more appropriate to work than to play. We talk about a Protestant work ethic. And idleness, as such, is the devil's work.

It's interesting to note that in early agrarian societies, where the image is one of people farming and working from sun up to sun down, there was commonly an extended time taken daily to relax or engage in playful activities. People have long understood that all work and no play makes Jack a dull boy. But it is much more serious than that. All work and no play will eventually take your health.

In American culture many women have been brought up to believe that their reason for being and their primary role in life is to get married and raise a family. For males, their greatest sense of self-esteem and meaning comes from being a provider for that family, or from their work. To do other than your learned and expected role is unacceptable.

I remember when my father would go deer hunting each winter. He *lived* to go deer hunting. Each Monday following Thanksgiving he would disappear for a week hunting buck with my Uncle Henry. Our family enjoyed his excitement and interest. But an interesting question is, "What would my mother have had to go through if she wanted to disappear for a week?" The real question is, "Who makes this stuff up?"

I'm not meaning to start fights among couples or families who have established certain roles and habits. And I don't mean to have my male readers question my sanity that I would dare risk that their wives would now stand up and assert their right to be themselves and pursue their own interests, needs and values. Or would I?

The problem is that if you don't get your needs met appropriately, you will get them met inappropriately. It is extremely important that people, all people, seriously consider their personal needs, even though at first it may sound selfish or go counter to their learned roles. For example, let's say that we have a school setting where a child is "acting out." We often say the real reason for a child's acting out behavior is that the child has an underlying need for attention. If we now are able to meet that child's need for attention in a more appropriate fashion, what tends to happen to the acting out behavior? It tends to lessen. You get your needs met appropriately or inappropriately, but you will get them met.

Similarly, chances are when you've had a cold or the flu you told yourself, or someone said to you, "See, your body's telling you that you need to rest or slow down." The implication is that if you had rested or slowed down, you might not have gotten the cold or flu.

Another example is from my clinical experience working with women with an overweight condition. If a woman is truly overweight and has eaten properly for an extended time period and still not lost weight, I have found that food for her can become a symbolic form of nurturing. Food is a way to fill an emotional void. And until the woman is able to get her need to be nurtured met in a more appropriate fashion, even if she continues her dieting, she is not likely to lose weight. You get your need met appropriately or inappropriately.

I want to give a couple more examples, hopefully to make my point emphatically. A more classic example of an overweight condition would be if a woman were in a relationship that turned out very badly. She might then unconsciously put on weight to make herself unattractive so that she never finds herself in a situation again where she can be "devastated." Understand that she did not consciously choose to overeat and gain weight, but her so-called "subconscious mind" or "defense mechanisms" functioned to protect her from future emotional pain.

One of the things you learn early in life is that if you want attention, get sick. We all want and need our parents' love and attention. I remember my father mostly as a strict disciplinarian, but my mother tells me that when I was sick with the croup or whooping cough, it was my father who would sit up all night with me. A primitive part of our psyche remembers this and understands it well. And so we know that people can contribute directly to the onset and duration of their illness because that illness is being rewarded. If people are widowed and lonely, one way to get their needs met (unconsciously) would be to get sick, because now they're going to get their "loneliness" need met. To be well or get better may mean people will come to visit much less often. You will get your need for love met appropriately or inappropriately, but you will get it met.

You surely can remember how you used illness to manipulate your situation and get your needs met in childhood. Remember when you had a test in school that you really didn't want to take? You really weren't prepared or just hated tests? So, very conveniently, you woke up the morning of the test with a sore tummy or sore throat. Do you really think that you didn't directly (unconsciously) contribute to your illness?

We commonly say people use their pain to manipulate people. I'll bet you know people who are usually in considerable pain, but when they really want to do something, somehow the pain subsides just in time. It's amazing how much pain they can have when they don't want to do something, or when they want your attention in some way. I remember a woman in therapy admitting that she knew she could get well, but she said, "I waited on my husband for years and years, and now that son of a bitch is going to wait on me!"

I don't mean to beat a dead horse, but I hope you get the point. If you don't get your needs met appropriately, you absolutely risk your health. So is it selfish to think about and make an effort to meet your needs? Or is it good sense and necessary for your health?

One very sobering rationale for not only meeting your own needs, but for being supportive of others in meeting their needs, is related to a common experience I had at funerals. I've attended a lot of funerals because of my work with cancer. And a very common event is to hear people say at the funeral that they wished they had done "this or that" for the person while he or she were still alive. Do it now. Part of loving is being supportive. Part of the fun of loving is seeing the joy and excitement in our partners when they are doing something they really enjoy.

Dr. John Gray talks about this with real wisdom and wit in his book, *Men Are From Mars, Women Are From Venus*. He explains how men and women are different in the way they do things. Men are problem-solvers and like to analyze and "fix" things. They don't particularly like to talk about their problems, or want advice necessarily. Their sense of self is defined through their ability to achieve results. A woman's sense of self is defined through her feelings and the quality of her relationships. She loves to talk. She wants to share her feelings, but God bless her if she mentions she has a problem. Her male partner, thinking he is helping, is prone to interrupt and offer any number of solutions and tries to "fix" things. Before very long, she'd like to give him a black eye. She didn't want to be fixed. She wanted to be listened to.

You Need to Feel Listened to and Cared For

This was my experience in working with cancer patients and their families. When I would ask what really helped them, of all the things I taught in my program, they would consistently say, "You listened, you cared, and you were sincere." This helped them more than any particular coping skill I taught. All people, not just women, need to feel listened to and cared for.

Another way to help you understand the wisdom of recognizing your needs and taking care of yourself is related to the experience of someone being homebound. When I worked in the rehab hospital with people dealing with strokes, prior to my work with cancer, oftentimes people were discharged to home and needed full-time care. This obviously was quite a setback for the patient, but was also a great adjustment for the caregiver. Commonly at this time family and friends phoned to tell the caregiver that they would come over to sit with the patient so that the caregiver could "get out of the house." You need to get to church, go to the store, and otherwise resume somewhat of a normal lifestyle. I think most people recognize that ignoring their personal needs, even at a difficult time such as this, is not in anyone's interest.

One time I walked into a hospital, and a young woman I knew was just leaving and said that she had just been up three straight days and nights with her mom. She seemed to be rather proud of what she had just done. I told her, "Keep it up and you'll be in there with her." I knew her well enough to say what could have sounded very direct and insensitive, but I hope you understand my point. There needs to be a balance between taking care of others and taking care of yourself. At some point if you ignore your needs, this will take a toll on your health, and you'll be no good to anybody.

When I was living in Cleveland, a severe tornado came through Ohio and into Pennsylvania. People were killed, and whole communities were destroyed. When people were interviewed on television about their experience, they all said it was the worst thing that ever happened or that they could even imagine happening. Then literally one year later, a television station from Cleveland interviewed these people again. And now these same people said that the tornado was the best thing that ever happened to them, their families, and community. What in the world happened in one year that made them change their minds so radically? The most significant thing was that they began to re-prioritize their lives.

It's usually uncomfortable to talk about death, but realistically, death is the only "given" in life. One day we are all going to die. But, of course, most of us don't spend time regularly thinking about this fact. What tends to happen is that we become somewhat numb to life and begin to take it for granted. When a tragic, life-threatening event like a tornado hits, it can remind us of the fact that one day "we're outta here". But what can also happen is that it can cause us to rethink: How do I want to spend the time I have left in my life? Dusting? Washing dishes? Working 10 and 12 hour days?

It's not that cleaning the house or your job is not important, it's just that the key, again, is balance. I believe the people in that tornado could look back and say, "That tornado was the best thing that ever happened," because now they were more starkly aware that one's lifetime is limited. And they started to do more of the things they loved to do and which mattered most to them. Their lives actually became richer and fuller as a result of the tornado. How do you want to spend the time you have left? What makes life worth living for you and for those you love? Make time and take time for the things that give your life joy and meaning and that we could say are life-giving.

Doctor's Orders: Have Fun 1x Daily

Many times people have told me that they're so busy that they don't have time to do all the things they already have to do, let alone take time for themselves. For those of you who ever had radiation treatments for cancer:

Remember when you didn't have time for your radiation treatments? You took off work, you canceled any other number of activities to make sure that you got these treatments. For those of you who ever had chemotherapy: Remember when the medical oncologist said that you needed chemo? Even though you expected to throw up and lose your hair, if your doctor told you that you needed the chemo you probably did it (even if you also knew these treatments were going to cost you a small fortune). So, if that's what it takes, I'll get your doctor to write you a prescription: You have to have fun 1x daily. We actually did this in the cancer centers where I worked. And, if it helps, we'll be glad to charge you a small fortune.

When older people are surveyed and asked to reflect back on their lives and what they would have done more of and what they would have done less, they almost always say they would have played more and worked less. It's not too late. Dr. Joseph Campbell, one of the world's greatest scholars on the wisdom of myths and parables, often exhorted people to follow an age-old dictate of the heart: "Follow your bliss."

3

Your Beliefs Are Potentially As Powerful As Any Medical Treatment

Probably the greatest example of a mind-body interaction is the placebo effect, which is based on one's beliefs or expectations. For example, if a physician prescribed a medication, and you took it, you would expect to get well. If you genuinely believe in the expertise of your doctor, and if your doctor told you to take these pills, you probably would take them and would feel better. However, if your doctor gave you "sugar pills" (fake pills, pills with no active substance in them), but you didn't know they were fake, you would still get better one-third of the time. Sugar pills or "placebos" work as well as the real medication one-third of the time. Most of you probably know about this phenomenon, but I'd like to emphasize its real implications.

In 1994, the *Journal of the American Medical Association* reported a major review of placebo effects in pain treatment and research, and concluded that the placebo effect consistently accounted for 35% to 75% of all pain reduction. Another review of research on all "double-blind" studies of pain medications reported that 55% of the therapeutic effect for these drugs was due to a placebo response. This means that 55% of the potency of morphine or aspirin or any other pain medication for one-third of all people is due to the power of one's beliefs! In fact, the more serious the illness is, and the more extreme the treatment is, the better the placebo effect works! *This means that your beliefs are potentially as powerful as any medical treatment.*

This placebo effect is so real that it must be controlled for in doing research, which, of course, is what science is all about. In testing the effectiveness of any treatment, it must be compared to yet another treatment because the *belief* that you are getting treatment will bring about the same results of the actual treatment to some extent. In research, treatments need to demonstrate that they are more effective than a placebo. If this "expectation effect" is not controlled for, the research and the effectiveness of the treatment are questionable and invalid.

This is why "double-blind" research is held in such high regard. In a "double-blind" study, neither the physician (nor anyone administering the treatment) nor the patient know which is the "active" or real treatment. This is because not only can the patients' beliefs affect the outcome, so can the doctors'. Isn't it interesting that we view the beliefs of the health professionals or the experimenters to be so real and powerful that they could contaminate and invalidate the research? We even create double-blind studies to eliminate any possible effect of their beliefs. Yet, knowing this, why don't we do everything we can to optimize the power of patients' beliefs to affect their outcome?

Varieties of Alternative Treatments

All oncologists (doctors who study or practice medicine with tumors or cancer) in all major industrialized countries have access to the same research. Yet treatments for cancer vary considerably in each of these countries. If you were diagnosed with cancer you would be treated differently in England, Germany, France, China, Japan, and so on. This is documented very clearly in Lynn Payer's book, *Medicine and Culture: Varieties of Treatment in the United States, England, West Germany, and France*. A summary of this book is in Michael Lerner's book, *Choices in Healing: Integrating the Best of Conventional and Complementary Approaches to Cancer*, which I strongly recommend you read as an excellent survey of the wide variety of choices of cancer treatments around the world. Another excellent resource is the video and book, *Bill Moyer's Healing and the Mind.*

Imagine that the president of the United States were in need of healthcare. Do you think he or she would get good care? Of course. What if the Queen of England needed health care, would she get good care? Of course, again. However, in this case, the queen would be offered naturopathic medicine and homeopathy as legitimate options in her care, along with the medical. This is the case also in France. China and Japan value and use acupuncture and herbs along with biomedicine, and all of these countries value spiritual approaches to their medical care. Germany probably offers the widest range of choices, which they consider valid cancer therapies. Dr. Simonton's psychosocial cancer program is seldom covered by insurance reimbursement here in America, but it is covered in Germany where Dr. Simonton travels extensively teaching his approach. And the use of surgery, chemotherapy, and radiation is much more aggressive and extensive in the United States than in any of these countries. This is not meant to have you think less of conventional medical treatment, it is to inform you of a much wider range of options in your health care.

Now in telling you that there is much more that you can do to treat cancer besides radiation, chemotherapy, and surgery, I know I may have opened a real "can of worms" for some of you. My experience with the cancer patients I've seen over the years, is that many of them honestly don't want to become actively involved in their treatment. They expect the doctor to tell them what to do, and, as I said before, if the doctor doesn't tell them to do it, then they assume it's not important.

The fact is, you now have some work ahead of you to identify the many different approaches which do exist. This really shouldn't be too difficult, however, for most communities today have wellness programs or holistic health centers where you can find these therapies. There are many books also documenting these approaches, some of which I've already noted. An excellent, recent book is *The Best Alternative Medicine* by Dr. Kenneth Pelletier.

Another real concern, though, is choosing a therapist. Even if you determine that a particular adjunctive therapy is for you, how do you know that practitioner is any good? I recommend, like in choosing anyone else to provide a service, that you ask around. In short time you'll find that one or a few people stand out. Ideally this would be the same in choosing a medical doctor.

A further concern is: How do I really know what all of my options are, and how can I possibly do it all? I have a fairly simple answer: Do that which you are attracted to, that which has meaning for you. I am relatively certain in my work and study that the greatest reason why any therapy works is because you believe in it. If you choose some treatment and don't really believe in it, you're likely to receive significantly less benefit. This, again, is related to the power of your beliefs. So if you believe strongly in a spiritual approach, but don't find yourself comfortable with a vegetarian diet, I recommend that you do what feels right for you, and not become concerned that you're not doing it all. This is not to suggest that a vegetarian diet is not a good idea; it is a very good idea. But if you don't really want to do it, your mindset or attitude will likely countermand a significant benefit and only cause you additional upset.

How Emotions Affect Your Health

Probably the greatest argument disputing the power of one's beliefs and a possible mind-body interaction has been the accepted fact that the immune system functioned independently of any other system. Until relatively recently, medical science believed that the central nervous system (which includes your brain and spinal cord) was not connected to the immune system, which is the primary mechanism identified for fighting disease. If the brain and immune system are not connected, how can one's thoughts, feelings, attitudes, beliefs, or any mental factor affect the disease process?

Forget the common sense that one's mental state and beliefs clearly affect physical structure and function, and in fact, I joke in science we don't use common sense. That's my way of saying, again, that in science, if it isn't supported with research it's not true or not worthy of our consideration. But in the 1970's a new field of study was born which would radically change the notion of mind and body being separate.

Dr. Robert Ader, a psychologist at the University of Rochester School of Medicine, and a colleague, Dr. Nicholas Cohen, an immunologist, found that if you paired a drug which suppresses immune function with a placebo, eventually the immune system becomes suppressed by the placebo alone. This is similar to Pavlov's pairing the ringing of a bell with presenting meat to a dog. Eventually the ringing of the bell alone, without the meat, caused the dog to salivate because of the association of the bell with food. He called this "classical conditioning," a form of learning. Learning does not take place without the use of a brain. In order for the placebo in Ader and Cohen's research to suppress immune function through this form of learning, the brain had to be connected to the immune system. Further research demonstrated that this same "conditioning" approach could enhance immune function and decrease the side effects of toxic chemotherapeutic drugs. Dr. Ader coined the term "psychoneuroimmunology" to account for the interaction between learning (psycho), implicating the physical brain (neuro), and one's immune function. He edited the now-classic text called *Psychoneuroimmunology* in 1981. Each chapter is original research clearly demonstrating a link between the central nervous system and the immune system. This confirmed the earlier research of Dr. George Solomon who coined the term "psychoimmunology" to explain how personality affects disease.

Much research has been done since to confirm that the immune system is capable of self-regulation. In 1985, *The Journal of Immunology* devoted a special issue just to research demonstrating the interaction of the central nervous and immune systems. One of these articles by Dr. Candace Pert and her colleagues attempted to explain a bodywide psychosomatic network of peptide substances, which distribute information throughout the body. Receptors for these substances (neuropeptides) are found principally in the limbic system, which is considered the seat of the emotions. Dr. Pert, who was then Chief of Brain Biochemistry for the National Institutes of Mental Health, concluded that these neuropeptides and their receptors are the molecules of emotion, the biochemical basis of how emotions affect health or disease. The immune system is in constant communication with the brain, endocrine and nervous systems by a system of neuropeptides, and every state of mind is reflected in the immune system. When people feel helpless, hopeless, and withdraw from life, the cells that fight disease become sluggish. When people are feeling hopeful and more connected to their feelings these cells become more active and increase in number. Belief truly does become biology.

This shouldn't be so surprising. People, including physicians, have talked about psychosomatic disease for quite a long time. This means that one's emotional or mental state can affect physical symptoms or disease. The term "hypochondriac" is often used to describe people who create through their beliefs a state of melancholy and any number of physical symptoms which we often say, "are all in their head." Of course these symptoms are real, but the idea is that their mental and physical health were directly caused by their beliefs.

The *Diagnostic and Statistical Manual of Mental Disorders* is the official guideline for psychiatrists and psychologists for evaluating one's mental health. One major category is called "somatoform disorders," which includes "hypochondriasis." "The essential features of this group of disorders are physical symptoms suggesting disorder (hence, Somatoform) for which there are no demonstrable organic findings or no physiologic mechanisms, and for which there is positive evidence, or a strong presumption, that the symptoms are linked to psychological factors or conflicts."

The Power of Prayer and Faith

Another strong example of the power of one's beliefs to affect a physical outcome is through the power of prayer or one's spiritual beliefs or faith. Dr. Larry Dossey is one of the leading experts on spirituality and medicine and the powers of prayer. In his best-selling books, *Prayer is Good Medicine, Healing Words: The Power of Prayer and the Practice of Medicine,* and *Be Careful What You Pray For...You Just Might Get It*, Dr. Dossey has given great comfort to many people grateful to discover that their belief in prayer could be grounded in science. In 1993, Dr. Daniel Benor reported in his book, *Healing Research*, that 131 controlled studies had been published testing the effectiveness of spiritual healing. The majority of these studies showed a statistically significant healing effect.

A national Gallup poll in 1989 reported that 95% of all Americans believe in God, 90% pray at least occasionally, and two-thirds consider prayer an important part of their daily lives. Dr. Herbert Benson has headed a number of Harvard Medical School conferences on spirituality and healing and reported that about 80% of Americans believe their religious beliefs can heal. This contrasts with a 1989 UCLA study which reported that only approximately half of all physicians believe that people's strong religious or spiritual convictions could contribute to increased longevity.

Medicine has worked hard in the last 100 years or so to break away from any concept of mysticism as part of medical practice, and this reliance on "science" has forced many physicians to be quite out-of-step with their patients. But according to Dr. Larry Dossey, the evidence for prayer and healing is so great that in the future, "The use of prayer will become the standard in scientific medical practice in most medical communities. So pervasive will its use become that not to recommend the use of prayer as an integral part of medical care will one day constitute medical malpractice."

I encountered a unique use of one's religious beliefs while I was working in cancer centers in Central Pennsylvania. Many rural Pennsylvanians are of German descent and some are referred to as "Pennsylvania Dutch." I found many of these people using a religious belief called "Pow-wow" for healing any number of ills. I felt proud when I was lent John George Hohman's 1920 book, *Pow-Wows*. It listed "a collection of mysterious and invaluable arts and remedies for man as well as animals with many proofs of their virtue and efficacy in healing diseases, etc." To be honest, on the surface, it reads like blatant superstition. But I can tell you sincerely that scores of people have told me how their unique beliefs in "calling on the Lord in their time of trouble" was the only and direct reason for their cures.

All major religions believe that faith can make one "whole" or healed. Christians commonly cite and believe, "With faith you can move mountains" (Matthew 17:20); and "Ask, and it will be given you; seek, and you will find; knock, and it will be opened to you" (Luke 11:9).

Following an apparition of the Virgin Mary in 1858 in Lourdes, France, millions (today, four million each year) of people suffering serious disease have traveled to Lourdes seeking a cure. Approximately 6000 claims have been made of extraordinary healing due to this religious experience. An International Medical Commission was organized in 1947 to examine these claims. Only 64 have been declared "miracles." The criteria necessary to be a "miracle" are borderline supernatural in themselves; it is very difficult to have a miracle, or at least to have it declared so by the Catholic Church.

In 1993 The Institute of Noetic Sciences published a major survey/book, *Spontaneous Remission*, reviewing incidents like the above miracle cases where people were cured from their terminal or incurable diseases with no known medical explanation. After examining almost 3500 articles from over 830 medical journals, the authors reported that, "people who remit have a very strong sense of self-sufficiency, and a central locus of control that is very internal. They feel in charge. These cases say something about the mind/body relationship which we believe is strongly involved here." These authors are convinced we all have a natural ability to recover from illness and disease.

Voodoo is just as real in its power to bring about negative consequences. In voodoo, the victims' beliefs in the curse made upon them are the foundation for what literally can cause their deaths. This brings up the ethics of what and how physicians tell people about their diagnoses and prognoses.

What about "False Hope"?

Many physicians are concerned about giving their patients "false hope." Norman Cousins proposes that doctors should be equally concerned about giving people "false fears." He encouraged people to, "Accept the diagnosis, but deny the verdict." The fact is that no matter how serious the illness or how close to death, someone has fully recovered. It is one thing to give a life-threatening diagnosis, or even to say that there is nothing more a particular physician/specialist can do within his or her expertise. But it is quite another matter to say something is incurable or that someone will definitely die within a certain time period. Many physicians understand this and will actually say to patients that they don't have a crystal ball and can't predict their outcome.

It makes more sense to talk about the challenge rather than the fatal outcome, and that the physician and patient are both going to do everything they can to increase the odds. Dr. Patricia Norris made this astute comment in this regard in 1986 in the journal of *Biofeedback and Self-regulation*:

> Some belief, hope, and confidence that what one is attempting is *possible*, even though not guaranteed, is essential. To learn to dive, tumble, win a swim meet, or eliminate a wart or tumor, one must believe it is possible. Suppose an athlete trying out for the Olympics was told by a coach, "Don't get your expectations up, I don't want you to have any false hopes. Don't forget, only one person can get a gold medal, and most people won't even make it past the trials. The chances of you winning, or even getting to the Olympics at all, are pretty remote." It's not hard to imagine what the effects of such "realism" would be on achievement.

This is, again, where many physicians understand that one's beliefs or "a strong will to live" can make a difference and would not risk creating yet another serious problem by dashing all hope. Depression is a common result of a serious diagnosis, and can compromise the immune system. How the doctor communicates information can be lethal. There are no guarantees at this time, only probabilities. Even a positive outlook is no guarantee. But to take one's hope away because it isn't realistic (as Dr. Norris explained in the above citation) is to risk creating hopelessness and pessimism. Is this advisable? Someone much wiser than I once said, "Without hope people perish."

I have physician friends who were born and trained in England. In their cultural beliefs and medical training doctors did not tell someone, "You have cancer." It was understood that people equated cancer with death, and to tell them they had cancer would almost certainly contribute to that outcome.

So the question is: How should doctors inform you of your diagnosis and prognosis so that you can make an informed choice regarding your medical care without contributing in a negative way to your prognosis?

Today with the frequency of malpractice suits, physicians have to be extra aware of what they say. I'm sure that many physicians are torn between wanting to be careful about how they tell you your medical condition and making sure they tell you in a way that they're protected legally. What an awkward position for the physician, patient, and family.

How does the doctor handle a situation where a family member says, "Don't you dare tell my father he has cancer; it will kill him"? The medical position of "informed choice" dictates that the patient must be told his or her diagnosis and prognosis. Patients must be told of their illness or disease, the medical facts about treatments and how these treatments will affect the course of the disease, including potential side effects of medical treatment. But the family insists that if their father knows the medical facts it will complicate and worsen their dad's medical condition. What are doctors to say? Who do they tell? How much do they say?

An article, "Breaking Bad News: Consensus Guidelines for Medical Practitioners" appeared in 1995 in the *Journal of Clinical Oncology* addressing this situation. The general recommendation was that the amount of information given and rate of this disclosure should be tailored to the needs of the individual. One strategy was simply to ask patients how much information they would like to know. But this article reported that only about one-third of practitioners feel competent at interactional skills. Given the power of one's beliefs, including belief in one's doctor, serious further attention is required in this regard in physicians' medical training for everyone's benefit.

I remember when I was getting ready for one of my classes and a man I had never met before came in crying. He told me that his doctor had just told him he had cancer, that he would die in a short time, and that he should go home and sell his farm. This man was truly devastated. Somehow he had heard about me, and now he was asking me what he should do.

Most importantly what I did at first was empathize with him. I'm never sure what was really said in any conversation that I haven't been part of, so I couldn't be sure what this physician actually said. But clearly this man was feeling totally hopeless and helpless.

Eventually I got around to explaining that even if he had been given this dire information, he could always consult another doctor to be sure, and it's just possible that he might have something different to say (or say it much more sensitively). I then explained about "a strong will to live," and how it could make a difference. All of this took time, and he went on to say how he had certain plans, but now was unsure what to do, "Would I live that long?" I would never tell someone what to do or how long they'll live, but I shared my experience how many other cancer patients and families consistently have chosen "to live like you're going to live." It may make good sense to put your affairs in order, but how do you want to spend the time you have left: withdrawn from life and waiting to die? Then he explained to me about "Goose Day."

In Central Pennsylvania there's a day in September that if you eat goose it's supposed to bring you good fortune. This was all new to me, but it's a very special day for this community. And it turned out that this man raised most of the geese in town for Goose Day. But it's Spring, and Goose Day isn't until Fall. He decided to buy the geese, and to shorten my story, lived to raise many more geese for more Goose Days. Everyone involved in his case was certain that a number of psychosocial factors like "a will to live," hope, and social support extended his life.

The Body Will Do What You Tell It

Probably all of you have seen or heard about circus-like performers and their extreme ability to regulate their bodies so that they can swallow swords, lie on a bed of nails, walk on hot coals, etc. While there are many who would try to "debunk" this ability, claiming that these performances are faked, the fact is that there are many, many people who legitimately can alter their bodily processes in the extreme, even if there are those who would fraudulently appear to do so.

I observed this first-hand at a conference in Phoenix, Arizona, in the mid-70's. A man who called himself Komar laid on a bed of nails while I was standing only a few feet away. Then another bed of nails was laid on top of Komar so that he was sandwiched between the nails. Then several men were invited to come up and sit on top of this "sandwich," so that there was now probably 1000 pounds of pressure exerted on Komar. One interesting aside was that while Komar was giving this demonstration, he was smoking an unfiltered Camel cigarette with one hand, and drinking a can of Coke with the other. Following this seemingly bizarre act, Komar had only minor dents in his body from the nails, and no bleeding. Later I saw him walk up a ladder of machetes. The blades of the machetes were pointed up, and Komar walked directly on the sharp edges exerting the full weight of his body and, again, experienced no bleeding.

This phenomenon has been studied widely in the laboratory demonstrating once again a clear mind-body interaction. Dr. Kenneth Pelletier, an associate professor at Stanford University Medical School, tested people like Komar back in the early '70s. A good account of this research is in his 1977 book, *Mind as Healer, Mind as Slayer*. According to Dr. Pelletier, these people had learned a deep meditative discipline that allowed them to train their autonomic nervous system in a way medical science today still cannot fully explain. Some of these people developed their skill because of life-threatening situations such as being tortured in a prison camp. Victor Frankl discusses his experience as such a prisoner in detail in his book, *Man's Search for Meaning*.

One example of this behavior is with religious practices where zealots act to demonstrate their faith publicly by abusing their bodies in some extreme way. They literally suspend themselves with meat hooks through the skin and muscles of their back, or skewer any number of body parts with needles or knives. This is a widely practiced phenomenon in many cultures noted regularly by anthropologists.

Less sensational examples of this type of body control, but just as unusual, have been demonstrated by yogi masters. In 1970, a yoga teacher from India named Swami Rama, allowed himself to be tested at the highly regarded psychiatric laboratories of the Menninger Foundation. Two true pioneers in the research of the mind's power to control the body are Dr. Elmer Green and his wife, Alyce. They have been Directors of the Voluntary Controls Program Research Department of the Menninger Foundation since the mid-60's. They are best known for their pioneering work in biofeedback, a type of self-regulation technique I'll talk more about in the next chapter. An excellent accounting of their work (including the research on Swami Rama) is in their 1977 book, *Beyond Biofeedback*.

Under strict laboratory-controlled conditions, Swami Rama demonstrated voluntary control of blood flow by causing the left side of his right hand to increase in temperature 11 degrees above the right side of the same hand. He was able to stop his heart from pumping blood for 16 seconds. He could kill a specific number of white blood cells on command. In other experiments he produced a cyst within four seconds and made it disappear as rapidly. He claimed that all of the soft tissues of the body are easy to manipulate including starving and eliminating tumors by voluntary control of blood flow. Swami Rama said that his yoga teacher in India was much more skilled and adept than he, but "his teacher had asked him to come to the United States to demonstrate to medical people that the mind can control the body."

Indian yoga, Tibetan Buddhism, and Sufism are very similar spiritual traditions whose followers have demonstrated unusual powers of self-regulation. The Sufi tradition is an esoteric branch of Islam, and one of its practitioners, Jack Schwarz, also allowed himself to be tested at the Menninger Foundation laboratories. He was very much like Swami Rama. Both seemed to need no more than two or three hours of sleep each night, both could regulate brain-wave activity and blood flow, both were quite skilled at pain control, in particular, and both believed everyone has this capability for psychosomatic self-regulation.

An interesting aside for me is that Elmer Green was early influenced by another Sufi practitioner, Arthur Green, and a spiritualist minister, Will J. Erwood, and others of various philosophic backgrounds. Elmer Green said that all were saying the same thing: "The body will do what you tell it, if you learn how to tell it. The way of telling it involves quietness plus a visualization of what you want the body to do."

Hypnosis

Tribal medicine people and spiritual practices have employed hypnosis under various labels since antiquity. In the late 1700's, Dr. Franz Anton Mesmer was able to "cure" physical illness through his system of "animal magnetism," a technique which came to be known as mesmerism. This gave birth to what is now called hypnotism. The value of Mesmer's work was the evidence that suggestion could produce physical changes. The term "hypnotism" actually came from Dr. James Braid in 1843 as his version of mesmerism, which now included putting patients into a trance or sleep state. Jean Martin Charcot, Hippolyte Bernheim, Sigmund Freud, and others added further theory and respect for the way the human mind could affect the physical body, and slowly hypnotism emerged as a science.

Unfortunately hypnotism has not been adopted into mainstream medical care even though it was formally recognized by the American Medical Association in 1958 as a valid medical treatment, and even though there are thousands of studies demonstrating the benefit of this approach medically. I felt fortunate to be able to see a "stage" hypnotist perform at a university function while I was in graduate school. While the use of hypnosis for entertainment seems to have trivialized the benefit of a serious therapeutic tool, I recommend generally that if you have a chance to observe a "stage" hypnotist that you give it a chance. It is captivating to see the power of suggestion and imagination at work.

Actually everyone has experienced hypnosis in so many ways daily. I was trained that hypnosis is basically suggestion, acceptance, and expectation. So when you wake up before your alarm clock goes off, it's really a form of hypnotic suggestion. When a mother awakens to a baby's whimper, but is not disturbed by other noises, her ability to minimize these other distractions and focus her attention on the baby is another demonstration of hypnotic suggestion.

A more medical understanding of how one's thoughts have the ability to affect the body is primarily by blood flow. Many so-called "incurable" and chronic conditions have been remitted or improved with hypnosis because of this ability to directly affect blood flow to all of the tissues and organs of the body. The important factors are motivation, belief, expectation, and imagination.

You Can Increase Your Odds

When I've taught my program for cancer patients and their families, the most common examples I've given supporting the power of one's beliefs are how they can use them to offset side effects of medical treatments. The most widely researched techniques with cancer patients are hypnosis and guided imagery, which have been used very effectively in preventing and reducing both anticipatory and post-treatment nausea and vomiting. In one very interesting case study, a person who was suffering from nausea was given a placebo and told that this would reduce these symptoms. Within 15 minutes the nausea disappeared and gastric motor activity resumed. However, the placebo was actually syrup of ipecac, which is normally taken to induce nausea and vomiting!

In another study, cancer patients were given their chemotherapy, and because of the toxicity of the drugs, all of them experienced nausea and hair loss. When these same patients were given a second round of chemotherapy, they were also given new drugs, which they were told would offset these side effects. Upon taking the new medication, *a placebo*, along with their chemotherapy, a significant number of patients now did not have nausea or hair loss.

Unfortunately chemotherapy can cause nausea and hair loss, but this depends on several factors, including the toxicity of the drugs. My experience is that most cancer patients *expect* these side effects.

So in another experiment testing the effectiveness of a new chemotherapy, patients were assigned to a treatment group and given the chemotherapy, or assigned to a control group and given a placebo. The patients did not know which group they were in. Thirty percent of the control group given the *placebo* lost their hair!

Many years ago I worked with a patient who had lung cancer, and I explained how he could use guided imagery to potentially offset the side effect of nausea from his chemotherapy. I didn't know that he was much more concerned about the potential for losing his hair. So, on his own, he imagined powerful figures protecting his hair follicles, and that they would easily withstand the effect of the drugs. When he didn't lose his hair, he told me that his physician was actually upset. "Everybody loses their hair from this chemotherapy." The patient needed more chemotherapy, so the physician told him he would certainly lose his hair this time. Again the patient did not lose his hair, and he said the doctor got even madder the next time.

Because I usually worked in radiation oncology centers, I regularly helped people use guided imagery to offset the side effects of their radiation treatments. A common side effect is the burning of the skin. In one instance a woman with an advanced stage of cancer was given very high doses of radiation in a shorter than normal treatment time due to the extreme nature of her case. She was certain to have a breakdown of her skin. Her doctors were very confused when she didn't have any signs of skin irritation. She explained that she told the radiation beam to go right to the tumor and not to stop at her skin!

Another woman was especially concerned that surgery for her breast cancer would disfigure her. She used guided imagery extensively prior to, during, and following her surgery. The surgery went well and she healed in a remarkably short time. After a number of check-ups, her physician asked if he could use her as an example of such a good cosmetic outcome of surgery. She was the best he had ever seen. He really was an excellent surgeon, who did most of the breast cancer surgeries in that hospital, but the woman and I were certain that her excellent cosmetic outcome was due to her use of imagery along with the benefit of the surgeon's skills.

Clearly people's thoughts or suggestions and their beliefs and expectations can cause direct physical effects. Your beliefs and expectations can definitely increase your odds. But I want to tell you now about the most dramatic example I know that confirms the power of one's beliefs.

In 1957, a drug called Krebiozen was actually thought to be a cure for cancer. Once it went through all of the drug trials necessary to be approved for testing with human subjects, it was distributed to 100 hospitals to be tested. In one of these hospitals Dr. Bruno Klopfer headed the study. One of Dr. Klopfer's patients was a man named Mr. Wright, who read in the newspaper about this new drug, which he now believed would save his life.

Mr. Wright had a very advanced cancer with huge tumor masses the size of oranges in his neck, axilla, groin, chest, and abdomen. He had developed resistance to all known medical treatment. His spleen and liver were greatly enlarged. His thoracic duct was obstructed, and his chest had to be drained of fluid every other day. He was on oxygen and not expected to live more than two weeks. While Mr. Wright was certain that the Krebiozen would save him, one of the criteria to be included in the study was that patients have a prognosis of at least three, and preferably six, months. Dr. Klopfer explained that there was only so much of the drug to be tested and, unfortunately, Mr. Wright did not qualify. As much as Dr. Klopfer tried, he could not dissuade Mr. Wright's enthusiasm for this "golden opportunity."

Dr. Klopfer thought that Mr. Wright wouldn't even live through the weekend, so he gave him the drug thinking it wouldn't be too much of a problem. On Monday, everyone who qualified for the treatment showed no change. But Mr. Wright, who had been completely bedridden, was now *walking* around the ward spreading "good cheer." His tumors were now half their original size. The regression could not be accounted to any treatment outside of the one injection of Krebiozen.

They continued to give Mr. Wright the injections three times weekly as the study stipulated, much to the joy of Mr. Wright, but much to the bewilderment of the medical staff. Within 10 days Mr. Wright was discharged from the hospital breathing normally, fully active and flying his own airplane at 12,000 feet with no discomfort.

About two months later Mr. Wright heard news reports that all of the clinics testing Krebiozen showed no improvement in their patients. Mr. Wright began to lose his faith in this last hope and, "after two months of practically perfect health, he relapsed to his original state." I now want to cite the original report on Mr. Wright:

> But here I saw the opportunity to *double-check* the drug and maybe, too, find out how the quacks can accomplish the results that they claim (and many of their claims are well substantiated). Knowing something of my patient's innate optimism by this time, I deliberately took advantage of him. This was for purely scientific reasons, in order to perform the perfect control experiment which could answer all the perplexing questions he had brought up. Furthermore, this scheme could not harm him in any way, I felt sure, and there was nothing I knew anyway that could help him.
>
> When Mr. Wright had all but given up in despair with the recrudescence of his disease, in spite of the "wonder-drug" which had worked so well at first, I decided to take the chance and play the quack. So deliberately lying, I told him not to believe what he read in the papers, the drug was really most promising after all. "What then," he asked, "was the reason for his relapse?" "Just because the substance deteriorated on standing," I replied, "a new super-refined, double-strength product is due to arrive tomorrow which can more than reproduce the great benefits derived from the original injections."
>
> This news came as a great revelation to him, and Mr. Wright, as ill as he was, became his optimistic self again, eager to start over. By delaying a couple of days before the "shipment" arrived, his anticipation of salvation had reached a tremendous pitch. When I announced that the new series of injections was about to begin, he was almost ecstatic and his faith was very strong.
>
> With much fanfare, and putting on quite an act (which I deemed permissible under the circumstances), I administered the first injection of the doubly potent, *fresh* preparation – consisting of *fresh water* and nothing more. The results of this experiment were quite unbelievable to us at the time,

although we must have had some suspicion of the remotely possible outcome to have even attempted it at all.

Recovery from his second near-terminal state was even more dramatic than the first. Tumor masses melted, chest fluid vanished, he became ambulatory, and even went back to flying again. At this time he was certainly the picture of health. The water injections were continued, since they worked such wonders. He then remained symptom-free for over two months. At this time the final AMA announcement appeared in the press – "Nationwide tests show Krebiozen to be a worthless drug in treatment of cancer."

Within a few days of this report, Mr. Wright was readmitted to the hospital *in extremis*. His faith was now gone, his last hope vanished, and he succumbed in less than two days.

In 1986 Dr. Ernest Rossi, a student of Dr. Bruno Klopfer, wrote this conclusion to the case of Mr. Wright in his often-cited book, *The Psychobiology of Mind-body Healing* (which also contains the above cited medical report):

We know today, for example, that cancer growth can be controlled by the person's immune system; if you can improve the immune system, it can destroy the cancer. Obviously, Mr. Wright's immune system must have been activated by his belief in a cure. The incredible rapidity of his healing also suggest that his autonomic and endocrine systems must have been responsive to suggestion, enabling him to mobilize his blood system with such amazing efficiency to remove the toxic fluids and waste products of the fast diminishing cancer. As we shall learn later in this book, we now know a lot more about the "limbic-hypothalmic system" of the brain as the major mind-body connector modulating the biological activity of the autonomic, endocrine, and immune systems in response to mental suggestion and beliefs. In summary, Mr. Wright's experience tells us that it was his *total belief in the efficacy* of the worthless drug, Krebiozen, that mobilized a healing placebo response by activating *all* these major systems of mind-body communication and healing.

When I've told people in my classes about Mr. Wright's experience with Krebiozen, and asked them if they believed that Mr. Wright's beliefs played a role in his recovery or demise, they almost always say, "Yes." But because one person had a particular experience doesn't mean that anyone else will have the same experience or outcome if they do the same thing. When scientists conduct research they usually need hundreds or even thousands of people to test. So how can one say scientifically that Mr. Wright's beliefs made a difference?

In research, (1) If you know someone's "baseline" condition, or current status, such as was the case with Mr. Wright medically; (2) Then you hypothesize that a treatment will have a particular outcome; (3) Apply that treatment and you get the hypothesized effect; (4) Withdraw the treatment and the person's condition returns to the original baseline; (5) Apply the treatment again, and you get the hypothesized effect again; (6) Withdraw the treatment and you go back to the initial condition – this is a statistically sound demonstration that the treatment (in this case, Mr. Wright's beliefs) made the difference, even though it was only with one person.

This suggests that one's beliefs can be powerful enough to reverse a terminal diagnosis. Understand, however, that just because this can be true doesn't mean that it always works. It would be highly inappropriate for me to tell you that if you believe in something strongly enough that you will be able to achieve whatever you want. The odds are that your beliefs will not win out most of the time. But how would you like to increase your odds?

Do you remember when your physician signed his or her name in blood guaranteeing that if you have a particular treatment that it would cure you? There are no guarantees. It is always about increasing the odds. The placebo effect (the power of your beliefs or expectations) is potentially as powerful as any medical treatment. You can use your beliefs, along with your medical treatment or whatever other "alternative" treatments you believe in, to increase your odds – sometimes dramatically.

4

Relaxation and Imagery Techniques

Mental relaxation and imagery techniques include meditation, prayer, autogenic training, progressive relaxation, hypnosis, and guided imagery. These types of mental techniques have played a major role in healing throughout history. Dr. Jeanne Achterberg gives a very thoughtful and scholarly review in her book, *Imagery in Healing*, how shamanism, "the most widely practiced type of medicine on the planet," relies particularly on the use of imagination. The early fathers of medicine such as Aristotle and Hippocrates clearly understood that people's imagination and beliefs could contribute to their health or disease. And until this century, psychologists including William James, Francis Galton, and Edward Titchener accepted imagery as a fundamental concept. However, the influence of behaviorism and the difficulty in measuring mentalistic events largely curtailed American mental imagery research and use until the 1960's.

Prior to this century, psychology was recognized as a philosophy and not a science. But with the advent of the scientific age, psychology was going to have to become objectively "measurable." For example, the concept of "mind" now had to respond to questions like: Where is it located? How much does it weigh? What are its dimensions? These are highly appropriate scientific questions, and, of course, psychology had no objective answers. The joke became that psychology lost its mind at the turn of the century. (Some would say they've been searching desperately for it ever since.)

The image of psychology as a "social" science or "soft" science remains to this day. Biology, chemistry, physics, and medicine are recognized as "hard" sciences, as though these fields of study are more rigorously studied than sociology or psychology. Interestingly, an M.D. degree is not a research degree, but the public image is that a physician has more training and understanding of research than a psychologist. In fact it is just the opposite. A Ph.D. degree in psychology is a research degree, and a psychologist generally has far more research training than a medical doctor. This is not intended as a slight to medical doctors; it is to point out a basic perception (or misperception) of psychology and psychologists. And so the jokes continue such as, "If you go to see a psychologist, it means you really do need one," as though psychologists are less stable than any of the people they work with. I'll admit I know quite a few strange and unusual psychologists, but if you think about it, I'll bet you've met your share of peculiar doctors.

We've come to believe that it's okay to be physically sick, but if you're mentally ill there's a very real social stigma attached. You could tell someone that you have to go to see a medical doctor due to any number of physical complaints, but you sure don't want someone to know you need a psychologist.

When I would go to cancer centers and be introduced as a psychologist who wanted to speak to patients and families, almost no one wanted to meet me. When we decided to introduce me as Dr. Shrock (without being identified as a psychologist) who was going to talk to them about their immune system, almost everyone wanted to speak with me. But it was usually a tough sell to help them appreciate that psychology had anything to help them with their cancer. Cancer is a very physical disease, so what do I need a psychologist for?

So I'd like to describe more in detail some of the research and clinical evidence for the uses of imagery in healing, which may help you appreciate further the role of psychology in health care, and how you can take more control of your health.

When You're Relaxed Your Body Works More Effectively

While psychology in the United States was becoming more scientific at the turn of the century, Europe continued to be more open to approaches which were not so easily "measurable." Perhaps the single most influential application of the use of relaxation and guided imagery in Europe on current behavioral imagery techniques in psychotherapy was the autogenic therapy developed by Dr. Johannes H. Schultz. Using a simple sitting posture the patient was verbally instructed to follow mental exercises such as, "My arms feel heavy, warm, and relaxed. My heart beat is calm and regular." One was to imagine a particular part of the body relaxed in a passive and casual manner. This approach is documented in the extensive writings of Wolfgang Luthe. One of these volumes by Luthe lists all of the disorders and diseases that autogenic therapy has been used with successfully. I remember thinking when I first read this book that there's more stuff that this approach has been found effective with than I've ever even heard of. How could simply imagining yourself to be relaxed in this way lead to the healing of so many conditions?

Stedman's Medical Dictionary defines relaxation as "lengthening or lessening of tension in a muscle." Muscle fibers have a response repertoire of one: All they do is contract. When you are relaxed, your muscle fibers lengthen. As a rule, do you think your body functions better when you are relaxed or tense?

Let's consider how a particular system in your body works, and how tension or relaxation would affect its function. The circulatory system carries blood, food, and oxygen to all parts of the body. It also carries away waste material and is part of the immune system and how the body functions to heal itself. If you are tense and your muscles contract, does this aid or hinder normal and healthy function of the flow of your blood? When you are relaxed and your muscle fibers lengthen, this enables normal, healthy blood circulation.

In Chapter 2 I explained how your immune system automatically monitors and controls any foreign substance, including cancer cells, when working properly. Your body is built remarkably well to keep you healthy or repair itself. If you were in the kitchen and cut your finger with a paring knife, would you stop at that time and order your blood to coagulate and a scab to form? Most likely you would wipe it off and maybe put a Band-Aid on it, and go about your business. Your full expectation would be that your finger would heal itself. Anything you can do, like relaxation that helps your body function normally, is clearly in your interest. So in the instance of autogenic therapy, if this approach can cause people to relax, it makes sense that it could have contributed to the natural healing of so many illnesses and disorders.

Dr. Edmond Jacobson's 1929 (and revised in 1938) book, *Progressive Relaxation*, is one of the earliest and most influential investigations of relaxation. With extensive research he demonstrated that when you imagine that you are relaxed, your body literally becomes more relaxed. This decrease in muscle activity commonly led to the reduction or elimination of many symptoms and disorders.

In a related study Jacobson had people lift a weight, and he recorded the electrical activity associated with this physical movement of the arm. Then he had these same people only imagine that they were lifting the weight. They didn't move their arm; only imagined it. Remarkably similar electrical activity was produced and recorded when they actually lifted the weight and when they only imagined it.

Sports psychologist, Dr. Richard Suinn, similarly tested the electromyograph responses of an alpine ski racer as he imagined a downhill ski race. Suinn reported, "By the time he finished this psychological rehearsal of the downhill race, his EMG recordings almost mirrored the course itself."

How could you explain that the body would produce the same

neuromuscular activity when actually active vs. only when imagining the activity? One way to explain this is with the idea, "thoughts are things." Remember the earlier discussion about thoughts appearing to be "nothing"? Thoughts must be something, some form of energy or vibration, in order to cause changes in the physical body. This is yet another example of a mind-body relationship, and the ability of thought to cause a physical, measurable response in the body.

Bud Winter was a legendary track coach at San Jose State College. His track athletes set 37 world records. Coach Winter had learned about the ability of relaxation to affect athletic performance as chairman of a research program in relaxation at Del Monte Pre-Flight School while in the Navy. Under his direction, 200 naval cadets were randomly assigned to a relaxation or a control group during their academic, military, and athletic training. The relaxation group out-performed the control group dramatically. Winter discussed this research in his book, *Relax and Win*:

> The piece de resistance (and I mean resistance) came the day a surprise test was given in Nomenclature and Recognition to both the control group and the experimental group. The cadets had to identify planes at a fiftieth of a second while the sound track of the movie Desert Victory was played backward as loud as possible. Almost none (17%) of the control group could finish the test. Many threw down their pens and said, "To hell with it." All of the relaxation group finished the test. Relaxation aiding the ability to concentrate was evident.

After six weeks, 99 of 100 cadets in the relaxation group could fall asleep in two minutes sitting up in a chair while a simulated cannon was blasting in the room. The average relaxation group cadets reduced sleep body movements from 153 to 39, and body turnovers from 48 to 13. Winter reported that there were even more dramatic improvements in their sports related activities, including reduction of injuries. He concluded that relaxation techniques such as progressive relaxation "could help virtually everyone" in (1) studying, (2) sports, (3) sleeping more soundly, (4) improving grades, (5) concentrating, (6) developing more endurance, (7) improving reaction time, (8) seeing more clearly, (9) taking examinations, (10) improving speed of hand and foot, (11) learning more rapidly, and (12) conquering fears.

Later, as coach of the San Jose State track team, Coach Winter trained his athletes to use progressive relaxation and guided imagery. He believed that relaxation led to more efficient use of glycogen in the body and more efficient use of muscles, which gave athletes more energy. He also taught his athletes that when they were relaxed their minds were more open to suggestion. Then guided imagery or affirmations could condition any "subsequent feelings, thoughts, and actions to follow the directions in the slogan you repeat over and over in that relaxed state." After years of coaching experience and interviewing great athletes in all sports, Coach Winter concluded that the most important requisite for being a champion is the ability to relax under major competition.

Dr. Herbert Benson, an Associate Professor of Medicine at Harvard Medical School, has studied and researched mental relaxation techniques extensively for the past 30 years. At first he studied the effects of transcendental meditation, which included the silent repetition of a sound called a mantra and a passive approach to any distracting thoughts. It was a gentle focusing or narrowing of attention. He found that this approach differed significantly from a normal, quiet, resting state, and also from sleep. By focusing their attention in this way people were able to decrease their oxygen consumption rate, lower blood lactate levels, produce more low frequency brain waves, lower heart and breathing rate, and decrease muscle tension all associated with relaxation, the opposite of a stressful response. His 1975 book, *The Relaxation Response*, details much of this early research and this approach which entails 1) something to focus your attention on which is non-threatening and, ideally, which has meaning for you like a personal affirmation, 2) a quiet environment, 3) a comfortable posture, and 4) a passive attitude. With your eyes closed, this is all meant to focus your attention.

Benson has found that many cultures have used this basic approach, which is rooted in religious practice and types of prayer. He has tested other mental relaxation techniques including autogenic training, progressive relaxation, hypnosis, Zen meditation and yoga, and found that all produce this relaxation response. To date the relaxation response has been tested successfully with a wide range of medical conditions including the treatment of nausea and vomiting related to chemotherapy treatment of cancer.

Meditation and Mindfulness

As mentioned above related to Benson's work, meditation has a rich history dating back thousands of years. It is usually associated with Eastern religions, but is in fact a form of prayer associated with all of the major religions including Islam, Judaism, Christianity, and Buddhism. It is a common tradition to use the repetition of a word, phrase, or prayer such as in Christianity the repetitious prayer, "Lord Jesus Christ, have mercy on me." However, today the use of meditation as a form of health care, as demonstrated by Benson, is not at all mainstream in Western medicine. But I want to tell you about two people and their programs where meditation has been used very effectively in medical settings.

Dr. Dean Ornish is a cardiologist, a heart specialist. He has been published in the world's most respected medical journals proving you can reverse heart disease without surgery or drugs. He would be certain to tell you that he is not averse to using surgery and drugs. Once a patient is stable, however, heart disease can be managed much more effectively with lifestyle changes such as diet, exercise, and stress management. I'll talk more about diet and exercise later, but I want to focus on one of Ornish's primary approaches to stress management in his program, which is the practice of yoga.

Yoga, he explains, is not just a collection of various stretching exercises and postures to limber up the body. It also includes breathing techniques, meditation, guided imagery or visualization, self-analysis, and altruism. Ornish teaches that both peace and stress begin in your mind and "meditation is the process of quieting your mind." Meditation, as practiced for thousands of years by different spiritual traditions, was not developed as a stress management technique. Its primary purpose was for the practitioner to experience inner peace and happiness. Greater health was a by-product. The challenge is that you must have the discipline to quiet, still, and focus your mind and attention. In his book, *Dr. Dean Ornish's Program for Reversing Heart Disease*, he states:

> You cannot force your mind to be quiet, any more than you can smooth out the waves in a tray of water by running your hand across its surface. And if you look at your reflection in a disturbed tray of water, then your face looks distorted. You don't have to do anything to smooth out the waves other than to stop disturbing them. When you do, then you can see your true self more clearly in the reflection.
>
> Similarly, meditation doesn't smooth out the disturbances in your life, as a tranquilizer might. Meditation allows you to go deeper, to where the disturbances begin. It helps you become more aware of how your mind becomes agitated and gives you more control to stop these disturbances. It doesn't *bring* you peace, for the peace is already there once you stop disturbing it.

Dr. Ornish believes that meditation allows one to rediscover and begin healing the inner self. Meditation is a tool for transformation where people can reconnect with themselves and their feelings, and also spiritually. A common occurrence in meditating is to experience a connection with something larger than ourselves, and a deep sense of peace and joy. Ornish proposes that healing is ultimately healing our sense of isolation. His

"Opening Your Heart" program attempts to integrate medical knowledge with a deeper, ancient wisdom.

He recommends meditation 20 minutes twice a day, but a few minutes on a regular basis that fits into your daily routine is what's most important. For him, some of the most simple yet powerful types of meditation are (1) focusing on your breathing, (2) focusing on a sound, (3) self-analysis, (4) prayer or devotion, and (5) mindfulness.

In a form of meditation called mindfulness you pay full attention to whatever you are thinking, feeling, or experiencing with no intention of being other than fully in the moment. This approach comes from the Buddhist tradition as a means of increasing one's awareness and wisdom.

Dr. Jon Kabat-Zinn has used this mindfulness practice effectively with a broad range of serious physical illnesses. He is Director of the Stress Reduction Clinic at the University of Massachusetts Medical Center, where he is an Associate Professor of Medicine. Thousands of people have been referred there by their physicians, usually because more standard medical care has been relatively ineffective with their various conditions. Interestingly, this program offers the same training in mindfulness and stress reduction to everyone. Kabat-Zinn explains that his program is a way for people to experience and understand the mind-body connection and to use it to deal more effectively with their life situations. Usually people come with no particular knowledge of meditation or interest in it.

Can you imagine that you have some serious chronic illness that has not responded particularly well to conventional medical treatment, and you walk into Dr. Kabat-Zinn's program and one of the first things you're going to do is take an extended time period to eat one raisin? You might have seen this on Bill Moyer's 1993 PBS special, "Healing and the Mind." It certainly can seem bizarre at first, and remember additionally the difficulty in disciplining your mind to focus your attention. In his book, *Full Catastrophe Living*, Kabat-Zinn explains his approach:

> For some people, the inherent difficulty of meditation practice is made easier by the profound states of relaxation and pleasant feelings it frequently produces. But mindfulness is about far more than feeling relaxed or tension-free. Its true aim is to nurture an inner balance of mind that allows you to face *all* life situations with greater stability, clarity, understanding, and even wisdom, and to act or respond effectively and with dignity out of that clarity and understanding.
>
> That means an integral part of mindfulness practice is to face, accept, and even welcome your tension, stress, and physical pain, as well as mind states such as fear, anger,

frustration, disappointment, and feelings of insecurity and unworthiness when they are present. Why? Because acknowledging present-moment reality as it actually is, whether it is pleasant or unpleasant, is the first step towards transforming that reality and your relationship to it. If you do not face things in this way, you are likely to become stuck and have difficulty changing or growing...

When thoughts or feelings come up in your mind, you don't ignore them or suppress them, nor do you analyze or judge their content. Rather, you simply note any thoughts as they occur as best you can and observe them intentionally but nonjudgmentally, moment by moment, as events in the field of your awareness.

Paradoxically, this inclusive noting of thoughts that come and go in your mind can lead you to feel less caught up in them and give you a deeper perspective on your reactions to everyday stress and pressures. By observing your thoughts and emotions as if you had taken a step back from them, you can see much more clearly what is actually on your mind. You can see your thoughts arise and recede one after another. You can note the content of your thoughts, the feelings associated with them, and your reactions to them. You might become aware of agendas, attachments, likes and dislikes, and inaccuracies in your ideas. You can gain insight into what drives you, how you see the world, who you think you are – insight into your fears and aspirations.

Kabat-Zinn recommends meditating for 45 minutes a day at least six days a week. The three most basic formal meditation practices used in his clinic are: (1) the body scan where you slowly and systematically move your attention through the various regions of your body, from your feet to the top of your head, noting any physical sensations, (2) a sitting meditation where you initially and primarily focus on your breathing, and (3) hatha yoga postures. He recommends the informal practice of mindfulness, also, where you remind yourself to be in the present moment during all your daily activities (like eating the raisin and paying full attention to it, rather than automatically reaching for more food).

This informal practice of mindfulness is really a lot like the idea, "Stop and smell the roses." It may be helpful here to discuss mindfulness and meditation in this way to help demystify their concept and practice. When you're sitting by a fire and watching the flames dance; when you're sitting on the beach watching the waves roll on shore; when you're watching a sunset, listening to music, or doing anything you love in this passive way, this is a form of meditation. It is a focusing and narrowing of your attention on something non-threatening.

Earlier I talked about relaxation as a lengthening of muscle fibers, which requires passivity. This is different generally from recreation or my idea of "going fishing." But going fishing is a very mindful activity. Ideally, going fishing is doing what you want with passion, fully immersed in that which makes you feel most alive and fulfilled. It is all about bringing more joy and meaning into your life. And as a by-product, it will bring you peace of mind.

Think about it: When do you have peace of mind? This may be a little scary to think about actually because my experience is that you're likely to find that you don't have it very often. You'll find, though, that you usually do have peace of mind when you're going fishing – when you're doing the things you love to do. As Martha Stewart would say, "This is a good thing."

Going fishing, what we talked about earlier as seemingly selfish behavior, is the one thing you do that can bring you peace of mind. Make time for it, for you and those you love. Only now, do it more mindfully. And ideally, you would do everything mindfully, slowly and with ease. As the Tibetan Monk, Thich Nhat Hanh, says in his book, *The Miracle of Mindfulness*, "Don't do any task in order to get it over with. Resolve to do each job in a relaxed way, with all your attention. Enjoy and be one with your work."

Relaxation and peace of mind are goals of mindfulness and meditation. And remember that when you're relaxed, your body functions more healthfully. But meditation is mostly about discovering who you are, and a deep sense of connectedness. I'll talk more about this in Chapter 10. But for now understand that meditation and mindfulness are excellent approaches to becoming more relaxed.

Guided Imagery Is Mental Rehearsal

Guided imagery is a form of mental rehearsal. It is the mental picturing or thinking of a desired outcome. In the same way that you could learn something by practicing or observing, you could learn by modeling or imitating this behavior symbolically through thought and imagination. As one of the positive-thinking mantras states: "If I can conceive it and believe it, I can achieve it."

When you experience something, that perception is then represented and stored in your memory. Thousands of the same neurons are stimulated when you experience the real event and when you only imagine it. Like the placebo effect, your brain doesn't differentiate between fantasy and reality. Your brain is an information processor, and when you perceive something, real or imagined, the body responds similarly in both cases. When you took the sugar pill, your brain didn't tell you that this was just a joke. It responded to your belief, a mental representation.

Remember, thoughts are things. How you perceive something registers in your body the way you observe or imagine it. When the person took syrup of ipecac, but believed it would soothe his stomach, the belief or expectation (thought or image) of this outcome actually brought it about and even overrode the biochemical effect of the ipecac.

Imagine that you are going to eat a lemon. Imagine a bright yellow lemon. Feel its texture in your hands. Now imagine you are cutting that lemon in half with a knife. Maybe some juice squirts as you cut through the rind and pulp. Now imagine taking this juicy lemon to your mouth and squeezing it gently. Imagine the cool, but very tangy lemon juice dripping onto your lips and tongue. As the citric juice hits your sweet and sour taste buds, your mouth will almost certainly begin to salivate, and your lips pucker or face wince. Your autonomic nervous system has just physically responded to your imaginary lemon juice. There's no lemon, just your imagination, which created the physical response.

Your imagination created the same response as the actual lemon would. Thoughts are "things," a form of energy or "thought waves." One way to help you appreciate that thought is real is through the understanding in physics that at the most basic level, all matter is really frequencies or waves.

In physics we know that all physical matter is comprised of so many molecules, protons, electrons, etc. These particles are actually waves, or frequencies, or vibration. The theory of quantum mechanics states that all of perceived matter is never static, but is in a constant state of movement and can only properly be defined in terms of force fields or abstract relationships that are part of an infinite source of energy.

Your body is actually energy fields. In fact anything which exists, as we know it, is some wave form of energy. In order for thoughts to be "things" then, thoughts also have to be a form of energy, or thought waves. This might help make thought more tangible for you, and help you to understand how something which is seemingly "nothing" is as real as something physical.

Theoretically, all sound is frequencies vibrating between zero and 20,000 cycles per second. You have senses (hearing) which resonate with this range of frequencies and allow you to hear or perceive sound. At the upper end of the spectrum of frequencies which humans can sense are colors. The difference between red and orange is the frequency of a wave, or how fast the wave is vibrating. The height of that wave is its amplitude, or how strong it is. So if you were to whisper something or shout it, the frequency would be similar, but the amplitude would change.

I say this because I believe that thoughts have to be some form of energy (like sound or color) in order to exist and interact with the body, but also to point out how the intensity of your beliefs would have a greater effect than a normal thought. If you believe something strongly, it sends an amplified thought wave through your body, and thereby, has a greater impact. So when you feel highly motivated, determined, have a strong will to live, believe with great faith, etc., these thought waves have a real and intensified effect on your body and behavior. Any thought, then, true or false, real or imagined, is perceived by the senses as real and has the same electrochemical consequences as the actual event. When that thought or belief has great meaning, emotion and intensity, it has even greater consequences.

Also, while this technique of guided imagery may suggest that you have to imagine it pictorially, that is, that you have to "see" it, this is not so. What matters is your intention and the intensity of your thought. Actually, all thought has an image component. If I said "umbrella" or "olive," when you thought of these words, was your umbrella open or closed? Was your olive ripe and black or green and stuffed with pimento? If you didn't see it, you couldn't say.

One therapist I know says that when people tell him that they can't image something, he asks them if they can imagine some sexually related scene or memory. You image whether or not you realize it. But the point is, again, that what matters is your intention or purpose or goal. The thought/image will automatically be processed by your brain, and your body or behavior will be forced to respond in kind.

Remember the TV commercial, "I want to be like Mike?" Children were saying and imagining that they wanted to be like Michael Jordon. Of course imagining it doesn't make it so, especially in the case of being able to play basketball like Michael Jordon. But the fact is that you can imagine, for example, shooting a basketball accurately and literally improve your ability.

Athletes from every sport regularly use guided imagery as a way to improve their performance. In one study basketball players practiced shooting foul shots as they would normally. Another group spent the same total time practicing their foul shots, but half of that time was spent only visualizing making the shot. When tested, the group using guided imagery had 25% better accuracy at making their foul shots.

Earlier I mentioned the remarkable success that coach Bud Winter had using guided imagery with his San Jose State College track team. Richard Cox stated in his 1985 textbook, *Sport Psychology*, that perhaps the strongest evidence of the use of guided imagery in improving athletic performance came from the research of Dr. Richard M. Suinn and his visual-motor behavior rehearsal program (VMBR).

In the early 1970's Dr. Suinn was asked by a ski coach at Colorado State University to help his skiers manage their competition tensions. Suinn's method of imagery rehearsal worked so well for them that the director of the United States Nordic Ski Team program asked him to become the sports-medicine psychologist for the 1976 Olympic ski team. This marked the first time that the United States used a sports psychologist on-site for their Olympic athletes. With the help of Dr. Suinn and his VMBR program, the team recorded what was then the best performance in the history of U.S. Nordic cross-country relay teams.

As a clinical psychologist, Suinn initially used this approach to treat people with depression. It is an adaptation of systematic desensitization therapy, where muscular relaxation and imagery techniques, such as used in autogenic training, are the key features. Since 1958, when it was developed by Dr. Joseph Wolpe, systematic desensitization has been used successfully in the treatment of a wide variety of problems, including phobias.

The procedure involves three steps. First, the person learns muscle relaxation, usually through a progressive relaxation technique. Second, the person develops a hierarchy of scenes related to the phobia, going from the least anxious situation to the most anxiety-arousing. For example, if the phobia were of snakes, the first scene might be to imagine yourself with a pair of binoculars looking at a picture of a snake, which is at a comfortable distance. The next scene might be to imagine yourself looking at a picture of a snake without the binoculars. This would progress to where perhaps you would imagine yourself actually holding a snake. The third step is the actual desensitization, where you combine the first two steps: Imagine yourself relaxed and visualizing your least anxious scene relating to your fear, and continue to imagine your next scene or scenes until your relaxation gives way to anxiety. Then practice your relaxation exercise again and reimagine the scene that produced the anxiety. Continue this process until you can visualize your last scene and remain relaxed.

The underlying theory of this therapy is based on the principle of reciprocal inhibition: One cannot be anxious and relaxed at the same time. Therefore, one is taught to prevent anxiety arousal by relaxing. When you pair your relaxed state with what would normally create a phobic response, eventually the anxiety becomes extinguished. This usually is accomplished in about 20 sessions, depending on the complexity of the fear.

Interestingly, desensitization is one of the most researched and effective behavior therapies, and this method depends essentially on the production of visual imagery. You imagine yourself to be relaxed. Then, you imagine yourself able to confront your fear. Within a relatively short time, you are able to alleviate a dysfunctional condition with the use of guided imagery.

Suggestions for Using Guided Imagery

Sit quietly in a place where there are few or no distractions, and make yourself comfortable (as discussed in Benson's suggestions for practicing meditation or the relaxation response). I recommend a sitting posture, because when you are in a focused state of attention this way, you will become more relaxed and have a tendency to fall asleep. If you want to relax and fall asleep, lie down to do your imagery. Even if you've had difficulty falling asleep, doing guided imagery will still cause some people to fall asleep quite easily.

The relaxation exercise I've used most is to have people imagine that they had all the time, money, and their health and that they could do anything. Most people I've worked with imagine they're on vacation; it tends to be warm weather and near water. You can draw on your experience or your imagination. That is, you don't actually have to have been there, you can imagine it. And I recommend you really let your imagination go if you like. You can imagine you're borrowing Donald Trump's yacht, being fanned on the beach by Mel Gibson or Cindy Crawford, all expenses paid, etc. Remember that relaxation is a passive activity, though, so see yourself on the beach sitting or lying down. And draw on all of your senses.

What would your beach look like: sand, seashells, driftwood, trees, flowers, the color of the water and sky? Anyone else on the beach? You can be by yourself or with anyone else you choose. What would you hear: the sound of the water splashing gently on shore, birds, children playing in the distance? What would you feel: the softness of the clothes you're wearing, the towel, beach chair, sand, water, Mel or Cindy giving you a therapeutic massage? What would you smell: the salt in the air, the scent of flowers, suntan lotion? What would you taste: a catered tray full of food, something special to drink? And remember that perception is reality. As you imagine yourself relaxed in this way, using images that have meaning for you, your physical body begins to relax.

Another thing you can do is imagine that you're on that beach doing the mental relaxation technique of progressive relaxation. See yourself seated very comfortably on the beach, and the sun and temperature are just perfect. Feel the warmth of the sun on your toes and feet. How does it feel? As the warmth of the sun is transferred to your muscular system, your muscle fibers begin to lengthen and you literally become more relaxed. Now feel the warmth of the sun on the calves of your legs. It feels so good it's as though someone is gently massaging your calves. Now imagine the warmth of the sun on your thighs. You feel so good that you feel your body sinking into your chair comfortably. Your legs feel warm and pleasantly heavy or light, and relaxed.

If you just tell yourself to relax, it doesn't work as well as when you imagine yourself in a relaxed setting. If you were an actor and I were the director and I told you to cry, even if you were a great actor, you probably couldn't just cry. But if I knew you well enough, and I reminded you of something very sad in your life, you are more likely to cry. So, when you want to relax, don't just tell yourself that you're relaxed. See yourself in some very relaxed setting, and then do your progressive relaxation. But remember, you're likely to fall asleep doing this unless you're pretty disciplined.

You can do your guided imagery with your eyes open, if you like, but it will be much more difficult to focus your attention. There's nothing mysterious about closing your eyes to meditate or do your imagery. It helps you focus and narrow your attention.

Probably the most important recommendation is that you "see" the end result. See yourself relaxed. See yourself completely well and healthy. See the basketball going into the basket. See yourself having won the game. Remember the old Johnny Mercer song that went, "Accentuate the positive, eliminate the negative, and don't mess with Mister In-between"? This is good advice in doing your guided imagery.

In my hypnosis training I also learned that "trying" implies failure to the subconscious mind. Don't say you're "trying" to do something; say you're doing it. If you're "trying" to do something, you haven't achieved it. You're in a state of "wanting." Your mind functions more literally when you're in a state of hypnosis or focused attention. For example, under hypnosis, if you ask people to raise their right hand, they would only raise their right hand, not their arm.

There's a statement in the Bible which suggests this same principle. In the book of Mark (11:24) Jesus says, "Therefore I tell you, whatever you ask for in prayer, *believe that you have received it*, and it will be yours." In the book, *Conversations with God*, the use of prayer is explained similarly:

> You will not have that for which you ask, nor can you have anything you want. This is because your very request is a statement of lack, and your saying you want a thing only works to produce that precise experience – wanting – in your reality.
>
> *The correct prayer is therefore never a prayer of supplication, but a prayer of gratitude.*
>
> When you thank God in advance for that which you choose to experience in your reality, you, in effect, acknowledge that it is there…*in effect*. Thankfulness is thus the most powerful statement to God; an affirmation that even before you ask, I have answered.
>
> Therefore never supplicate. *Appreciate*.

And so with your guided imagery, you want to state or imagine the end result as though you have already achieved it. There is some logic to this. If your brain is an information processor, it is going to process and produce that which it is processing, just like the computer-related expression "GIGO": garbage in, garbage out. Your brain doesn't differentiate between fact and fantasy. Why would you present your brain-computer with anything less than the best or optimal outcome for it to process? This doesn't mean you will automatically achieve this ideal state, because you have years of beliefs of "not having" that now have to be balanced.

Imagine a see-saw. One end is loaded with years of experience, expectations, and beliefs that are less than perfect or ideal. In order for you to have more of what you want, you're going to have to load the other end of the see-saw with a conscious application of your new expectations.

In this regard it is also recommended that you focus on what you *want*, not what you don't want. For example, if you want to manage pain, your emphasis would be seeing and saying you feel well and improved vs. that you don't have pain. As Freud said, "There are no negatives in the unconscious." This can take great discipline. If you really are in pain, being able to imagine yourself pain-free can be difficult.

When I worked in a pain management program, people who came to it had experienced an average of five years of considerable chronic pain. We were usually their last stop. Medical approaches had been ineffective. And one of the tools I was going to teach them was guided imagery. It was usually difficult to convince them.

Imagine having five years of extreme pain, and medical treatments have not worked. Then you meet me, and I'm going to tell you, as people tended to say it, that "you can imagine your pain away." I would joke that I was glad my desk was as wide as it was, because people would have reached across to slug me for proposing something so stupid. "For all these years I've suffered, and nothing has worked, and you're going to tell me to imagine my pain away?"

I can remember a man named Bud. He had a very advanced cancer and was in a lot of pain. When I first met him and his wife, Shirley, at one of the cancer centers, and explained my program, I was sure he wouldn't attend because his energy was so low and he had considerable pain. But he came to the first evening class. I could see him in his wheelchair, shifting his body often, trying to be comfortable. As I was explaining how to use guided imagery, he leaned forward with real disgust and said, "You mean to tell me that I can imagine my pain away?" He was quite upset at this seemingly preposterous idea.

As it turned out, I didn't have to say anything in response; the class did. I was surprised how many people that night knew something about the power of the mind to heal, and began to cite many examples, including some of the research, especially with athletes. Bud settled back in his wheelchair, but I was sure he wouldn't come back to the next class, either because he thought I was crazy or because his physical condition wouldn't permit it.

At the end of class I gave out an audiotape of a mental exercise to have them imagine themselves well. They were to practice their guided imagery at least once each day. The next class, Bud showed up. He was still in bad shape, but actually feeling a little better. He came back to all six classes. But now Bud had a real dilemma: His prognosis at the beginning of the class series was that he would live only two months; now his two months were almost up and he was feeling pretty good. "What should I do?" he asked.

Bud and Shirley literally loved to go fishing. And now Bud wanted to buy a new boat! Can you imagine this? Medically, Bud was supposed to be dead in a matter of weeks, and he wanted to buy a ten thousand dollar new boat. With all of his medical expenses, and the fact that he was supposed to die, that's what he wanted to do. What would you have said to Bud?

Obviously I didn't recommend he buy the boat, but I couldn't tell him not to. They bought the boat, and Bud didn't die. They told me time and again that that summer was the best time of their lives. And while this is one of those special stories, the real point of this was how dedicated Bud was to doing his guided imagery. He took his audio tape and tape player with him everywhere. He used it daily on the boat or wherever he went.

Not all of Bud's days went well. He had some ups and downs along the way. When Bud finally did die, Shirley buried him with his audiotape and player. They were so grateful to have learned about guided imagery, and were certain that it was why Bud lived so long and did so well. I, too, believe that Bud's belief in imagery and use of that tape made a difference.

Another recommendation for doing guided imagery is that you use images that have meaning for you, real or symbolic. For example, if you wanted to imagine your immune system functioning properly, you could look up in a book what white blood cells look like, and imagine/think about them in an anatomically correct way. But your symbolic representation of them would work equally as well. Remember it's your intention that is most important.

I remember having a woman in class who was a cell biologist. She knew what white blood cells and cancer cells looked like, so I thought that when she did her guided imagery she would imagine their biologically correct function. She said she imagined PAC MAN™! She said that PAC MAN™ (the computer game where the pie-shaped figure chases the dots and invariably gobbles them up) was a perfect representation of how the immune system works in the body. Once the immune system identifies a foreign substance (and it always does when working properly) it then seeks it out and "eats" it.

Your immune system basically does three things: (1) It works like a perfect radar system; it knows what should and shouldn't be in your body. (2) Once it identifies the foreign substance, it seeks to neutralize it as white blood cells in great numbers surround and destroy the foreign substance. (3) Then the mop-up crew comes in. Another part of your immune system functions to clean up the debris created from this violent activity and eliminate this waste material from the body primarily through the urine and stool. So, another way you could imagine your immune system working to keep you well is in this "militaristic" way.

I remember when I had an Amish woman in one of my classes, and she said that she didn't want to imagine all of that violent activity in her body; could I suggest another image? Because of her religious beliefs, I thought she might appreciate a prayerful use of imagery. Prayer is actually a form of guided imagery. Remember when I cited Jesus' statement, "Pray believing you've already received"? It's an excellent description of guided imagery.

I asked this woman if she could imagine when she prayed that God's perfect healing energy would come in through the top of her head and begin to fill her body. Then, like progressive relaxation, she could systematically imagine it going through her body. She also thought of this energy as a translucent blue-green light. Once her head was filled with this light energy, I told her then to imagine what it would feel like to know that her head was filled with God's healing energy. Then imagine this energy filling her entire body. Her belief in God and God's power to heal (it was meaningful for her) would contribute to the effectiveness of the guided imagery.

When I worked at the rehab hospital, I often would pray with my patients (only once I knew this was okay with them). What I actually did was use guided imagery, but within the framework of a prayer. I would "pray" and have patients imagine God's healing energy coming into their bodies, and then see themselves getting better. I went to one of the medical directors to explain what I was doing and why. I knew word would eventually get out that I was praying with patients (who loved it!) and that I would be criticized for doing something inappropriate. Kind of sad, isn't it? But I knew if patients believed in "prayer" it would function like a placebo and contribute to their healing.

If you believe in prayer, as most people do, I strongly encourage and recommend that you pray. For scientific reasons alone, because of the placebo effect, if you believe in the power of prayer it probably will help you. Please remember the earlier comments about prayer of gratitude vs. prayer of supplication, however. Pray in the present or past tense, knowing, not hoping, that God answers prayer.

I noted earlier that Dr. Larry Dossey is one of the leading experts on the power of prayer and the practice of medicine. I strongly recommend his book, *Healing Words*. In this book he talks about the use of prayer, and concludes that the best way to pray is that which "intuitively *feels* best." Some people are more comfortable "telling God what to do," a more directed, guided imagery form of prayer. Some prefer to pray deferring the outcome to God, "Thy will be done," vs. praying for a specific outcome. The Spindrift organization in Salem, Oregon, has researched various forms of prayer such as the more directed or nondirected forms of prayer, and found that both work. Dr. William Braud, professor and director of research at Palo Alto's Institute of Transpersonal Psychology, has concluded that there are five things which generally could contribute to the effectiveness of prayer: (1) relaxation and quiet, (2) training in some focused-attention technique, (3) guided imagery, (4) intentionality, and (5) positive emotions.

5

Explanations for the Effectiveness of Guided Imagery

When I wrote my doctoral dissertation about guided imagery, I surveyed the literature and found 10 hypotheses to explain the effectiveness of guided imagery. I presented this information at The Institute for Guided Imagery Conference in Toronto in 1987, but it has never appeared in print except in my dissertation. I'd like to list and describe these hypotheses now for a couple of reasons. I believe that giving people a rationale for how guided imagery works can build their belief, confidence, and expectations, and therefore affect a greater outcome. Also, because I am not aware of anywhere else where this information exists, I think it could give some direction for future research to delineate and examine further the interactive nature of mental processes, physiological systems and self-regulation.

I have tried purposefully to not be too technical in explaining these 10 hypotheses, but some of you may find this section tedious. You may want to jump ahead to the next section on biofeedback on page 63.

1. **Guided imagery is a form of modeling based on learning theory.** Individuals need not experience an event directly to learn from it. They can view others and learn vicariously via live models, film, or imaged events. You can model your own imagined behavior.

2. **Guided imagery is mental rehearsal of alternate coping strategies.** Rehearsal of a behavior generally leads to improved performance of that behavior and the probability that the behavior will become a more pronounced alternative. Mental practice allows for re-examining one's options, which enhances a position of flexibility in dealing with future situations and decision-making, and produces a more adaptive pattern. One's coping ability determines the relationship between stress and disease; therefore, mental rehearsal of constructive coping skills

could contribute to one's health.

3.   **Guided imagery gives a sense of self-control and confidence.**
The things we fear in reality, we also fear in our imagination. If
we no longer fear something in imagination, it follows that we
could have a greater sense of self-confidence and control in the
actual situation. The image that one can be personally effective
and competent would balance thoughts of hopelessness and
helplessness. Guided imagery gives individuals the feeling that
they can rely more on themselves to control their own destiny,
and a greater sense of self-control and independence.

4.   **Guided imagery is a form of positive distraction or healthy
escapism.** The use of imagery with chronic pain is strong
evidence that one can distract one's self very effectively to
inhibit a pain response. When you're busy doing what you like
to do in reality or imagination, you tend to forget your aches and
pains. Imaging something positive would keep one from
thinking or worrying about negative consequences or pessimism.
Focusing on positive accomplishments can reduce self-critical
attitudes and feelings of depression or helplessness.

5.   **Guided imagery acts as a placebo or expectation effect.** If one
believes or imagines that something should have a certain effect,
this attitude can lead to real behavior or physical health changes.
Autogenic approaches clearly have been demonstrated to self-
regulate health, and the belief alone that guided imagery is
effective could have self-fulfilling consequences.

6.   **Guided imagery is a form of information processing.** Imagery
is an innate way that the brain processes information. The central
nervous system appears to convert mental images into nerve
impulses, which then affect physical functioning. Every
experience is transposed into thoughts and images and influences
our actions. The brain processes verbal information sequentially
and less efficiently than visual images which are parallel in
processing form. Thus, the autonomic nervous system responds
more readily to imagery than to verbal instruction alone.
Research with deaf subjects, who never received any language
training, supports the brain using imaginal processes. These
subjects who had no speech or verbal capacity learned to
associate one picture with another (implying the operation of
imagery) as well as children who could hear, tested with similar
materials. It follows that one could change behavior or physical
functioning by altering the cognition or image process that
guides behavior or function.

7.   **Guided imagery has somatic and emotional components.** There

is now substantial evidence that the nervous and immune systems are interconnected, and that both mundane and severe stress can alter immune responses. Stress is often a perceptual event; that is if you think something is stressful, the body tends to respond stressfully. It's like the saying: "What's one man's meat is another man's poison." The meaning or emotion that accompanies the thought/image determines if or how much the perception affects a somatic response. Many studies document the effectiveness of imagery producing the same autonomic and affective responses as a real stimulus would, such as Jacobson's and Suinn's research cited earlier. When people imagined bending an arm or lifting a weight, in each instance the same neuromuscular response was measured as occurred in actual performance. The same thing happened when an Olympic skier actually skied downhill or only imagined it. In their book, *Beyond biofeedback*, Elmer and Alyce Green concluded that this affirms the psychophysiological principle:

> ...Every change in the physiological state is accompanied by an appropriate change in the mental-emotional state, conscious or unconscious, and, conversely, every change in the mental-emotional state, conscious or unconscious, is accompanied by an appropriate change in the physiological state." This principle, when coupled with volition, allows a natural process – psychosomatic self-regulation – to unfold.

8. **Guided imagery affects brain wave production and states of consciousness.** States of consciousness include more obvious subsystems such as the waking state, hypnagogic state (between waking and sleeping), sleeping and dreaming. Altered states of consciousness include those one does not commonly experience and that do not occur spontaneously such as in meditation, hypnosis, and states induced through psychedelic drugs. Focused attention techniques such as meditation, hypnosis, and guided imagery produce greater amounts of the lower brain waves, alpha and theta. Normal awake and alert behavior tends to produce mostly the higher range of beta brain waves. The production of the lower brain waves is associated with decreased oxygen consumption, blood pressure, muscle tension, and respiratory and heart rate. These are the opposite of a stress response. Guided imagery and altered states of consciousness, then, could promote

wellness through stress reduction.

Elmer and Alyce Green have developed and tested a theta-training program at the Menninger Foundation for use in psychotherapy. When one is awake, theta brain waves are associated with a state of reverie and feelings of psychological well being. Using a blend of yoga (a breathing exercise), autogenic training (relaxation and guided imagery), and biofeedback training (knowledge of the results), they have found that this theta-training technique produces a deep sense of reverie and psychological integration (reduction of neurotic and psychosomatic symptoms).

9. **Guided imagery involves greater right hemisphere brain use.** It is generally recognized that the left hemisphere of the brain is more involved in processing verbal and logical information, while the right hemisphere is involved more in the processing of spatial, intuitive information. The right hemisphere also appears to dominate during dreams, hypnosis, meditation and related altered states of consciousness. Dr. Arnold Lazarus proposed that our schools and culture have imposed more logical, analytical, and verbal methods of learning, and have suppressed right hemispheric intuitive abilities causing detrimental imbalance in one's functioning. Deliberate use of altered states of consciousness, such as in deep relaxation and guided imagery, could be a way of creating a better balance and harmony between the left and right hemispheres of the brain. Any enhanced harmony of functioning, as such, could contribute to one's increased feeling of well-being and health.

10. **Guided imagery is consistent with holographic theory, quantum mechanics, and theoretical physics.** Dr. Karl Pribram, Professor of Neuroscience at Stanford University, suggested that like the hologram, every brain cell contains the pattern of the total organism, which is stored throughout the brain in waves and images. Some believe, therefore, that imaging is the "language" of the brain, and guided imagery would be a very effective and efficient means of communicating within the brain's frequency domain.

Dr. David Bohm, Professor of Theoretical Physics at the University of London, believed that there is an infinite sea of energy that unfolds to form space, time, and matter. All of reality is a manifestation of a deeper energy, order, and reality, which is not manifest. Physical matter is a very gross form of energy, but there are other subtler forms of energy that interrelate with all other forms of energy/matter. He further postulated that underlying all of these energy patterns or vibratory rates is a "Primary Reality" which is the source of all other realities.

Dr. Pribram suggested that our brains mathematically construct "concrete" reality by interpreting the frequencies or vibratory patterns of this primary reality. Like Bohm, he posited that without a brain and physical senses to interpret reality within the limits of these senses, that the world would be an organization of frequencies flowing out of an underlying energy matrix or force field of harmony and order. This correlated with the theory of quantum mechanics that all of perceived matter is never static, but in a constant state of movement and can only properly be defined in terms of force fields or abstract relationships that are part of an infinite sea of energy.

According to Marilyn Ferguson, implicit in this theory is that harmonious states of consciousness are more attuned to this primary, underlying reality. Attunement, then, would be difficult in states of anxiety and stress, and be facilitated by such states as relaxation and meditation.

Similarly, since thoughts are things (a wave form of energy of some kind), when one is in a deep state of relaxation and imaging a particular outcome, these thoughts while in a state of harmony would resonate with the underlying energy matrix of harmony and order (Primary Reality) and could become manifest in reality. The thought/image/prayer could actually potentially create reality, or the visualization could act as the guiding form or pattern for the energy to materialize.

Biofeedback Is Essentially Guided Imagery

Biofeedback is essentially guided imagery with biological feedback to build your confidence that your guided imagery is working. A common question regarding guided imagery is, "How do I know it's working?" You need some kind of feedback or indication that it is. Feedback is essential in learning and mastering any skill.

Earlier we talked about relaxation techniques and how they affected blood flow. When you're more relaxed, your muscle fibers lengthen and your blood circulates better. This can be easily demonstrated. If you were to hold a thermometer between your thumb and forefinger, you would get biological feedback of the temperature of your thumb and finger. Hold onto the thermometer until the temperature reading stabilizes (as you would if you were going to check your core body temperature by putting a thermometer under your tongue). Then record the temperature (which will be considerably lower than your core body temperature of about 99 degrees, and, therefore, much easier to change). Now close your eyes and do some mental relaxation technique. After a few minutes I will almost guarantee you that the temperature on the thermometer will have raised. You became more relaxed, blood flow increased in the extremities of your body, and the temperature went up in your thumb and finger. You now know that the relaxation technique works.

This is how biofeedback works. By measuring an external, biological change, you come to know and believe that your use of guided imagery can affect a physical outcome. The most common ways to measure this change are with skin temperature and muscle tension. Sensors are placed on a finger tip (as above) to measure skin temperature as an indication of the dilation of blood vessels, or placed on the skin to detect electrical activity related to muscle tension in that area.

As explained before, the effectiveness of guided imagery is affected by the intensity of your belief. When you first hear about the power of beliefs, mind over matter, guided imagery, etc., and are given the evidence that it works, it builds your belief and confidence. You now *hope* that it works for you. But there's a big difference between hoping and knowing. Biofeedback gives you the direct feedback that you can do it. You now *know* that it works. You did it and got the immediate feedback that you can use your mind to affect your body.

One story I often tell is about patients I worked with in the rehab hospital. While most people came in because of having had a stroke, people were admitted regularly due to amputations and the need for physical therapy. People commonly had a leg amputated due to diabetes and poor blood circulation. They usually were concerned that because of the diabetes and poor circulation that they could lose the other leg, too. I was glad then to be able to explain how they could learn to voluntarily control and increase their blood flow.

Actually I found that people usually were quite skeptical about other than medical approaches. The fact is that most people didn't even give me a chance to demonstrate biofeedback with them and how it might "save" their other leg. I tell you this again as a reminder to be gentle with yourself and others when you don't do everything you could do to help yourself. It is important that we respect our individual differences and choices.

When I was given the opportunity to help, I usually began by explaining that biofeedback is just a scientific way to explain some common sense. I would remind them about when they learned a very important medical technique called, "Kissing it and making it better."

We have all learned as children or as parents this medical marvel. If a child fell and skinned a knee or elbow, for example, Mom or Dad said to come home so that they could kiss the "boo boo" and make it better. It works beautifully. However as adults, we've become too clever and we think this only works for kids. You can relearn that this works as well for adults as it ever did for children.

The technique I used then was to have patients imagine that they had all the time, money, and their health, and what they would do if they could do anything. I mentioned this technique before when I talked about relaxation and guided imagery. In the meantime, I would have placed a thermometer between the toes of the good leg, and got a stabilized temperature reading and recorded it. Following the imagery exercise we would check the thermometer reading again. I never had an instance where the temperature didn't raise a minimum of four degrees. Norman Cousins, doing research at UCLA using a more hypnotic technique, said the temperature would raise a minimum of 10 degrees.

If you had just lost a leg due to poor blood circulation, do you think this would get your attention? The biofeedback, which was the thermometer reading, would build your knowledge, confidence and belief that the guided imagery could work. Chances are you would approach the use of guided imagery the next time with a much greater confidence and expectation of its benefit, which would only tend to enhance its effectiveness.

When I lecture I find that most people don't know what biofeedback is, and almost no one has ever used it. This is interesting because there's so much research demonstrating the use of biofeedback with a large number of physical illnesses from migraine headaches to cancer. According to Dr. Jeanne Achterberg, in her book *Imagery In Healing*, "Biofeedback is even more thoroughly documented and studied than most medical protocols, including drug and surgical procedures." The extensive clinical and research evidence is "that every physical function that can be measured...[with biofeedback] can be controlled or regulated to some extent."

In 1963, Dr. J.V. Basmajian published research in the highly respected journal, *Science*, demonstrating that you can affect the function of a single cell in the body with biofeedback. Some of you may be familiar with the early research and pioneering work of Dr. Barbara Brown and her books, *Stress and the Art of Biofeedback*, *New Mind, New Body,* and *SuperMind*. Earlier I mentioned the research of Elmer and Alyce Green at the Menninger Foundation. The 1974 film, *Biofeedback: The Yoga of the West* by Hartley Productions, documents some of their research and the unusual abilities of Swami Rama, Jack Schwartz, and others. All of these resources document extensively the effectiveness of biofeedback.

One of my favorite books which has influenced me is *Why Me* (It has been retitled, *I Choose Life*), written by Garrett Porter and Patricia Norris in 1985. Patricia Norris is a psychologist at the Menninger Foundation and daughter of Elmer and Alyce Green. Garrett Porter was then a 10 year-old boy with an inoperable brain tumor. In their book Dr. Norris explains how she taught Garrett biofeedback and how to warm any part of his body, which led to the remission of his cancer:

> It was not hard for him to believe that since he could send blood where he wanted it, and since white cells travel in the blood, he could send white cells wherever he wanted to also. It was not hard for him to direct his internal states, but then came many months of practice and hard work. And Garrett and I both came to know that what he learned to do others can also learn to do. That's why we wrote our book. Garrett resents it greatly when others call his elimination of his brain tumor a miracle. I wrote in the book of a number of other cases of the same sort of psychophysiological healing, and there are hundreds, probably thousands, of others across the country, written about by other people, recognized and unrecognized. I think if our cultural beliefs supported it, and people were taught how, almost everyone would be able to reverse many illnesses, including cancer, soon after they were diagnosed. Unfortunately, many patients are not encouraged to try self-regulation therapies until all else has failed.

As Dr. Norris said, "Some belief, hope, and confidence...are essential." Biofeedback and learning how to self-regulate the body give one a sense of control, optimism, and decreased feelings of helplessness. Biofeedback is simply the body responding to your thoughts and feelings in a measurable way.

I have one last suggestion related to your use of guided imagery in biofeedback. Earlier I said that I believe it is important to imagine the end result, such as, "Pray believing you have already received." While this is recommended, another approach may also be helpful.

Another common practice in biofeedback is to see your condition improving gradually so that the guided imagery doesn't seem unrealistic, "crazy," or "too good to be true." If you're in great pain, imagining yourself now pain-free may be too much of a leap for you. A realistic sense of control may be more believable. And this is the key: Do that which feels right and has meaning for *you*, that which you can believe in.

Trigger Mechanisms

Another way to enhance the effectiveness of guided imagery is through the use of "trigger mechanisms." These "triggers" are a form of conditioning, which was demonstrated in the classic experiment by John B. Watson, the founder of the behaviorist movement in psychology. In this experiment Watson conditioned a fear of furry objects in a young child.

The child enjoyed playing with white laboratory rats, but as part of the study, when the boy now reached to play with a rat, Watson made a loud noise. After seven pairings of the rat and the noise, the boy began to react to the rat with fright but without the noise. Later testing demonstrated that this fear of rats could be generalized to other furry objects. Without any further conditioning, this same boy also produced frightened behaviors in response to other similar stimuli such as a rabbit, dog, fur coat, and a Santa Claus mask. A conditioned fear reaction had been established through this process of respondent conditioning, which is similar, of course, to the research of Ivan Pavlov where he paired the ringing of a bell with a salivation response in dogs.

I want to give other examples of this type of conditioning to help explain the effectiveness of guided imagery and trigger mechanisms. If someone were bitten by a dog, the next time that the person sees a dog, he or she is likely to feel threatened and move away from the dog. Dogs now could become a trigger mechanism causing feelings and behaviors such as fear and withdrawal.

Imagine that someone took a child for a doctor's appointment, and the doctor was wearing a white lab coat. Whatever the child's experience or reaction to the person, the child now is likely to respond to other people similarly who are wearing white lab coats.

If a person were to receive chemotherapy and have a nausea reaction to the drugs, anyone or thing associated with the administration of those drugs could now become a trigger mechanism for a nausea response. In fact an example of the term "anticipatory nausea" could be where a person driving a car to the doctor's office to receive chemotherapy could become nauseated before even getting the drug treatment. The association between the drugs and nausea were so well established that simply anticipating his or her treatment and reaction to the drugs could nauseate the person.

A similar example of this was with a woman I knew who would become nauseated from receiving chemotherapy for treatment of her cancer. One day she was shopping in a grocery store, and normally she wouldn't expect to see her doctor in this setting. But she said that when she turned the corner of one of the grocery aisles, there was her doctor, at which time she proceeded to throw up. This medical oncologist became a trigger mechanism for her nausea.

I'd like to give one last example before I explain how you can create your own trigger mechanisms to bring about more of what you want in a very positive way. In a true case study, a woman worked as a secretary, and was normally quite competent and productive. But she would cry occasionally at work, and eventually she went to her supervisor and asked to resign because her crying was interfering with her work. The woman was granted a leave of absence and began to see a psychologist to help her understand this crying behavior.

As part of her treatment the psychologist asked the woman to allow her subconscious mind to recall an experience that could account for her crying. (I'll explain this therapy in more detail in Chapters 9 and 12.) The woman remembered herself as a young girl going to church one Sunday morning. Following the church service, the girl returned home and witnessed her house burn to the ground. This was a very traumatic experience for her. However, what the psychologist also discovered was that a church bell was ringing in the distance as the girl watched her home being destroyed.

As an adult, where this woman worked as a secretary, there were numbers of churches which rang bells throughout the day. At a subconscious level, whenever the woman heard these church bells, it triggered the recall of the early traumatic event related to her home burning down as a child. Church bells became a trigger mechanism for her crying behavior.

Clearly we can become conditioned by any number of trigger mechanisms to respond in a conditioned way, whether or not we realize it or are conscious of it. So, why not create our own trigger mechanisms to bring about more of the responses we would like to have happen? With the use of guided imagery or self-hypnosis, you can tell yourself that whenever a certain event takes place, it now triggers a particular response.

Whenever I would work with athletes using guided imagery to mentally rehearse their performance, I would include a trigger mechanism related to the sport. For example, golfers could tell themselves that whenever they grip the golf club it triggers the perfect performance. Baseball pitchers could say that whenever they touch the baseball it reinforces their throwing the perfect pitch. Similarly, you could say whenever you see your team's colors, that it brings about your ideal athletic performance.

Remember that perception is reality. You can perceive something to be true, whether or not it really is true, and create that reality. That's how "sugar pills" or placebos work. Your brain doesn't distinguish between fact and fantasy; it responds to your perceptions and beliefs. If unwittingly you can be conditioned through your experience and perception of dogs, lab coats, and bells, then you can create your own trigger mechanisms to bring about what you want.

In the guided imagery exercises that I used in the "Taking Control of Your Health" program, which I've included in the Appendix in the back of this book, I included a trigger mechanism to reinforce each exercise. The guided imagery script for the first class included the statement, "And anytime you smile or see anyone else smile, it reinforces this renewed enthusiasm for life you now have, and strengthens the patterns and expectation of improved health and control over your life." The guided imagery script for the second class states, "And anytime you think of water in any way, it causes you to become instantly relaxed and calm, and everything about your body now functions and continues to function in a perfectly healthy, normal and balanced manner."

I suggest that you use a particular trigger mechanism for only one result. For example, you could say that "water" triggers you to become relaxed, but you wouldn't use water to trigger a perfect athletic performance also. You don't want to dilute the effectiveness of a trigger by pairing it with more than one outcome.

I also recommend that you closely tie your trigger mechanism to the subject of your guided imagery. If you want to lose weight, your trigger mechanism may be "anytime you think about food." If you want to have less stress at work, your trigger could be "anytime you hear a telephone ring." If you want to improve your golf game, your trigger might be "every time you grip the golf club."

If you take guided imagery and trigger mechanisms seriously, there likely are many things you'd like to change or reinforce. However, if you don't tie your trigger closely to that outcome, you risk becoming confused. Was "water" used to reinforce relaxation or for something else? Was "hearing a telephone ring" a trigger for weight control or stress management or to stop smoking? You will find that guided imagery and trigger mechanisms are excellent tools you can use to affect every aspect of your life.

6

Simple Recommendations for Nutrition and Physical Exercise

Nutrition – You'll Feel Better

Considerable research exists confirming the benefit of nutrition in health care. Some confusion has been created, however, with the seemingly endless number of new diets that we hear about so often, especially those promoted for losing weight. If we really knew what was right to eat, especially to lose weight, there wouldn't be so many new books promoting everything from eating only grapefruit and hard-boiled eggs to any number of liquid concoctions.

Part of the problem, I believe, is related to psychological factors. As I said earlier, an overweight condition may be an inappropriate way to get your needs met. If being overweight is some kind of protective or coping mechanism for you emotionally (unconsciously), then eating properly is not enough to lose weight. You're going to have to deal with the underlying psychological causes, too.

The approach to diet or nutrition that has always made sense to me is one followed by diabetics. These people clearly have to watch their sugar or calorie intake, in particular, and this condition has been studied at great length. So, a good basic nutrition plan would be to follow a diabetic diet.

Every major health group tends to recommend a similar diet. The American Cancer Society, The American Heart and Lung Associations, etc. all follow similar dietary guidelines. However, Dr. Dean Ornish's research with heart disease suggests that these conventional guidelines of 30 percent fat and 200 – 300 milligrams per day of dietary cholesterol are not enough. He found that the more people changed their diet by lowering their fat intake, the more improvement they showed in their coronary artery blockages. The diet he recommends is only 10 percent fat and five milligrams of cholesterol per day. This low-fat, vegetarian diet is considered relatively extreme by many, but Dr. Ornish's research showed that all but one of his patients were able to stop or reverse their heart disease. The comparison group, which received standard medical treatment and followed the conventional dietary guidelines of the American Heart Association, all got much worse.

Dr. Ornish believes that "eating fat makes you fat." He believes it can also give you heart disease and is associated with other diseases including cancer, strokes and all other causes of death.

All foods are made up of fats, proteins, or carbohydrates. Each gram of fat has twice as many calories as protein and carbohydrates. A diet higher in calories is linked to increases in many diseases, including cancer. Low fat foods, which are high in complex carbohydrates, are very filling. High calorie foods such as sugar and alcohol are simple carbohydrates and are not as filling, and you're likely to eat more food (and calories) when your diet has more of these. Also, our body converts high fat foods more easily into body fat and increases your blood cholesterol level. And this seems to be key: It's not the amount of food or calories you eat that's the problem, it's how many of those calories come from fats, especially saturated fats such as tropical oils, whole milk and whole fat dairy products, and red meats.

A vegetarian diet has no cholesterol and usually has few saturated fats. Cholesterol comes from animal products such as meat, chicken, fish, and dairy products. A diet low in cholesterol and saturated fats will reduce your blood cholesterol and blood pressure and your risk of heart disease (which kills more people than all other diseases combined). But even if your blood cholesterol is low, eating high cholesterol foods still increases your risk of disease and death.

While Dr. Ornish's research clearly supports a role for nutrition in reversing heart disease, his program is much more comprehensive, including exercise and stress management. Exercise and stress management also lower blood cholesterol and blood pressure, and are major factors in health and disease. While it is difficult to say how great a factor this low fat, vegetarian diet was in reversing heart disease compared to the other components of the program, eating a healthier diet certainly played a role and *just makes good sense.*

People from all walks of life, and certainly athletes, know that if you eat a high carbohydrate, low-fat diet you feel better and have more energy. A big problem for people, though, is that we have grown up eating a high fat diet, usually four to five times more fat than Dr. Ornish's "Reversal Diet." We've become conditioned to believe that fatty foods taste good, and it is difficult for many people to adjust to eating a more vegetarian diet. "Rabbit food" is what a vegetarian diet is. Who wants to eat that, rather than a good steak, butter, pastry and ice cream?

Many times, unless your back's against the wall (you've just had a heart attack, for example), you won't really alter your diet much. Change itself is difficult, and you've become conditioned to like the higher sugar and fatty foods. The fact is, though, that you can learn to like more healthy foods if you'll give them a chance.

Chances are many of you used to drink pop or soda, which has a very sugary taste. And today you drink diet soda. The regular soda now seems excessive, too sweet. Similarly with milk: You used to drink whole milk. Now if you drink 2% or 1% or skim milk, the high fat milk tastes especially thick and heavy and not as good. As you decrease your use of sugars and salts to flavor your food, your taste buds become more sensitive and you can savor the subtle favors of the natural food, which can become very appealing and delicious. You will learn to dislike the taste of fats and sugars, which will seem too rich or oily.

But you have to want to do it and give it enough time. Don't wait until you have a heart attack or cancer to begin to eat a healthier diet. I strongly recommend the book, *Dr. Dean Ornish's Program for Reversing Heart Disease*, as one of the best books and programs for preventing or reversing any disease. It has excellent guidelines for nutrition, and also for exercise and stress management, which I'll talk about later. But I want to say more about the psychological part of nutrition, and that I believe no one diet is right for everyone.

I mentioned early in this book that I have experimented personally with a number of nutritional approaches, including vegetarian, fruitarian, raw foods, and fasting. I became convinced that all of the approaches had or could have benefit, but not for everyone. And they didn't affect the physical symptoms (my hay fever) for which I was most motivated to change my diet. I believe too often that there are exaggerated claims made for a particular diet and how it can cure any number of things. This is not to say that certain diets and foods cannot have benefit. The American Cancer Society and the National Cancer Institute recommend a low fat, more high fiber diet, including foods rich in vitamins A and C. They also recommend you minimize your consumption of salt-cured foods and alcohol.

Dr. Andrew Weil also has become a well-recognized expert and proponent of natural approaches to health, including a low-fat, vegetarian diet. These approaches are documented in his best-selling books, *Spontaneous Healing* and *Eight Weeks to Optimum Health.*

Dr. Weil believes that cutting our fat intake is important, but maybe only to 20 to 30 percent of total calories. Actually, Dr. Ornish says that you don't have to cut your fat intake to 10 percent if you don't have heart disease. His prevention diet allows for 15 percent fat intake. But both are clear about saturated fats: Reduce them. This is primary.

The second most important consideration is fiber, which is found in all whole grains, fruits and vegetables, and is not in any animal products. Refined foods like white flour and white rice are less healthy because much of the important fiber has been removed in the refining process. Fiber is important in the function of elimination (bowel movements) and in the absorption of cholesterol and carbohydrates so that our blood cholesterol and sugar levels stay at a healthy level. But before you increase your fiber intake, check with your doctor or nurse if you have a digestive-related disorder. A high fiber diet is not recommended for some intestinal or bowel conditions.

The next most important element in nutrition, I believe, is your approach to it. If you approach dieting with the attitude that, "Now I have to give up everything I like," you're off on the wrong foot. And I believe this is why most diets don't work – you've taken the fun out of them.

You don't have to give up everything. Moderation is the key, usually, even with sugar, salt, and caffeine. You definitely want to lower your saturated fat intake, and this is becoming easier to monitor since most foods list the amount of their saturated fats. But there's a time and a place to cheat.

I had a great friend, Dorothy, who had seemingly every known medical problem. I first met her in the rehab hospital when she was admitted for a stroke. But she had had cancer, diabetes, arthritis, etc., and she was overweight. Over the years we became very close, almost to the point of dependence. I made a point to phone her every week and she seemed to "live" for my calls. I mean that in a good sense. Dorothy responded very well to my friendship and support.

At one point she was making an extra effort to diet and lose weight, especially because of diabetes and a heart problem. She had eaten as recommended by her physicians, but she wasn't losing weight. And the following week was the family reunion, which meant there was going to be lots of food, most of it not on her diet. Relatives came from considerable distances for this affair, and usually visited for about a week, even though the actual reunion was just one day. They were full of fun. And, of course, joy stimulates digestion (it makes you want to eat), and eating is usually a big part of social gatherings.

Well, Dorothy decided that she had tried hard and long enough to diet, and now she was at least going to enjoy herself for a week. The following week she said that she ate everything wrong – and lost weight! Now, I'm not suggesting that you can eat anything you want, just because you like it and feel good, and that you'll lose weight as a result. I'm trying to make the point of not taking the fun out of dieting or nutrition. Again, I believe that moderation is the key. But on special occasions, the psychological benefit of "cheating" may outweigh the seeming advantage of never eating high fat or high calorie foods.

Remember, if you eat healthier, you'll feel better. It's really that simple. You're changing the way you eat to feel better. Give it a chance. And enough time. But don't make it so restrictive (unless you have a significant reason like a heart attack) that it's hard to follow and stay on. It is excellent preventive medicine and will reduce the amount of disease by allowing your body to function efficiently and more healthfully.

Billions of dollars are spent each year on fad diets, vitamins and supplements. The fact is that if you eat a wide variety of foods (particularly fruits, vegetables and whole grains), you will have limited need for supplements.

Eat more slowly. It takes 15 to 20 minutes for your brain to get the message that you are no longer hungry. This way you'll eat less food. It is also a good occasion to practice mindfulness. Take your time and appreciate each bite of food. And eating mindfully will have greater benefits than just sound nutrition.

Eat when you're hungry rather than sitting down to a more traditional large meal. Keep nutritional snacks handy. Have carrot and celery sticks ready to eat in the refrigerator. Keep a dish of raisins or other dried fruit near your favorite chair where you tend to sit. Don't buy foods you don't want to eat. One woman told me how she eats a bag of potato chips while watching TV. If you don't have them, you can't eat them.

Dr. Michael Lerner, one of the leading authorities on complementary cancer treatments, has written a wonderful book, *Choices in Healing*. He summarized the nutritional literature: "nutrition appears to hold considerable promise in cancer prevention, in reducing the side effects and augmenting the benefits of conventional treatment, in enhancing general health and quality of life, and in some instances in extending life with cancer." If you are under treatment for cancer (chemotherapy or radiation), he recommends that you eat a nutritious diet for strength and energy to deal with both the cancer and the therapy. A multivitamin and the antioxidant vitamins A, C, and E may be helpful "to ensure your nutritional needs are met, especially as you go through hospitalization and treatment, which may cause nutrient deficiencies."

Michael Lerner reports that most of the research on nutrition and cancer has been done supporting its role in prevention. And, unfortunately, believe it or not, studies have not been done testing the therapeutic benefits of nutrition with cancer. This lack of scientific evidence and the fact that physicians have little or no training regarding nutrition usually results in cancer patients being given little information or support when they ask their doctor about diet or nutritional supplements.

Physicians are appropriately concerned when claims are made suggesting that nutritional approaches can cure cancer. That research has not been done. (Note that there is also no research showing that nutrition doesn't have therapeutic value.) But given the extensive existing research demonstrating nutrition's role in preventing cancer, the same dietary approach would seem to be reasonable for treatment as well. Perhaps, as Michael Lerner proposes, we should not dismiss nutrition's role in cancer treatment because it hasn't been demonstrated to cure, and it is reasonable to consider nutrition as a complement to effective cancer and patient management.

Physical Exercise – Use It or Lose It

The benefit of physical exercise for health-promotion is well-researched. Aerobic activity and yoga practices have been proven consistently to increase health. But, again, with cancer, Lerner reports that the research has been focused on prevention:

> *One very striking gap in the literature on exercise and cancer is that there are no studies that I have been able to find assessing the effect of exercise on an existing cancer – only cancer prevention.* Indirect evidence, however, shows the benefits of physical activity for people with cancer. The line of reasoning is that enhanced functional status or performance status is a predictor of better outcomes in some cancers, and "functional status" is a synonym for capacity to be physically active. Similarly, most oncologists regard a person who is in good physical shape as potentially more resilient to treatment.
>
> The absence of studies of the effects of exercise on survival in people with cancer is as striking as the paucity of psychological and nutritional cancer survival studies. It reflects the same astounding medical assumption that what we eat, think, feel, and do while we have cancer can have no possible effects on the outcome of established disease, and therefore that the subject is not worth studying.

Research with athletes suggests that as one becomes more lean and fit, it can protect against cancer. Non-athletes can have twice the risk of breast and reproductive system cancers. This effect may be modulated by reducing estrogen levels. Exercise can also reduce depression, which is common with cancer. Depression normally compromises immune function. Therefore, exercise could lower cancer risk because of its anti-depressive effect.

Scores of studies confirm that physical activity has dramatic health benefits. And you don't have to do extended, prolonged aerobic exercise to make a difference. Aerobic exercise is any activity that is continuous and vigorous. A good measure of aerobic activity is if it elevates your heart rate, but you are able to carry on a conversation while active. If you get out of breath, slow down or rest. People who are physically inactive have about twice the number of heart attacks and heart disease as those who spend half an hour a day walking, swimming, golfing, bowling, gardening, dancing, or doing daily work around the house. Some activity is definitely better than none.

This moderate level of activity is also associated with the reduction of a number of other diseases. Exercise burns off calories, lowers blood pressure, increases blood flow and oxygen and energy levels. It also makes you feel better about yourself. When you're doing something, you generally feel better than when you're the stereotyped "couch potato." Physical exercise will also help to metabolize the excess hormones released into the blood during stress. I'll explain in the next chapter how these stress-related chemicals literally can kill you.

If your physical condition is such that you can't exercise much, do what you can. And if that activity includes an element of fun, you'll find that it will be easier to do and for longer periods. Remember my early example of my friend who normally couldn't walk across the room without getting out of breath, but when he would look for his favorite mushrooms, he could walk for hours without difficulty? Walk with a friend or your dog. Play with your children or grandchildren. Walk in a flower garden or any other setting where you forget that this is exercise. It's fun.

The shopping mall is a good example of combining a chance to be physically active and window-shopping or socializing. Walk leisurely until you're tired. Then sit and rest on a bench and talk with friends. When you feel rested, walk to the next bench. Socializing has additional benefits beyond the physical activity. I'll say more about that later, too.

Your body is a lot of muscle. This suggests that you were meant to be physically active. And the feedback your body will give you if you're not relatively active is that your muscles will weaken and your health will decline. You use it or lost it.

7

Stress and Stress Management

Medically, stress is the rate of wear and tear on your body. It is the response of your body to any demand. In fact, stress is all about change and adjustment. The greater the adjustment you have to make to any life situation, the greater the stress reaction and potential for the harmful effects of stress.

Your body produces extra hormones like adrenaline as a survival mechanism. Dr. Walter Canon, a physiologist from Harvard University, proposed in the 1930's his "fight or flight" theory as a way to explain this natural response to stress. Whenever humans feel threatened or stressed, the endocrine system automatically produces extra hormones, which put the body into a heightened state of arousal. In the most basic way, this prepares you to protect yourself, to fight or run away. This would have been especially useful for early human beings like cavemen and women. As hunter-gatherers trying to survive in the wild, having an automatic response to perceived threats would have been very helpful. But what happens in a more sophisticated living situation where fighting or running away is not usually the optimal way to solve problems?

Imagine you're driving a car, exceeding the speed limit, and get stopped by a policeman for speeding. Your endocrine system automatically responds to this stressful situation by pumping extra hormones into your blood as part of the fight or flight response. So, now imagine that you either punch the policeman or speed away. Not so clever. But what happens to these hormones which have been produced by your body as a response to your upset if you are not physically active at that time? You may be surprised to know that most are eliminated within hours primarily though your urine and stool, once you settle down and feel less stressed.

But according to Dr. Hans Selye, a neuroendocrinologist and one of the foremost pioneers in stress research, some of these hormones are insoluble and remain in the body. The evidence of this is what you call "liver spots" or "aging spots." It is a form of chemical scarring whose direct cause is the stressful event. But remember it's not the stress, but how you coped with the stress that caused these "spots." We tend to think that these so-called aging spots are age-related, when, in fact, they are stress-related. It's just that the longer you've been alive, the more chances you've had to deal with stress and accumulate these stress marks. I call it "keeping score."

According to Dr. Selye, another novel example of how we know stress registers in the body is the loss of the elasticity of the skin. Again we tend to think that as our skin and parts of our body begin to sag, it's due to the aging process. But according to Dr. Selye's research, the primary reason for this sagging is stress-related.

Any number of products are promoted commercially to help you make those aging spots disappear or to tighten your skin. I, of course, support you however you choose to conduct your life, including things that might appeal to your sense of vanity. But, with all due respect, if you really want to reduce some of the physical evidences of aging, GO FISHING.

When you "go fishing" you have less stress for more than the obvious reason that you're enjoying yourself. I'd like you to make a list of all the things that irritate or upset you. Your list will tend to be quite long in a relatively short time. One of the things that used to be on my list was the smell of cigar smoke. One day when I was going over my list, I got to thinking about how an old friend I called Uncle Jack used to smoke cigars all the time. I loved being around Uncle Jack. He told the greatest stories. Then I got to thinking how I would normally not like being around cigar smoke, but when I was with Uncle Jack, who always smoked cigars, I wasn't even aware of the smoke.

When you feel better about yourself or your situation, the things that "bug" you will tend to "bug" you less – or maybe not at all. When you "go fishing", you will be less aware of the things that normally irritate you. And if you're not aware of them, they can't upset you.

One of the unique features about stress is that stress usually isn't stress unless you think it is. Imagine that we were going to test whether or not a stressful event actually affected the body. We could draw blood from a room full of people and measure their hormone levels. We could check muscular tension, also, to know their current state of relaxation or tension. Now imagine that we introduce a stressor, a great big menacing snake. The probability is that this would be unsettling, and these people would try to get away from the snake. Once we isolate the snake safely from the people, and draw blood to check hormone levels again, do you doubt that there would be elevated amounts of hormones associated with a stress reaction?

But what if someone in that group were deaf and blind, and didn't know that there was a snake or that the others were alarmed? The probability is that this person's hormone levels or muscular tension would not have changed. And, what if some of these people were actually fond of snakes? Maybe they're wildlife enthusiasts and even have pet snakes. Do you think these people's hormones or muscles would have responded like the rest of the group?

It wasn't the snake that caused the stress reaction. It was their perception of the snake. If you don't think something's stressful, it isn't. And if you're not aware of it, it can't affect you. So, when you're fishing, when you're feeling more at ease, things that bother you won't bother you as much or maybe not at all.

Learning to Roll with the Punches and to Keep Perspective

Another key to stress management is learning to "roll with the punches" and be more flexible. Stress is a given. When do things stop changing in your life? You are constantly adjusting to or coping with any number of problems or concerns. Therefore, you can't eliminate stress, but you certainly can learn to manage it better.

Remember when you were raising your children? How many times, literally or symbolically, did you throw your hands up in the air and say, "I have no idea what I'm doing"? The kids could be so challenging and so stressful that you nearly went out of your mind. But somehow, some way, you managed. You learned to take the good with the bad, and realized that things have a way of working out. And it went better as you realized that you weren't always in control. And even better, if you realized you couldn't always be in control, and that it didn't matter. Often when you tried to insist on your way, it only tended to increase the resistance from your children. So you learned to roll with the punches, when to back off, and what it would take to coexist more peacefully.

When you have good days, do you tell yourself that things will always be good? When you have bad days, do you tell yourself that things will always be bad? In my experience you're more likely to tell yourself when things are bad that they're going to stay bad. But, in reality, you know that on the way from point A to point B, it's never a straight line. You have good days and bad days. And, hopefully, in time, you discern how to have more good ones than bad. One way you discover this is by learning to roll with the punches and keeping perspective.

Another way that you can help yourself to manage stress, then, would be to try to catch yourself as early as possible when you're feeling stressed, and remind yourself that it's only temporary and that your fretting about it is not helping anything. Dr. Richard Carlson makes this point very well in his book, *Don't Sweat the Small Stuff...and It's All Small Stuff*. We have a way of blowing things way out of proportion, and living our lives "as if they were one great big emergency!"

One thing I tell people to say to themselves when things are not going the way they think they should is, "Tell God the next time to check with me first." If there's an all-knowing and all-loving God, and God has a unique plan for all of us, do you think that God doesn't have a pretty good idea how things are going? And what's best for us? Did God make a mistake? "God, how come you didn't do it my way? You should have checked with me first!" Hopefully, you see how silly this seems, and the need to keep perspective. Remember the serenity prayer (my paraphrased version!): "God, grant me the wisdom and courage to change the things I can, but that I not get too goofy when things don't go the way I think they should." Keep perspective. And remember that it's easier said than done. Be gentle with yourself and each other when you're not always "whistling while you work."

Stress Can Kill You

But back to the seriousness of not managing stress so well: It can kill you. I tell you this, not meaning to scare you, but to help you understand the importance of learning to cope with stress. Remember that your doctor isn't likely to prescribe stress management as part of your medical treatment, so you tend to think that it isn't that important. Think again.

When I was writing my doctoral dissertation, I read a book called *Is It Worth Dying For?* by Dr. Robert Eliot, a cardiologist and one of the world's most respected stress medicine specialists. As a cardiovascular consultant to the U.S. government in Cape Canaveral in 1967, Dr. Eliot found aerospace workers dying of heart attacks at an alarming rate. He proposed that this was due to the stress of being fired and having no transferable job skills. As the government started to make the space race a lower national priority, these highly specialized professionals didn't know, day to day, whether or not they would have a job.

> Physical and laboratory exams of engineers at the Cape showed no unusual levels of the standard coronary risk factors. What I found instead were anxiety and depression and a universal, pervasive feeling of hopelessness and helplessness. Cape Canaveral families led the nation in drinking, drug-taking, divorce, and sudden heart attack deaths. The space workers were a whole population suffering from the acute stress of knowing that at any moment they could lose their work, income, status, and identity as skilled professionals.

What Dr. Eliot found was that adrenaline and other stress chemicals were in all autopsies of sudden cardiac death. These excess hormones, produced by a constant fight or flight response, literally had ruptured the muscle fibers of their hearts and killed them.

The importance of job satisfaction is demonstrated similarly in what Dr. Larry Dossey calls the "Black Monday Syndrome" in his book, *Meaning and Medicine*. Most heart attacks take place at nine o'clock Monday mornings, "the very hour on which the new workweek begins."

> The health risk of being chronically unhappy in a job has been known for some time. In 1972 a study done in Massachusetts for the Department of Health, Education and Welfare found that the best predictor for heart disease was not any of the major physical risk factors (smoking, high blood pressure, elevated cholesterol, and diabetes mellitus) but *job dissatisfaction.* And the second best predictor was what the researchers called "overall happiness." This finding fits with the fact that most persons below the age of fifty in this country who have their first heart attack have *none* of the major physical risk factors for coronary artery disease.

Dr. James Muller of Harvard Medical School did an extensive survey and found that not only do most heart attacks tend to occur around 9:00 A.M., but that the data with strokes was even stronger. Most strokes happen between eight and nine in the morning, and happen the least between three and four in the afternoon. "Sudden deaths" in general happen twice as often at 9:00 A.M. than at 5:00 P.M. when they're the lowest. The best explanation reported seemed to be related to job satisfaction and what Dossey calls "joyless striving." When people feel trapped, helpless, hopeless, and their lives or jobs become meaningless (or worse, their jobs mean something they despise), their health is at risk.

Dr. Eliot came to the same conclusion about what he called a "joyless struggle." Many people get to a time in their lives when they become quite disillusioned, like the old Peggy Lee song, "Is That All There Is?" Dr. Eliot believes that when people work to gain what society values rather than developing their own sense of identity and self-esteem, they feel a loss of control over their lives. Dr. Eliot said that when he had a heart attack himself, he became acutely aware of what causes chronic stress:

> It took a heart attack for me to make some new choices, to get out of the trap of joyless struggle. Now after twenty-two years of research on stress and the heart, I am convinced that the question "Is that all there is?" is the best clue to the cause of harmful, long-term stress: the sense of being

trapped, hopeless, and helpless to get what you really want
out of life.

How Stress Contributes to Chronic Disease

While chronic (long-term) stress clearly can have serious health
consequences, so can short-term or acute stressful experiences. Dr. Hans
Selye believes that when one experiences stress, it affects the body in a
different way than just the fight or flight response. When you perceive
something as stressful, it manifests itself in the body by picking on the
weakest link in the chain of the body.

For example, imagine that there were a room full of people, and a man
came into the room and began to terrorize them. He started shooting a gun
and threatening, although no one was actually shot or even touched. But
these people genuinely feared for their lives. In this example I'm trying to
create a situation where you could imagine everyone truly would be stressed.
According to Dr. Selye, these people are all likely to develop physical
symptoms as a direct result of excessive stress. Their endocrine systems
would have been forced into over-drive, and these people would also require
medical attention related to the weak links in their bodies breaking down.

If one of those people's weak link were the respiratory system, that
person could now develop asthma, hay fever, or some other lung or bronchial
disorder. If another person's weak link were the digestive system, that person
could develop ulcers or some other kind of digestive distress. If someone's
weak link were his or her derma or skin, then this person could develop
symptoms of eczema or psoriasis or some other skin-related condition.
Everyone could have developed specific symptoms as a result of this very
stressful event, and all of their symptoms could have been different
depending on their "weak link."

To help me make a point, and to develop Dr. Selye's theory further, let
me give another example (with a bit of a sense of humor). Imagine I stepped
on a nail and it really hurt. Now imagine I went to the doctor who examined
my foot and he said, "No wonder your foot hurts! You've got a nail sticking
through your shoe into your foot!" So now the doctor gives me my medical
options for treatment: (1) He could anesthetize my foot so I didn't have to
feel the nail or pain. (2) He could put a thick pad in my shoe to distance the
nail from my foot. (3) He could cut my foot off, or (4) He could pull out the
nail. What is going to happen to my symptoms, once we pull out the nail
(assuming no other complications like infection)?

The point is that if the people who were terrorized are going to change
their symptoms, they could go to the doctor, which would be advisable.
Make no mistake, I would encourage them to seek medical attention for their
symptoms. That's what medicine really is: symptom management. But if

these people don't "pull out the nail" (that is, if they don't deal with the precipitating event of the stress of the fear for their lives), their symptoms will continue. They'll be anesthetizing their foot indefinitely.

Many people in the mind-body medicine field today agree with Dr. Selye's theory. Again, if someone develops medical symptoms, medical attention is recommended. But you may want to think about what was going on in your life at the time of your first symptoms. Actually, symptoms don't usually manifest overnight. So it is usually suggested that you think back over the last 18 months. Was there any major stress that went unresolved? Until you pull out the nail, you risk chronic symptoms.

For example, when I ask people when they first became aware of their symptoms/condition, I'm careful to note what they say in addition to mentioning a particular date in time: "It was two weeks after my younger brother died," or, "It was when I got engaged to my wife," or, "During my first final exam at college." In theory, unless you deal with the psychological factors underlying your physical or emotional symptoms, the symptoms will continue and require regular and indefinite medical management to suppress them. The problem won't just go away, and you'll be left with chronic disease.

Many people think that if they just put enough time and distance between themselves and major stressful events in their lives, that the problem eventually does go away. Nice try. To that I say, "Your memory is perfect; your recall is faulty." Everything that you have ever experienced is in your memory, whether or not you remember it consciously. And it continues to affect you all of your life, unless that experience is modified therapeutically, which I'll talk about in Chapter 9.

The Most Stressful Thing You Can Do or Have Done to You

I want to tell you now what I think is the most stressful thing you can do or have done to you. But I want to preface it with a story that I hope will help me make my point.

One day a man was watching television. During a commercial he had the remote control and was "clicking" around to other channels. He came across a talk show, and the guest was a 100-year-old man. The gist of the conversation was "To what do you attribute your longevity? How is it that you have lived to this ripe, old age?" If you've watched enough of these shows, you have to wonder about the interviewers, guests, and their responses, and God only knows what they might say. But when the old man was asked how he had lived to be 100, he said, "Because I've never had an argument with anyone in my life."

You could see the surprise and disbelief immediately in the interviewer's face. "Did you really say that the reason you've lived this long is because you've never had an argument with anyone?" And the old man said, "That's right." The host responded incredulously. He clearly didn't believe this could be true, and began pointedly to analyze the seemingly preposterous response. "One hundred years, times 365 days, times 24 hours, times 60 minutes, times 60 seconds; you mean to tell me in all that time that you've never had an argument with anyone?" And, again, the elderly man said, "That's right." The interviewer became quite upset. His face reddened, his posture became aggressive, and, basically, he yelled at his guest, "You can't tell me that in 100 years you've never had an argument with anyone!" And the gentleman said, "You may be right."

What's the moral of the story? One way to say it is, "If you argue with a fool, it's hard to tell who the real fool is." What did the older man have to gain by arguing with the interviewer? And what I'd really like to have you think about is this: When was the last time you had a major disagreement with someone and you said, "You may be right"?

When you really disagree with someone, you're prone to argue. Yet chances are you saw the wisdom in the elderly man when he chose not to argue with the host. Actually, if you think about it, when was the last time you had a serious disagreement with anyone and got them to change their mind? You'd think we'd catch on.

What I think is the most stressful thing we can do, or have done to us, is criticism. It is the epitome of, "Don't be yourself." Chances are you know people, who make you feel when you're with them, like you're "walking on egg shells." You're never quite sure if you're dressed the right way, saying the right thing, etc. How do you feel then? Not relaxed or at ease. Hopefully you also know people, who when you're with them, it wouldn't occur to you to think about how to be. You can be yourself. How does that feel?

If I could speak for all of us, I'd say that the one thing we're looking for is peace of mind. How do you get peace of mind? By running around trying to please everyone else? Or by being yourself?

As I said before, you're likely to find that you don't have peace of mind very often. It's the one thing we all want, and we don't have it much of the time. My experience, though, is that the one time you *do* have peace of mind is when you "go fishing," when you're doing what brings you the most joy and meaning.

Now I'd like you to think about any subject that you think you know a lot about. When will the day come that you'll know everything about the subject? Most people respond, "Never." This suggests that not only can you never know everything about a particular subject, but that you can never have complete knowledge about any subject. You were born to screw up. The crazy part about this, though, is who knows what "screwing up" is?

Remember the fable about a father and son loading their donkey to go to market? They have a great distance to travel, and they'll pass through many small villages along the way. They start off walking. When they get to the first village, they hear someone say, "You'd think one of them would ride that donkey; they have such a long distance to go." So, the father puts his son on the donkey, and they proceed. When they get to the next small village, they hear someone remark, "Look at the young son riding the donkey making his older father walk." So, the boy gets off the donkey, and the father gets on. When they get to the next village someone says, "You'd think they'd both ride that donkey." So, they both get on the donkey. In the next village someone comments, "Look at that poor donkey all loaded down with the father, son, and their goods for market!" Now imagine the next scene. The father ties the front legs of the donkey together. The son ties the back legs of the donkey. And they carry the donkey to the next village. What's the moral of this story? (*You can't please everyone.*)

But another very interesting question is, "Which villager was right?" Most commonly, people say, "None of them." But what I'd like you to consider is that all of them were right. Every villager had a different opinion, and yet they all were right. How could they all be different, and all be right? Because everyone has a different truth. Everyone is different, and has had a different life experience about what he or she believes is right or wrong. Who has the truth?

In my seminar, "Taking Control of Your Health," I ask someone to volunteer his or her phone number. I don't need a name, just a phone number. The reason why I don't need a name is because we'll call him or her, "Mr. or Mrs. Know-it-all." The next time any of us want to know what to do in a particular situation, we'll just call Mr. or Mrs. Know-it-all, and they'll tell us what to do! Hopefully you realize how preposterous this is that anyone could be so unreasonable as to think that he or she could actually know it all and could feel good about advising everyone else about what they should do. Actually, the scary part is that we probably do know people who really do think they know it all – and are not reluctant to tell you how to do anything.

I'd like to offer my own words of advice: Peace of mind comes when you realize you'll never have it figured out, you'll never be in complete control, and it doesn't matter.

If you'll never know everything about a particular subject, which means you'll never know everything about any subject, then, hopefully, you can appreciate the folly or arrogance of criticism. The fact is that you can't even know for certain what's right for you, let alone for someone else. The only thing that's crazier than criticism is paying attention to the person being critical. They don't know any better than you what's right for you. They just think they do. And the really good news about this is that if nobody's got it all figured out, then why be so concerned and upset when others are critical of us? It's laughable. Criticism isn't criticism unless you think it is.

Remember Archie Bunker from the "All In The Family" television show? We could laugh at his being so opinionated and his belief that everyone should think like he does. Who still wants to volunteer their phone number and be Mr. or Mrs. Know-it-all?

Now this doesn't mean that people can't offer "constructive" criticism, but, as the saying goes, "It's not what you say, it's how you say it." What is your real intent when you're critical? Is it to be genuinely helpful, or a conscious or unconscious effort to control others? Why do we have a need to be right?

I'd like you to think of someone who is really expert at what he or she does, someone who is truly the best at something. For example, imagine someone going up to Michael Jordon and saying, "You're the worst basketball player I've ever seen." What do you think Michael would say at that time? Do you think he would argue? I think he'd probably smile and say something like, "Yeah, one day I'm going to finally figure out how to play this game." Food for thought: When you know, and you know that you know, there's no reason to quarrel. When you're not sure is when you're prone to argue.

Another thing you may want to think about is something I learned early in my psychology training: What people say about others, says much more about them than it does about others. Think about the infinite things people could state about others. Why do they say a particular thing? Because it has special meaning and relevance to themselves. You've heard about the psychological concept of "projecting" your perceptions onto someone else. One example of this is "scape-goating," where people blame others rather than taking personal responsibility for themselves. Similarly, there's the concept of "mirroring," where others reflect back to you your own issues. Think about the things that "bug" you, or that you love about other people. That's you. You may want to consider this.

Sometimes criticism is misplaced aggression. Remember the line in the song, "You always hurt the one you love, the one you shouldn't hurt at all"? When you're stressed and unable to get what you want, frustration builds. Eventually it becomes the proverbial "straw that breaks the camel's back." Then you're going to strike out at the most convenient target. And that's usually the person who's around the most, your husband or wife, for example. When a husband yells at his wife, it has nothing to do with her. She's just the most available prey for his venting. He's likely frustrated out of his need to be in control, and now he's going to express his frustration. Ideally, she would see the situation for what it is, and not be upset by his temper tantrum.

But being yelled at is not fun or funny. How does it feel to be criticized, especially if it's done in a mean-spirited way? You feel hurt, belittled, disempowered, and resentful. What if at the moment of being criticized, however, you could have the poise and remember it's not about you? It's all about the person who's being critical. What if the next time someone was truly critical of you, you remembered the 100-year-old man story, and said, "You may be right"? How would you feel then? Chances are you'd feel much more empowered and much less stressed.

This doesn't mean that you can't or shouldn't speak up and assert yourself. Remember it's not what you say, it's how you say it. Let me recommend a diplomatic way to be assertive.

Imagine that you are attending a class in international diplomacy. Because of different cultures, people are going to have different ways of doing things, and different beliefs. Since your way, your cultural conditioning, is different, imagine being taught immediately to establish that your way is right and theirs is wrong. I hope you see how silly this last statement is. Diplomatically, you would be taught to be respectful of their ways. In the same way that you have come to believe what you believe through your family, community, and cultural training, so are other people exposed to and shaped by their culture. Which is right?

So, start by first acknowledging their beliefs or way of doing things: "I understand and respect why you believe or do what you do." Also, if you will never know everything about anything, you need to understand that they really may be right. Even if you totally disagree with them, they may be right. Scary, isn't it? But true. Once you acknowledge their position, then state your own: "And this is what I believe, or what I would do." You start by respecting their position, and then state your own (no yelling, swearing, name-calling, etc.). This doesn't mean that they're automatically going to respect your position, but you increase the odds that they will. You have a perfect right to speak up for yourself, and it will go better if you listen and attempt to understand their point of view, rather than assuming and insisting that your way is better.

Our concern about wanting to be right or to criticize others or ourselves comes from our own insecurities. You learned this primarily in early childhood, and I'll talk about how this happens and what you can do about it in Chapter 9.

One of the things I grew up with was the value placed on deer hunting. I mentioned this early in the book. I'd like to use deer hunting as an example of cultural conditioning and how we learn "rights" and "wrongs." Just because we learned to value something, and think it's right, doesn't necessarily make it so.

When my sister got married, she moved to Ft. Lauderdale, Florida, to raise her family. Ft. Lauderdale does not close public schools to allow deer hunting. Actually, there are places in Florida where they close public schools for the first day of the rodeo, but nowhere in Florida do they value deer hunting like they do in Pennsylvania, where the Monday following

Thanksgiving is the opening day for buck season.

My sister came home one Thanksgiving holiday with her two young daughters. My nieces were surprised to hear their uncles and others talking with such excitement about deer hunting. This was new to them. Finally, my youngest niece spoke up and said, "Do you mean you're going to shoot Bambi?" She was a little disturbed and distressed.

Now, is deer hunting right or wrong? If you're thinking anything other than it's a learned value, and has nothing to do with right or wrong, you will have missed my point. If you were born and raised in Central Pennsylvania, you're likely to think deer hunting is very right. But if you're from another place where deer hunting is not such a big deal, then you're more likely to question the rightness or wrongness of deer hunting. I know there is clear logic in wanting to control deer herds, but my point here has to do with the fact that your beliefs and values are strongly conditioned by your society, and these values can be very different (and not right or wrong) depending on your cultural conditioning.

I used to work at the Schuylkill Cancer Treatment Center in Pottsville, Pennsylvania. Many of our patients came from a nearby town, Higgins. Every year Higgins, Pennsylvania, makes the national news: the pigeon shoot! Every Labor Day weekend people gather for this traditional event, and many attend to protest what they believe is a very inhumane event. Is pigeon shooting right or wrong? If you were born and raised in Higgins, do you understand that you're more likely to think it's right? But if you were raised in another part of the state or country, you're less likely to think shooting these birds in this way is a good idea. Learned values.

One more example: toilet paper. Which is the right way to put the toilet paper on the roll when it has run out? When I ask this question in my classes, I always get a variety of responses, often split between the toilet paper rolling "over" or "under." I remember when an engineer tried to explain, based on the law of gravity, why it should roll a certain way! People usually have pretty strong feelings about the right way to put the paper on the roll. In fact, a great number of people are so invested in their ways, that even when they're a guest in someone else's home, they turn the toilet paper around! You may laugh, which usually happens in my classes, but this is not funny. Imagine someone turning your toilet paper around!

Now let me tell you the right way to place the toilet paper on the roll. (This usually evokes even more laughter.) Of course the right way is *your* way. If you really believed that there were a better way to do it, you'd switch. But what happens when your "right" way differs from someone else's "right" way? At some point we need to learn respect for individual differences. People are different. Who really knows the right way? Mr. or Mrs. Know-it-all? How are we going to learn to get along with one another if we keep insisting on our way? And this is the crazy history of our world:

People are so invested in their way of doing things, that, at the extreme, if you do it differently, they'll kill you! Think about wars and what has gone on for all of recorded history. People's cultural conditioning is often at the root of war. "My way is better than yours." When will we learn?

Some Additional Things You Can Do to Defuse the Stressful Effects of Criticism

There are tribes around the world where, often at puberty, adolescents go through any number of rituals. And as odd as they may seem to someone whose culture does not practice that particular ceremony, please appreciate that their way is as right and has as much meaning for them as any ritual you may practice.

I'm sure you've seen pictures of tribes' people with any number of kinds of markings on their bodies, objects through their noses, unusual forms of dress, etc. In one tribe in Brazil, adolescents have a very large disc inserted in their lower lip. I'm sure many of you have seen this. What was your first reaction when you first saw this approximately six-inch in diameter disc in their lip? ("Isn't that interesting." "What a creative way to adorn your body." "I'm going to have to ask my plastic surgeon if I can have that done.") I don't think so. People usually make a face and say something derisive like "that's stupid," "ridiculous," or some other critical statement. But understand if you were born and raised in that tribe, you'd have such a lip, and think it was the right thing to do.

Please understand in my next suggestion that I am in no way meaning to be insensitive or demeaning or in any way disrespectful. One way you could remind yourself that people are different, and that it's perfectly okay to be different and to be yourself, is to see that person who's being critical of you standing there with a six-inch disc inserted in his or her lower lip. Remember that this is related to people now being mean-spirited and critical of you. Again, where normally you would feel demeaned by others being critical of you, how would you feel now? You'd probably smile instead, and their criticism would be like so much "water off a duck's back." We want to stop the stressful effects of criticism right in their tracks.

My next recommendation is the most popular for people in my classes. Earlier I talked about the folly and arrogance of criticism, that some people actually believe they know everything and what's best for you: "Why can't everyone be like me?" The next time someone is critical of you, and you don't want to feel belittled, under your breath, say, "You have no idea how arrogant and stupid you really are!" This usually makes people smile. Instead of feeling demeaned and stressed, you could really feel empowered and see the situation for what it really is. But, remember, don't say this one out loud, say it silently to yourself. While this may not be the most ideal and loving thought you could have at this time, the point is to stop the stressful effects of criticism. I'll give a more loving alternative later.

One time I was on the radio being interviewed and a woman called the show to say that she was recently divorced, but that her ex-husband was still going way out of his way to interfere and make her life miserable. "What should I do?" she asked. My first thought was, "I have no idea what you should do." I say this because it was true, but, also to remind you that if you think you should always know what to do at any moment, it's just not realistic. When will you know everything? What did occur to me to say, however, because she really did sound upset and angry, was "Chances are he's the last person on earth you want to let you feel this way." "That's right," she said. So, I told her, "The next time he does something that would disturb you, tell him, 'You're the last person on earth I'm going to let turn me upside down like this!'" How do you think that would feel? Rather than getting frustrated and angry, you could put the situation in perspective immediately, and stop the stress and distress.

If you think about it, it is *we* who give others the power to make us feel bad. And it's usually the people or things that we would want to bother us the least that we let get to us! Think about the people and things that annoy you the most. They can't upset you unless you let them. Rehearse saying, "You're the last person or thing I'm going to let affect me this way!"

Another example is a story about a friend, Mike, who used to work for a "boss" (I hate that word) who seemed to enjoy being critical. One day at work he started yelling at my friend, and was so loud and "carried on" so much, that a crowd actually gathered to watch this "boss" berate him. Apparently he called him every name in the book, and Mike just stood there and took it. This went on for some time before the boss finally stopped and stomped away. Then another person went up to my friend and said, "He was so out of line. Why didn't you just knock his block off?" Mike said, "I guess he had to blow off a lot of steam, so I thought I'd let him blow it off on me. If he had done this to someone else, that person might have knocked his block off." What do you think about how he handled this? Was he a wimp? Or did it take real courage and insight to resolve the matter this way? Had he yelled or fought back, what would likely have happened? Remember the 100-year-old man story?

When I was growing up, one of the dumbest things I thought I ever learned was in Sunday school. I was taught that if someone hit me, I was to turn the other cheek. I never could figure out how this possibly made sense. Now I don't pretend to understand fully the point of turning the other cheek, but the above story would seem to be such an example. The psychology of aggression is that a bully needs someone to squirm. What if you don't squirm? Eventually the bully will leave you alone. And isn't that the point?

I was also taught in Sunday school that there was a Jewish law that said,

"An eye for an eye, and a tooth for a tooth." Moses said that you were to return evil for evil. Then Jesus showed up and said that this was not such a good idea. You were to return good for evil: "Love your enemies, do good to those who hate you, bless those who curse you, pray for those who mistreat you" (Luke 6:29.)

I've tried to think about what it must have been like during the time of Jesus. For generations there were established laws, which you would assume were wise and had served some good purpose. And then comes along this upstart, Jesus, who some claimed to be the Son of God. For all of your life you've believed one way, and overnight you're supposed to change completely, even if this is the Son of God? In real life, how do you think this is going to work? Do you think that people are going to be able to just transform and return good for evil? Change can be difficult.

So imagine Jesus instructing his disciples, and explaining about this new way of doing things, because he really believes that there is wisdom in returning good for evil. But if he were the all-knowing Son of God, he would certainly know that this is not going to be easy. They've believed this law of Moses for a long time. But, having the Christ Awareness, he wants to pass along what he believes will make life better and easier. So he says to his disciples, "It is important, and a loving thing to do, to teach them a new way of living. But, of course, they're not likely to just buy into our new teaching. But, because I'm the Son of God, and I know what's right and true, if they don't accept this new way of doing things, argue until you're blue in the face. And, if necessary, beat it into them!" What do you think?

Interestingly, immediately following the verses about turning the other cheek is another well-known verse, "Do unto others as you would have them do to you" (Luke 6:31.) As this chapter of Luke continues, Jesus tells his disciples again to "love your enemies...and you will be sons of the Most High...Be merciful...Do not judge, and you will not be judged. Do not condemn, and you will not be condemned. Forgive, and you will be forgiven" (Luke 6:35-37.) You reap what you sow. So, another way to handle criticism is to be loving, in spite of the ill will directed at you. "Can a blind man lead a blind man?" (Luke 6:39.)

I remember a story about a man who would buy a newspaper each day from a newspaper stand. The man who sold the paper was always gruff, but the man purchasing the paper was always pleasant. One day a friend was with the man while he was getting his paper, and he observed how kind his friend was, while the vendor was anything but amiable. As they walked away, the friend asked, "Why were you so nice when that guy was such a creep?" The friend responded, "I guess I never want anyone else to decide how I should act." Who do you want to determine how you should act? Who do you want to control you and how you want to be?

So, another way you could respond to criticism is to say, "I love you." It will drive them crazy. And because their behavior will not have been reinforced (you only participate in behavior that is rewarded), eventually they will leave you alone. And, again, isn't that the point?

This will require practice. It's normal when you're criticized to feel belittled, put down, hurt, disempowered, and resentful. You're then prone to cower or to argue. This is not going to change without your rehearsing handling the criticism differently. Imagine someone being critical of you, and now see yourself responding in a way that feels right for you (here are some examples):

1. "You may be right." (Remember the 100-year-old man story.)
2. "It's their issue, not mine. What people say about me, says much more about them than about me."
3. Listen to the person being critical, and then calmly acknowledge the other person's position and state your own.
4. See the person who is being critical with a large disc inserted in his or her lower lip. People are all different, and we need to respect our differences.
5. "You have no idea how arrogant and stupid you really are."
6. "You're the last person on earth who's going to make me feel like this."
7. You can stand there and take it. Let them vent.
8. You can say a prayer for them that you hope they'll soon realize the consequences of their behavior. Is that behavior causing people to want to connect with them and be with them? Pray they'll recognize their own fears and insecurities, and understand their misplaced aggression.
9. "You reap what you sow."
10. "I never want anyone else to decide how I should act."
11. "I love you."

8

Some Big Questions and Answers

Did I Cause My Illness?

This is a very sensitive and controversial subject. Did you cause your illness? I don't have a simple answer to this question, but let me try. Most illnesses have many factors as a cause. We know today that poor nutrition, lack of exercise, and inadequate stress management are all major contributors to disease. We used to think that smoking and drinking alcohol were actually glamorous and "cool." We now know that exposure to any number of environmental pollutants like car fumes, factory emissions, chemicals, etc. all can compromise our health.

A July, 2000 study published in *The New England Journal of Medicine* analyzed almost 45,000 pairs of twins in order to assess the risks of cancer at 28 anatomical sites for the twins of persons with cancer. The authors of this research, headed by Dr. Paul Lichtenstein, reported, "We conclude that the overwhelming contributor to the causation of cancer in the populations of twins that we studied was the environment." It was suggested that cigarettes, poor diet, lack of exercise, radiation and pollution were the likely environmental factors. While many people believe that hereditary or genetic factors are the primary cause of cancer, this study concluded that they contributed only about 10 percent for nearly all sites of cancer.

Clearly heredity can predispose people to certain kinds of ailments. For example, predisposition to diabetes can be inherited, but according to Dr. Selye, "it depends largely upon the ways the body reacts to stress whether or not a latent diabetic tendency will develop into a manifest disease." We know that heredity can play a role in breast cancer. Women who have a close female relative, such as a mother or sister, who has breast cancer, are more likely to develop breast cancer themselves. The interesting part of this is that the great majority of women who have this family history of breast cancer will not develop breast cancer. What causes a predisposed genetic factor to result in the actual disease?

It's very interesting to realize that of the major risk factors for heart disease (smoking, high blood pressure, elevated cholesterol, obesity, and diabetes mellitus), the best predictor for heart disease, as I said before, is job dissatisfaction. Several major studies report that people's opinions of their health (is it good, fair, or poor?) is a better predictor of who will live or die over the next decade than objective medical data such as physical examinations, lab tests, symptoms and even cigarette smoking. The subjective meaning you give to your job or your health is a better diagnostic tool than medical technology.

Remember how I said earlier that we probably have cancer cells in our bodies all of the time? We have hundreds of viruses and bacteria in our bodies all of the time, as well. Why aren't we always sick? Medically we know that the immune system normally identifies and keeps these foreign substances from getting out of control and becoming a disease. But the research is very clear that stress can compromise the immune system. If your immune system is suppressed by stress, and stress is largely only stress if you think it is, then clearly you can play a role in affecting how your body resists disease. You may not like the idea that how you managed the stress in your life could really lead to your risk of disease, but it's a fact. Most of the major diseases of humanity are controlled by your immune system. And your lifestyle dramatically affects immune function.

Chances are you never had any systematic training in stress management, largely because our understanding of stress and its role in health is relatively new. When you were younger and learning lots of social behaviors, eating whatever you wanted and smoking cigarettes, they were thought to be relatively benign habits. So now that you do know that these things can take your health, do you want to feel guilty for increasing your risk for disease when you didn't know any better? But ignorance is no exception to the law. Your life history of poor nutrition, exercise and stress management can contribute to the onset of illness.

The very positive part of knowing that there are lots of things you can do to affect your health, is that now you can begin to take control of your health. By eating and exercising and managing your stress better, you can help yourself get well and stay well.

The most common approach to health care historically, over time and across cultures, is shamanism. When people get sick they go to the tribal medicine person (shaman) who prays about what they need to do to heal. The answer is always related to people being out of balance spiritually or with community values. Sickness is thought to be a positive messenger that says you need to re-balance spiritually. This suggests that spiritual factors could also affect the disease process.

This belief is practiced commonly today in many cultures and religions around the world. Illness is looked at as a blessing in disguise because it forces you to pause and reassess your life. It's a form of biological feedback suggesting that you need to change. Buddhists, for example, pray thanking their illness for contributing to their spiritual growth. And, it is the tradition of all major religions, and even of psychology, that life is all about personal growth and development.

But if anyone or any group thinks that they really understand disease – medically, psychosocially, or spiritually – think again and again. Please excuse my warped sense of humor with the following example, but I'm trying to make what I think is an important point. Most people sincerely believe that their spiritual beliefs can affect their health. So, the idea is that if you were spiritually attuned, you would have less illness or less serious illness and you wouldn't die (or, at least, live longer).

Then think about this: Firstly, all of the great spiritual teachers who have ever lived – have died (and many at a premature age). And secondly, most of them died horrible deaths. If you think that all you have to do is "get right with God," and then you won't have any health crises, maybe you need to think again. Even the saying goes, "God helps those who help themselves." I believe strongly that your spiritual beliefs really can and do make a difference in your health. But do you understand that they alone are no guarantee?

Earlier I mentioned that a major study examined "spontaneous remissions" and concluded that people's sense of control over their lives and a strong will to live appear to be significant factors in overcoming poor medical prognoses. Yet when one of the people who survived his terminal illness was interviewed as part of this research, he said that he had totally given up. He was certain that the doctors were right, and that he would die as they explained he would. He said he became very morose, withdrawn, and waited to die. And he waited. And waited. And waited. And he didn't die. So, finally, he decided to go back to living. Clearly a strong personal locus of control or strong will to live can affect one's health, but there are always exceptions.

And Dr. Larry Dossey talks about "healthy reprobates." Dr. Dossey said that one day a patient came to him already diagnosed with advanced lung cancer, and wanted another opinion. Dr. Dossey, in fact, confirmed the original diagnosis. The patient then reported that the other doctor said he should stop smoking. He smoked three packs of cigarettes a day. Dr. Dossey agreed it was a good idea to quit smoking. The patient was incensed, "If I'm going to die in two months, why do I need to stop smoking?" Dr. Dossey said that the patient then actually began to smoke four packs a day. It was one of his real pleasures, and "If I'm going to die anyhow, then why should I stop?" He didn't die. Dr. Dossey said he still smokes three to four packs a day, and he's going strong. While smoking can be a cause for disease, this suggests that other factors can complicate our understanding of the disease process.

None of this excludes the probability that if you have a great deal of stress in your life and don't manage it well it will put you more at risk for disease. In fact, a good definition for health, in general, is the ability to adjust to your environment (your ability to cope with and adapt to physical, psychological, spiritual, immune and social challenges). It's all about probabilities. And there *are* things you can do to increase your odds.

Research in psychoneuroimmunology suggests that most illness is psychosomatic as its root cause. Dr. Eugene Pendergrass, the president of the American Cancer Society, stated 40 years ago, "There is solid evidence that the course of disease in general is affected by emotional distress...[and] the distinct possibility that within one's mind is the power capable of exerting forces which can either enhance or inhibit the progress of this disease." The National Cancer Institute of the National Institutes of Health in 1976 issued an overview of cancer research and announced that stress emerged as the single most probable cause of cancer. Dr. Candace Pert's extensive research, when she was Chief of Brain Biochemistry for the National Institutes of Mental Health, concluded that the endocrine, immune, and central nervous systems are essentially all the same. They are more than just linked. And no state of mind is not reflected by the condition of the immune system. She believes the progression of cancer can be directly affected by one's emotional state.

But remember, also, that Dr. Pert's research concluded that when you are in touch with your feelings, rather than trying to suppress them, immune function is actually increased. We used to think that so-called negative feelings like depression and anxiety would be unhealthy and suppress the immune system. But, in fact, when you express your feelings, rather than "stuff" them, you actually enhance immune function. This research suggests that your suppression of emotions can directly contribute to the onset of illness.

When you have cancer or any major disease, having to adjust to the diagnosis, treatments, side effects, changes in lifestyle, etc. are all stressful by definition. So, based on the above research conclusions, you could easily think you're killing yourself because you're feeling stressed. Go easy on yourself. You're human. You are almost certainly going to be stressed. And if you're able to acknowledge your feelings, rather than think you're "screwing up" because you're stressed, you'll actually be helping yourself.

Imagine you went to the doctor, who now told you that you had cancer. Could you possibly imagine at that time that you would or should feel positive? It would make no sense at all. If your very first response was something like, "Thank you, God, for this opportunity to learn and grow,"

I'm greatly concerned about you. Your normal, human, and healthy response is that you're scared, confused, frustrated, angry, and pretty overwhelmed. Be yourself. You're human, and it's okay to be you.

If your best friend had just gone to the doctor and were told that she had breast cancer, and now she's telling you that she's depressed – if you had your wits about you, you might say something like, "What did you think you'd feel like?" Actually, you would likely be remarkably sensitive and understanding of her emotional upset. But when it happens to you, you think you have to play Superwoman or Superman.

Whenever I've talked with a woman recently diagnosed with breast cancer, she begins to cry. And, in very short order, she then apologizes for crying. And then comes my mini-lecture, "What are you apologizing for? For being human?"

We've been brought up to believe that big boys don't cry, and girls are always supposed to act like little ladies. These early-learned behaviors disconnect you from your feelings. They also keep you from experiencing peace of mind or being yourself. And eventually these types of socialized behaviors will compromise your immune system. This suggests that your childhood conditioning can also be a cause of illness.

The behaviors you learned early in your life like stuffing your feelings, only feeling good about yourself when you're conforming to arbitrary social conditioning, poor nutrition and exercise, stress and exposure to environmental pollutants can all put you more at risk for your health. You could have had more control over these factors, but you didn't know any better. These poor health patterns became strong habits and difficult to break. So, did you cause your illness?

The issue of whether or not sickness can be a form of feedback that you're out of balance is a major belief and consideration for many people. It may not be your belief, but it is and has been for many millions of people throughout history. And, similarly, today people often say, "The best thing that happened to me was that I got sick."

Is illness good or bad? Is your health a form of feedback telling you that you need to change? I can't say what you should believe. The personal responsibility aspect of health, and that it may cause some to feel guilty, is a very sensitive and controversial issue. The facts would seem to support that you could, in fact, directly affect your state of health or disease. My encouragement and recommendation is that you view your ability to affect your health as a "positive." Many of the things we learned early in life were health–destructive. We can't change that. But we can begin to take more control of our health now by establishing new health habits based on recent and greater knowledge and insight.

What Will Bring Me the Greatest Peace of Mind?

Very simply, the single greatest suggestion I have for making a decision is to ask yourself, "What will bring me the greatest peace of mind?" Remember that right and wrong are relative, and that everyone has his or her own truth. What feels right for you?

I'd like to tell a story that might help to clarify this point. Many years ago I met a woman who told me that she drove her car four hours (two hours each way) to clean her mother's house every weekend. This had been going on for years. When the daughter developed breast cancer, the mother insisted that she still come every weekend to clean her house. What should the daughter do?

Whenever I've told this story and asked this question, I've gotten a wide range of responses mostly suggesting that they find another way to get Mom's house cleaned. It seemed advisable for the daughter to take time to care for her own health. And, yet, for two more years the daughter continued to drive each weekend to clean her mother's house.

I'd like to tell you why I think that this was the right decision for the daughter. *The right decision is what you can live with.* The guilt that the daughter would have experienced at that time would have been greater than the benefit of using that time to take care of herself. Until the daughter was able to deal with the guilt that she should abide by her mother's wishes, the decision which would bring her the greatest peace of mind was to give in to her mother.

Let me complicate this story. Let's say that the mother also had some illness or limitation, and that it wasn't easy for her to clean the house herself. And what if soon after the daughter decided not to go each weekend to help her mother, Mom became sicker or even died? How would the daughter have been able to live with the thought that she contributed to Mom's poorer health or death?

My experience is that your second-guessing yourself and believing that if you had only done "such and such" you would have saved someone's life, etc. is remarkably egotistical. People have their own ideas about everything, and chances are you tried to help those you love in any number of ways, and they resisted your efforts many times. Almost certainly there were lots of other things this person could have done to help herself, and she chose not to do them. And chances are she did other things, including medical help. Sometimes despite our finest efforts, things don't always turn out the way we'd like. And if your best laid plans go awry, it is illogical and unhealthy for you to hold yourself accountable for every outcome.

You are a very small speck in an infinite universe with infinite possibilities and an unknown life plan. To be sure, you are a very special and important speck. But to believe that the one or few things you might have done could have saved the world is not realistic, to say the least.

Add things up, make a choice, act, and experience the consequences. You're human and fallible. Do the best you can. But please don't kick yourself when you're down. It doesn't help anyone or anything.

Be Gentle with Yourself and Each Other

I'd like to expand on the concept of doing what feels right for you. As part of growing and learning, we've come to believe certain things, and then we learn some more, and discard some of our former beliefs. It's a natural part of life. In fact, learning may be the whole point of life. Understand, then, that what you believe now isn't what you've always believed.

If you recognize that many of the things that you used to think were true are no longer true, because you've learned differently, then is what you believe today true? If you're going to continue to learn, and never know it all, then chances are that much of what you believe today you won't believe in the future. Actually, hopefully you won't believe the same things tomorrow as today if life serves the purpose of learning.

My point is to help you understand, again, the idea of many truths. Everyone has his or her own truth. Would you have wanted someone to be critical of your beliefs before you were ready for another understanding? It is so important that we be respectful of others' beliefs and ways of doing things. And their readiness to do it.

I'd like to tell another story to help make this point. I had a patient who was especially bright, assertive, and otherwise someone who was quite interested in becoming an active participant in her healing. We determined that one major concern for her was her relationship with her husband. We thought it would be helpful, if not necessary, for her to confront her husband if she were really going to get well. She said, "I'd rather die." As intelligent, informed, and motivated as she was to increase her odds in dealing with her cancer, she clearly was not ready to do what she really believed she needed to do.

As extreme as this example may seem, that someone would rather die than do what they know or believe would help, I think it's imperative that we respect their choices. Please be gentle with yourself and each other when you don't always do what you think you should or could. Readiness is very important.

Don't Let the Bastards Wear You Down

Another consideration is to realize that sometimes it's okay to quit fighting City Hall. Let's say that you're upset because you're being discriminated against for some reason. For example, you're a female and not getting a fair wage compared to males in the same job. It's not fair, make no mistake. But what are you going to do about it?

I would advise you, firstly, to assert yourself in a way that makes sense to you. But I would also recommend that you take into account the realities of the time. This is a very patriarchal society and time in history. It is out of balance. Do what you can to create a more fair and equitable situation, but, as the saying goes, "Don't let the bastards wear you down."

To clarify this point, imagine that you were sailing. The skies were clear and the wind and water were calm. Things were going smoothly. Then the skies darkened, the wind picked up, and the waves became choppy. Soon the wind and waves became so great it looked like you might capsize. You could stay out to sea and fight the conditions. You could use all your skills and all your determination to fight the elements. Or you could pull into a safe port.

Sometimes it makes good sense to pull into a safe port. You might not like the reality that life is at times difficult to navigate or stay afloat. Do what you can, but don't risk your situation or your health and sanity unnecessarily. Remember my misparaphrased version of the serenity prayer: Do what you can, but don't get too goofy when things don't work out the way you think they should. Discretion is truly sometimes the better part of valor.

Remember, also, the idea of one day at a time. What if it's going to take 10 years to get what you want? You can fret and stew, or you can begin to take steps in that direction, even if they're baby steps. Where will you be in 10 years if you do nothing? I'm reminded of the little song, "Ninety-nine bottles of beer on the wall, ninety-nine bottles of beer... If one of those bottles should happen to fall, ninety-eight bottles of beer on the wall." Just because things didn't work out the way you hoped they would, doesn't mean that you haven't succeeded. You're learning.

It's Normal to Question Your Faith or Spirituality

This is a good place to remind you about the possibility that life serves a purpose, and how your spiritual beliefs can help you during times of crisis. Most Americans believe that God is intimately interested in their well-being and is always available to help. My experience is, however, that when things become bad enough long enough, you will likely question your faith. How could an all-knowing and all-loving God allow bad things to happen?

I'd like to cite a story called "Footprints" to help answer this question:

> One night a man had a dream. He dreamed he was walking along the beach with the LORD. Across the sky flashed scenes from his life. For each scene, he noticed two sets of footprints in the sand: one belonging to him and

the other to the LORD. When the last scene of his life flashed before him he looked back at the footprints in the sand. He noticed that many times along the path of his life there was only one set of footprints. He also noticed that it happened at the very lowest and saddest times in his life. This really bothered him and he questioned the LORD about it. "LORD, you said that since I decided to follow you, you'd walk with me all the way. But I have noticed that during the most troublesome times in my life., there is only one set of footprints. I don't understand why when I needed you most you would leave me." The LORD replied, "My son, My precious child. I love you and I would never leave you. During your times of trial and suffering, when you see only one set of footprints, it was then that I carried you."

If God is all-knowing and all-loving, and has a unique plan for each of us, do you think that God doesn't have a pretty good idea about what's in our best interests? One question that I think you could ask yourself at a time of spiritual crisis to help you keep perspective is, "Do I think God could ever intend harm?" If God could never intend harm, or as you tend to say it, "God would never give me more than I can handle," then your perspective of a situation as "bad" and that God is indifferent or less powerful than some other force is a loss of perspective.

In Chapter 10 I'll talk more about the role that suffering may play in helping us fulfill a life purpose. As I said earlier, many groups, especially Buddhists, pray thanking times of suffering for helping them to develop spiritually. But I'd like to introduce another related consideration here as "food for thought."

In the book, *A Child of Eternity*, a mother and her autistic daughter, Adri, wrote about their experience with autism. At age four Adri was diagnosed as a "low-functioning" autistic person and unable to speak. When she was nine years old she began to learn a method of "facilitated communication" where she could type words and sentences on a small computer. Adri soon typed a wisdom and knowledge far beyond her condition, age, and any conventional way to explain her way of knowing. Within months she typed that she chose to be autistic, and explained how she created this condition for herself within the womb before she was born. She claimed to have a "network of spirit guides" with whom she was in regular communication. She was told that her life purpose was "to show the world the will of God," to "open people's hearts for God," and to help her mother, more specifically, to develop an ability to heal people through touch or laying on of hands.

Adri said that one of the reasons that she chose to be autistic was to demonstrate that one's spirit or mind is separate from the body. Her mother, Kristi, chose as her life purpose to learn about patience. Adri chose to take on her autistic condition, additionally, to learn humility and to help her mother learn patience.

Let me ask you two very elementary questions: "If you gave birth, and the child were autistic, would you think that this were good or bad? Would you have chosen to have an autistic child?" Most people surely would not choose their child to be autistic.

Yet when we read Kristi's and Adri's story, autism would appear to be a spiritual blessing in disguise. They believe that autism afforded them the unique opportunity to develop qualities such as patience and humility. In this process they realized a much greater spiritual perspective personally, and were able to demonstrate this so that others might similarly learn to open their hearts to God. They have also been able to help thousands of other parents and autistic children to develop richer and more fulfilling lives. They are convinced, and communicate eloquently, that "Things happen for a reason."

A related consideration is that thousands of people have been declared clinically dead only to miraculously recover and tell a remarkably similar story. Dr. Raymond Moody was one of the first to research and document these near-death experiences in his book, *Life After Life*. Two of the most detailed accounts are in Dannion Brinkley's book, *Saved by the Light*, and Betty Eadie's book, *Embraced By the Light*.

As part of the "near death experience" it is common to be told by a spiritual being of light that life serves the purpose of learning to love. During Betty Eadie's time "in the light," as she questioned the purpose of life on earth, she was shown a scene from earth of a drunken man. It was explained to her that this "drunken bum" was actually a great spiritual being who "came to earth as a teacher to help a friend that he had spiritually bonded with." This friend was a prominent attorney who had an office a few blocks from where the drunk was lying on a street corner. The drunken man chose this life and experience as a reminder to the attorney of the needs of others. It was explained that the attorney would recognize the drunken man at a spiritual level "and be moved to do much good."

Again, if we could think of this man's situation as good or bad, we would be hard-pressed normally to find the value or benefit of this ""drunken bum" lying on the street corner. Like the question about autism, is being a drunken bum good or bad? (Please understand that I am not attempting to justify any and all conditions as spiritually ordained. My interest is to present "food for thought" regarding times in our lives where we feel God surely is not present. Otherwise, how could God let these "bad" things happen?)

The common spiritual theme is that life is about learning to love, which is exemplified by the demonstration of compassion and the admonition, "Do unto others as you would have them do unto you." Many of life's challenges will almost certainly make you bitter at times, and cause you to question your faith. But by experiencing the "bad" you will almost certainly also come to appreciate the "good" and to love mercy.

People's spiritual beliefs are very personal and very meaningful generally. I would not presume to suggest what you should believe spiritually. My experience, however, is that if you can make sense of your personal tragedies and crises, they will go more smoothly than if you view them as meaningless and serving no purpose.

Ask How You Can Help, Then Listen

I've been asked many times by friends and family members of someone who has cancer, "How can I help?" This may sound too obvious, but I have found it very nurturing and important: If you really want to support someone, ask him or her how you can help. They usually will tell you, if you ask sincerely, but my experience is that you usually don't listen. You have your own ideas about what will work, and you may be prone to insist on your way rather than be respectful of another's approach, especially if it differs significantly from yours. Remember, again, what works for you may not work or be right for someone else.

From the patient's point of view there is a fine line between what you view as helping and what they interpret as antagonism. Actually, one of the greatest things you can do is to listen. I've said this before, but it's very important: People want to be listened to more than they want to be fixed. You don't have to say anything. But if you do feel compelled to speak, my next suggestion is that you be genuine. If you don't know what to say, you can say, "I don't know what to say." People generally like and need to know that you care. And when and however you express your caring sincerely, it contributes more than I think most people realize.

Of course it helps if the person in need tells you how you can assist, and I recommend that this person or friend or family member make a list and communicate to others how they can help. Let's say that someone is in the hospital and would appreciate a hospital visit. If you knew this, you would almost certainly go visit this family member or friend. What if you also knew that after 20 minutes your visit would become counter-productive; that is, the person wants you to visit, but begins to tire after about 20 minutes. Would you want to stay longer if you knew that this wasn't helping? Of course not. So, again, I recommend that the patient or someone communicate to others how to lend a hand. In this case, "Please come to visit, but please don't stay longer than 20 minutes." It's a rather simple, but sometimes difficult, thing to do because you think that it would be socially inappropriate to tell someone to leave after they've made the effort to come visit. They need to know. They want to know. They want to help.

Am I a Burden to Others?

Sometimes people don't want to let you help or tell you how you can be of assistance because they feel they're being a burden to you. I'd like to address this next comment to the patient. Let's say that someone you loved dearly were in your position: They were sick or disabled or whatever. And when you wanted to aid them, they shut you out. How would you feel? You wouldn't like it. It can be helpful in dealing with this situation "to put the shoe on the other foot" and imagine what it would be like to be in the other person's shoes.

Not only can the so-called patient feel helpless at times, but so can the friend or family. First of all they want to support you because they love you. But they also need to do something as a way of dealing with their own sense of helplessness. Don't shut them out. They need to help.

You don't want to be sick. And your friends or family don't want you to be sick. But the reality is that now people want to be of service. Rather than seeing yourself as a burden to others, please allow them to love you. They need to.

I'd like to address this next comment to the friends and family. Lets say that the person you love says, "I want to die." The most common response from friends and family is something like, "Don't say that."

I'd like to recommend a different response, and, again, it's that you listen. When someone is really sick, in a lot of pain, etc. a common thought is that you'd like to throw in the towel. If you feel bad enough long enough, and there isn't any apparent relief in sight, who wants more of the same?

When you say to people, "Don't say that," however, you're forcing them to be doubly strong. Sometimes they really do wish they were dead, but facing death is usually a scary proposition. They need to express their feelings. When you say something that disconnects them from their true feelings, they realize that it is you who is having the problem. And now they can't talk about what is really on their mind and what they're really feeling. They are now forced to be "strong" for themselves and for you, too. Is that what you really want?

I am not proposing that you should endorse their wanting to end their lives. I am suggesting that you try to be more understanding and empathetic with their situation and condition. When people feel listened to and are able to be in touch with their feelings, their physical bodies respond more healthfully. And they will also have a greater peace of mind knowing they have your love, support, and concern.

This doesn't mean that friends or family shouldn't express their fears, upset, etc. when a loved one says they'd like to die. But do it in a way that firstly acknowledges the legitimacy of a person's right and need to be real and genuine.

The Four D's to Problem Solving

When Ken McCaulley developed his self-help program called PROBE, he included a problem-solving model that he called the 4 D's. Actually there are five D's, but I think you'll soon see why he said only four. I think you'll find this a good general approach to answering many of your questions and concerns.

The first *D* is to *define* the problem. But, very importantly, you need to define the problem in terms of the cause and not just the effect. For example, as I mentioned in an early chapter, if a child is "acting out," the real reason for this behavior is often a need for attention. In order to change the acting out behavior long-term, you've got to deal with the cause of the problem, the need for attention.

Similarly with a health concern, you need to define your diagnosis not just in terms of the symptoms, but to consider the potential underlying causes. Remember the example I gave where someone came into a room full of people and started shooting a gun. No one was shot, but the stress of fearing for their lives almost certainly led to physical illness. Dr. Selye's theory proposed that everyone could have developed different symptoms or illnesses depending on their weak links physically, but the real cause was the stress of fearing for their lives. Until you deal with the stressful event, you'll be managing the symptoms of the illness, the chronic condition, indefinitely.

Food for thought: what you're upset about is usually not what you're really upset about. You bring a rich history of experience to any given situation, and if it weren't that person or that thing that triggered your upset, it would have been someone or something else.

Throughout life as you experience dissatisfaction when you're not able to achieve what you really want, the frustration builds eventually to a breaking point. And the straw that breaks the camel's back is where you're likely to focus your anger. You need to refocus your attention on dealing with the unresolved frustrations that led to this current upset, or the situation will continue until you do.

The second *D* is to *delineate* the problem. Many times what we think is our problem is really someone else's. So often people think they should, ought, have to, or must do something, but not really because they believe it, but because someone else thinks they should. Remember the idea that you'll never know everything about anything? Remember how silly or arrogant it is to think that there's a Mr. or Mrs. Know-it-all who really knows what's best for everyone? The next time someone says (or you find yourself thinking) that you "should" or "have to," etc., stop and ask yourself, "Who said so, and based on what?"

Life's tough enough as it is. You don't need to take on someone else's problems, too. As demonstrated in the fable where the father and son loaded their donkey and went to market, everyone had a unique idea how to do it. If you try to do what everyone else thinks, you will go crazy, because everyone has at least a little different idea about how to do everything. Respect their advice, but understand that everyone is different, and what works for one person may not work for another. Everyone has his or her own truth.

People can have a way of making you feel guilty about what they think you should do. Children *and* adults can be especially manipulative and throw any number of versions of temper tantrums. You do not want to reinforce this behavior. In this case you are not helping them or yourself by giving in.

Also, be careful about trying to solve others' problems. I don't mean that you should be insensitive or indifferent about someone else's concerns. Remember the parable about the man who was hungry and asked for a fish? If you just give the man a fish, he'll likely be back for another fish. But if you give the man a fishing pole, he can catch his own fish. Indeed, sometimes it's most advisable for someone to learn personal responsibility, and your helping (or how you help) may not be in his or her best interest.

The third *D* is to *determine* alternative solutions to the problem. List as many things as you can think of that are possible ways to solve the problem, even ones that may sound crazy or unacceptable at first. Sometimes these "crazy" ideas can be amended to become realistic and creative solutions. Then prioritize them either in order of what seems to be the best solution, the most practical, or whatever order makes sense to you that you want to try first.

The fourth and fifth *D*'s are *desire* and *do*. Ken McCaulley believed strongly that desire is the energizer for getting things done. Necessity is not the mother of invention; desire is. So *do* is made a part of *desire* so that it does not become neglected and sidetracked.

Once you have defined your problem and determined where you want to start, it is essential that you now act. Doing nothing is not an answer. And please understand that if plan A doesn't work, then go to plan B. It doesn't help to wonder whether or not plan A will work. It may not. But then you go to plan B, and C and D or E as necessary.

If one plan doesn't work, it doesn't mean you've failed. An anecdote is told about Thomas Edison when questioned about all of the failures he experienced in inventing the light bulb. He replied, "What failures? I learned that hundreds of things didn't work!"

If at first you don't succeed, try and try again. It may sound a bit philosophical, but the process is actually more important than the goal. Do the best you can with whatever information, insight and ability you have at the time. Try not to "second guess" yourself or hold yourself accountable "down the road" for not knowing or doing something you didn't know about at the time you initially assessed the problem. Again, just do the best you can; no one can ever ask more.

9

Self-Esteem: How Do You Feel about Yourself?

In Chapter 6 I said that stress is change or adjustment. The greater the adjustment you have to make to any life situation creates a greater risk for the unhealthy effects of stress. I'd like to consider now the significant changes we have to make in childhood, and how this affects our self-esteem or sense of self-worth and our health.

Human beings have awareness prior to birth. Before you are actually born, your basic senses are operational for several months, and experiences prior to birth can be sensed as stressful. Think about your sense of temperature. The only temperature you would have known prior to birth is your mother's core body temperature, about 99°. The temperature in the delivery room of the hospital is about 68°. There's at least a 30° drop in temperature, then, that you would have experienced upon being born. And someone once reminded me, because of the evaporation process, there's going to be a wind-chill factor, too, so that it would have felt even colder to you. For however long you had awareness prior to birth, and only knew 99°, how do you think it would have felt to be delivered into a 68° room? Stressful. Change, by definition, is stressful unless you've learned to roll with the punches. And you hadn't learned that yet.

Think about your sense of lightness or darkness. You would have known only darkness prior to birth. However, the delivery room in the hospital is very bright in comparison.

How about sound? Do you think you perceived sound differently pre- and post-birth? Buffered in sacs and solutions, sound would have been relatively muffled prior to birth. But upon being born, any sound is going to appear highly amplified.

What other fun things happen at birth? Many people reflect about getting whacked on their bottom. Or having some apparatus forced into their mouth to extract mucous. Do you believe that you were thinking, "Thanks, I needed that?" How do you suppose you felt when they whisked you away from Mom to weigh you or stretch you to see how long you were?

We tend to think of Mom and how difficult it can be for her with labor pains and all. But how much fun do you think it was for you to go through her vaginal canal? For a number of months you've had all of your needs met by the mother organism. You were feeling relatively secure. Upon being born, you're not independent, but compared to your prior experience in the womb, you are relatively independent. Again, a major change.

If you could have vocalized your experience upon being born, what do you think you might have said? (No swearing!) Most people say, "Put me back." You're not exactly thrilled about your new circumstances. And just because your conscious mind may not remember this experience, your subconscious mind does. Your memory is perfect; your recall is faulty. And these earliest experiences stay with you and continue to affect you the rest of your life.

By now you know that your thoughts can dramatically affect your health and behavior. One of the most indelible experiences you had upon being born were feelings of insecurity. Again, for however long you had awareness prior to birth, your experience was one of relative security. But the experience of birth is usually a very traumatic and stressful experience. You now feel relatively insecure. So, day one, you start off with a pretty big case of insecurity and don't feel particularly good about yourself or your situation.

It gets worse. But I want to tell you about two things, in particular, to help you appreciate why these early life experiences are so impactful and erode your self-esteem.

When you are very young, your mind functions literally. It's no secret that you don't have use of reason and logic at first; they're not fully developed until you get through your teenage years. When you were being born you didn't have the use of reason and logic to be able to think, "You know, I'm not the first child ever born. You'd think they'd have figured this out a whole lot better by now." Your thoughts and feelings are literal, and affect your experience literally.

Let me give you an example. I have a good friend who said that he was in school during the time of prohibition, and one day during elementary school, a woman from the Women's Christian Temperance Union came into his school to talk about the evils of alcohol. She set up in front of the room and pulled out two jars. She asked one of the children to go out into the hall to fill the first jar with water. She filled the second jar with alcohol. Then she went into a third jar and pulled out two night crawlers. She dropped one into the water, and it appeared to be okay. She dropped the other worm into the alcohol, and this worm was in trouble. Then she asked the class, "What does this prove?" And the little fellow she called on said, "If you've got worms, drink!" She didn't realize that the children were incapable of abstract reasoning at that age. Their minds functioned literally.

Another example would be if you telephoned someone and a very young person answered the phone. You said, "Hello, is your mother there?" And the child said, "Yes." End of conversation. You expected the child to be able to reason beyond your literal question, "Is your mother there?" But the inability to reason abstractly kept the youngster from understanding that he or she was now supposed to tell Mom to come to the phone.

The other thing that makes early life experiences so important in shaping the individual is emotion. How much emotional control does a young child have? Not much. For example, if you try to take a toy away from a child, how does the child respond? Perhaps a mini temper tantrum. Children are very self-centered at first. Everything revolves around them. And when things don't go the way they think they should, they have a very limited and very effective way to get your attention. They're prone to cry and scream, as necessary.

This emotion is what "charges" the experience and makes it so significant. Emotion is the one sure way we know that an experience has meaning for someone. If you didn't care, you wouldn't emote; it wouldn't affect you. We know when something really affects us, or has meaning, because of the accompanying emotion.

Meaning affects everything. Let me show you how it affects your memory. What if I asked you, "What did you have to eat for dinner 10 years ago today?" Firstly, you'd probably think I was crazy, but then you probably would say that you didn't know. But if I asked, "What did you have to eat for dinner on some special day like your 25th Wedding Anniversary?" you probably could tell me. Unless you're suppressing or repressing memories because they're traumatic and threatening, you remember things partly because they have meaning. And this meaning or emotion amplifies that thought, and causes it to have greater impact.

You've probably heard psychologists say that the earliest years of one's life are so important in shaping the adult. And this is partly why: Your mind functions literally and you have little emotional control as a child.

Raising children is difficult business. This may sound trite, but raising children is probably the most difficult thing you'll ever even think about doing. No matter how much you love your children and how well prepared you thought you were to have them, raising children is largely on-the-job training. And the first child is the grand experiment.

After your second child, do you remember when your first child came to you and said, "How come I wasn't able to do that when I was that age?" And you wished you could have said, "Because I didn't know what the hell I was doing. And I don't know a whole lot better now!"

I believe that parents mean well. Two examples of parents' fine intentions to develop their children's well-being are teaching them to walk and talk. Most parents actually boast about when their children took a first step or said a first word. But as soon as they could walk and talk, it was, "SIT DOWN!" and "SHUT UP!" How do you think you felt as a child when this happened to you?

I remember asking a young boy about his first day at school. He was really upset. "They made me sit down and be quiet." I mean this sincerely, he was truly distraught. It seemed to have drained the life right out of him.

You Think You're No Good and Unloved

Let me take you through a day in your life as a child. Try to remember that I'm talking about you. At your current age you may be prone to think more as the parent or grandparent. What I'm about to say happened to you, and has set you up for any number of limitations including low self-esteem, stress, and poor health.

Imagine that your parents had to go somewhere and were going to leave you with the neighbor. It had been raining, and the yard was wet and muddy, so your parents told you that you had to walk around on the sidewalk to go next door. You couldn't take the short cut through the yard that you would normally take because your parents didn't want you tracking mud into the neighbor's house. They were very clear about this. And then when your parents returned home, they would phone you and you could come back home.

Now imagine that your parents went away, came back, and phoned you. "We're back. Come on home." But they were very clear, once again, to remind you about the muddy yard. Just as they didn't want you tracking mud into the neighbor's house, they didn't want you bringing mud into your house. So you were instructed to make sure you walked on the sidewalk.

But, in a case of terrible timing, your parents got an important long-distance phone call, and they weren't able to meet you at the door. When they finally got off the phone, they didn't have to wonder where you were, they followed your mud tracks through the house. What would your parents have said (or done) to you once they caught up with you if you had "disobeyed" and brought all the mud into your house?

You probably got an ear-full. "Don't you listen?" "How many times do I have to tell you something?" "What's wrong with you?" "What am I going to have to do with you?" Etc. Chances are this was said in an unpleasant voice. And maybe you got a spanking. How would you have felt?

You probably would cry, mostly because you felt hurt, and not just because of a spanking. You would have felt the disapproval of your parents. And at a young age you were unable to separate the behavior from the person. That is, when you were told that you were "bad," you took it personally. As adults we can love people and disapprove of their behavior. But they know we still love them. As a youngster, you were unable to differentiate between the person and the behavior. So when you were reprimanded, you perceived that you were bad or unloved. It wasn't that the behavior was unacceptable, you interpreted your parents' disapproval with your behavior as, "They don't love me."

I know there has been a time that you remember when you had to reprimand your children, and some later time they came to you and asked you, "Do you still love me?" Children greatly need your love and support, and when they feel "abandoned," it can erode their sense of self-worth. When children feel ashamed for not being good or doing what's right, or letting their parents down, they come to feel flawed, inferior, no good, and not worth loving. They learn to think less of themselves and feel no one could love them. And if their parents don't love them, they need someone or something to make them feel good about themselves. And this is the root of addictive behaviors: They're going to do whatever they need to do to find self-respect and a feeling of connectedness or belonging. Or they'll do whatever necessary to numb or repress their feelings of low self-worth and the shame and pain of feeling unloved.

Imagine that a child is crawling on the floor and about to stick a finger into a wall socket. If a parent were there, he or she would rush to make sure the child didn't stick a finger in that socket and get a terrific electric shock. How do you think the child would respond to this behavior? "Thanks, I needed that?" Again, children are very self-centered by nature, and when they're thwarted, when they can't have their own way, they emote. But they're also feeling that *they* are not acceptable, rather than that the behavior is not acceptable. So even when children are reprimanded for the finest reasons, they are prone to interpret the loving act of the parent as a signal that the child is bad and unloved.

So, back to the mud story. You probably cried because you felt hurt emotionally, and then you "skipped town." You wanted to get away from feeling bad. You may have wanted to get away because you feared getting hit, also, but mostly you were pained by feelings of rejection. But, now, who's going to clean up the mud?

Many times parents will say that the children have to clean it up. But often they realize that the children will only make a bigger mess, so the parents are left to tidy up. They're mad because you didn't listen and created the mess, and now they have to clean it up, too! That night everybody goes to bed mad.

Continuing this saga of a day in your life, you wake up and go downstairs to breakfast. And you get a ringside seat, the highchair. You have the best seat in the house, and are focused on Mom preparing something for you to eat. Imagine that she bangs a pot or pan in the process. This gets your attention, not just because it's a loud sound, but you're probably thinking something like, "Boy, would I like to get my hands on that pot or pan and do that, too." And God knows your time will come. From the parents' perspective, you're always getting into things. "I turn my back and you're into something else!"

From the child's perspective, it's simply exploring your curiosity. I believe curiosity is an instinct which drives us to learn. And if life serves the purpose of learning, it makes sense that we would have some inborn mechanism to help us learn or do whatever we need to do to grow and develop personally.

Now imagine that Mom leaves the kitchen to do the laundry, and you manage to slip out of the highchair. No matter how good or clever parents are at locking things up or putting things out of reach, the day comes when you're going to get into something (or everything). And now, as you're crawling on the floor, you come to the kitchen cabinets, and one is left unlocked. You open the door, and, lo and behold, there are the pots and pans.

Your tactile senses are a great way for you to experience and learn. So you get hold of the first pot. It feels cool, smooth, and firm. Then, in the mouth. Chances are you didn't like the metallic taste, and down goes the pot. But you didn't know that every pot, pan and lid would feel and taste the same. You're about to find out. Pot number two gets "thumbed up" pretty good. Then in the mouth, and on the floor. Pot number three. Number four. Five. Six. Seven. And then Mom shows up. How do you think she's going to handle this one? And, remember, she's probably not gotten over the mud incident from last night.

Actually, this is a neutral experience. That is, you and Mom are going to interpret whether or not your playing with the pots and pans is a good idea. From your point of view, you're exploring and learning; she likely has a different perspective. But the experience itself is neutral. For example, Mom could say, "Thank you. House cleaning is my hobby, and now I get to do it all over again. Thank you very much." What do you think she said (or did)?

Chances are she's thinking something like, "I had 100 things to do today, and I didn't need a 101!" It's just possible that she loses her patience a bit, and says something that suggests her disapproval. You feel "bad" and unloved again. You cry and crawl away from the scene of the crime. And maybe Mom adds, "Good, get out of my sight!"

Now Mom's left to put away the pots and pans. But while she's doing that, of course, you're into something else. It's your curiosity and drive to learn. You can't help it. And, before long, it occurs to her, "Oh, my God, I wonder what you're up to now?"

But in the meantime, while she was busy doing dishes, the mail came. When the mail is delivered, it's strewn across the foyer, and guess who's the first one to discover today's mail? And what is the mail going to look like in very short order? It's not that you're a bad kid, you're simply going to exercise your curiosity. You pick up each letter, crumple it, chew it, and them Mom shows up. How's she going to handle this one?

She may try to exercise a sense of humor: "You're going to grow up and be like your father's side of the family!" This may help Mom cope, but it's not likely to feel good to you. Her voice was probably not a pleasant, soft and soothing one. Again you feel inadequate, rejected, and unloved. You cry and crawl away. And Mom's left to resurrect the mail.

Let me complicate this. Imagine that one of those pieces of mail was Dad's favorite magazine. If this had been my dad, when he got home, he was going to say to my mom something like, "What were you doing all damn day long while you were supposed to be taking care of the kids!" So, not only does Mom have the task of making the mail and magazine look more presentable, she has the rest of the day to think about facing Dad when he gets home from work. How do you think she's going to handle your next exercise of curiosity? She's human, and chances are that her patience is wearing thin.

While she's repairing the mail, guess what? You've found her favorite plant. Imagine that it's one with very fuzzy, soft leaves. You touch the first leaf, and think, "Boy, what a nice, soft, fuzzy leaf." Remember, you don't know that they're all going to feel and taste the same. Chances are you don't like the taste of the leaves, and you spit them out, but you keep it up. Then, here comes Mom again. She's had it. And you're about to get it! Whatever she actually says, and in a raised tone of voice, you're interpreting that you're no good, unloved, and, maybe worst of all, that you only feel good about yourself when you're pleasing her (or Dad or other authority figures).

You Only Feel Good about Yourself When You're Pleasing Others

The research and common sense are that you feel best and are most healthy when you are able to be yourself, when you are being unique. You didn't learn to be unique. You learned to conform – to the arbitrary values of your parents. (I say arbitrary, because your parents' values are learned and formed by their parents, community, and culture, and everyone's experience is different.)

And, also, you're not stupid. If you're going to be yelled at and hit everytime you don't do things the way your parents would like, you're soon going to catch on. You're going to be like your parents. This may be flattering to some of you, or very scary to others: You are a lot like your parents. You've modeled and been strongly conditioned by them. And you've had your uniqueness, your spontaneity, your joy of exploring and learning sometimes squashed almost to extinction.

This is not to suggest that your parents didn't also act very lovingly. My presentation of a day in your early life is admittedly and purposefully biased, focusing on the experiences that eroded your self-esteem. And this is not intended to "blame" parents. If anything, it's acknowledging the need to forgive them (and yourself).

Your parents were the "victim" of their parenting, also. Not only were your parents and their parents human and affected by their humanness (the difficulty in raising children and not losing patience, etc.), but your grandparents had their own conditioning and beliefs, and were going to shape the beliefs and values of your parents. And, of course, this was passed on to you.

My father sincerely believed that he did his job well in raising his three children. He said publicly that he didn't care if we ever regarded him as a friend. He was going to teach us discipline. If this was my father's God-given life purpose, I assure you that he is in heaven.

My father was a perfectionist. God bless any of you who live with or work with a perfectionist. There's a saying about the military that there are two ways of doing things: their way and the wrong way (which really means that there is only one way to do things). This was my father to a T. He knew the right way to do everything, and he was not reluctant to tell his children (or wife). Can you imagine what it was like for my mom to live with my dad? She gave in at every turn to try to keep peace. What do you think was the quality of that relationship? And what was being modeled for me in terms of how a marriage should be?

I remember when I was in my teens and fantasizing about marriage. I was certain that I would and could never argue with my wife. But I went so far as to ask, hypothetically, what if we did disagree on something like raising children, how would we settle it? At first I drew a blank. But before long it became very clear: The man would decide! Where do you think I learned that? And how do you think it affects my conduct in relationships?

Deep within me is the strongly conditioned idea that I have to be perfect in order to feel loved by my father. I have to be right. What are my chances for peace of mind? Peace of mind comes from being yourself. But deep within all of us is the idea that to feel loved we have to please our parents and conform to their values (this happened before you had reason and logic to rebut them).

So, for you to go fishing, to do more of what you would really like to do, means that you will be unloved. I believe this is perhaps the greatest reason why you find it difficult to really be yourself and have peace of mind. At a deep psychic level you equate conforming with being loved.

It Gets Even Worse

But I haven't finished with what happens in childhood to erode your self-esteem. It gets worse. Understand, again, that I have purposely focused on the experiences where you learned to feel inadequate and resentful. But it isn't because you were a bad child or your parents didn't love you that caused you to develop your lowered self-esteem. Perception is reality. You regularly perceived yourself as flawed and unworthy. Your parents' humanness and values conditioned you to believe certain things and behave in certain ways. And your uniqueness and creativity were buried as you perceived that you had to conform to earn their love.

For about five years or so, you were learning your parents' values. Now you're going to go to school and learn a whole new set of values: your peers'. And this presents its own feelings of insecurity. You've learned at home to be more self-conscious about your behavior, and how to act. This is how you feel good about yourself. But now you have to leave your parents and learn how to fit in with your schoolmates.

In therapy a woman told me about her first day at school. She had been a "war baby," and because of so many children her age, they had mid-year entrance to school along with the normal time around Labor Day. So her first day of school was in January in the middle of winter.

As she walked up to the school, she said that everything seemed so big. And all or most of the children were bigger, too. She felt all eyes were on her. Actually children are still remarkably self-centered at this age, and they were probably busy playing and couldn't have cared less about her. But she was feeling very self-conscious (related to her learned insecurity).

As she approached the main door she said that there were a number of children waiting to go in. The sidewalk was slippery because of some snow and ice, and in front of what seemed to be a cast of thousands, she did a belly flopper. She was mortified!

But a very unusual thing happened. The other children rushed over to help her. They expressed any number of things, "Isn't this awful? Here it is your first day at school, and you've fallen. Did you hurt yourself? Please don't feel bad. We want you to know how much we love you and want you for a friend. Let's get you brushed off and inside where it's nice and warm. We hope you have a great first day at school." Fat chance! Everybody knows what really happened. They laughed. And she couldn't have felt smaller.

When she returned home that day, she said that she told her parents that she wasn't going back to school again. She was crushed. I know that most of you understand how badly this little girl felt. But I don't know if you fully appreciate how this kind of experience really could be so damaging psychologically. I want to explain this by digressing and telling another story before I come back and talk more about the effects of your childhood peers.

This is a true case study. A woman had suffered for most of her life with severe depression. She had seemingly every type of therapy, including shock treatment, which is usually a "last resort" approach. However, under hypnosis, she remembered a very traumatic event from her childhood.

One day when she had been outside playing, her mother called to her and said that it was time for dinner. She came in through the kitchen door, and Mom had just finished making cookies. Her mother was quick to tell her not to touch the cookies, "You'll spoil your dinner. Go wash your hands." Mom turned to do something else, and the little girl took a cookie. But Mom turned around again and caught her eating the cookie, and said, "God sends little girls to hell who disobey their parents." For the rest of her life this woman believed that she had nothing to look forward to except going to hell and burning forever! Fortunately this misperception could be changed and the woman was able to break free of her depression. But that single traumatic experience was the precipitating event for a life-long major depression.

I hope you can appreciate, then, that when the little girl fell in the snow, it really could have been traumatic. But I want to give this story a unique twist. Imagine that when the girl got home from school that she told her parents, "I'm, not going back...unless I have a new pair of $100.00 Nike tennis shoes."

What do Nike tennis shoes have to do with this? Everything. It's all about fitting in. In order to feel a sense of security, self-worth, and love, you've got to conform now to the values of your classmates. You're going to learn how to dress, how to talk, what music to like, etc. You've got to be "cool."

I don't know what the "in" words are today for kids. I'm sure they don't say "cool" anymore. I remember when the word "awesome" became the thing to say. Except that I'm using "awesome" here as an example of a learned way to appear that you fit in, I don't think I've ever used the word "awesome" in normal conversation. Yet young people couldn't go two sentences without saying "awesome." What's so special about the word "awesome?" To show you fit it. To hide your fear of being rejected for who you really are.

I remember when I was a boy that it was important to wear black, high-top KEDS tennis shoes. There's something about tennis shoes. I remember when it was really important in high school to wear PF FLYER tennis shoes. And they had to be really scruffy looking. You held them together with adhesive tape if necessary.

But, of course, this wasn't okay with my dad. I'd have to throw my old sneakers out of the bedroom window into the yard, and walk out of the house in a new-looking pair. But I wouldn't be caught dead in the new ones, so I'd quickly change into my old pair before I left the yard. Silly, isn't it? But if you think about it, you did the same kind of things so that you would fit in with your friends.

It was very important for most of you to fit in – in grade school, junior high and senior high. All of your formative years, before your reason and logic were fully developed, you learned to conform. And so we all wear masks, ways of presenting ourselves to the world so we'll feel accepted. An excellent discussion of how we find our security in pleasing others is in Dr. Joan Borysenko's book, *Guilt is the Teacher, Love is the Lesson*:

> In the childhood need to please parents and keep safe, the developing psyche splits into a public self, or mask, and a private self, or shadow, unknown even to ourselves. In this split, we lose our authentic sense of self and the ability to express our natural impulses. We lose the peace and power that are our birthrights. We become anxious, guilty, empty of vitality, and prone to thinking and acting like victims, and often we become physically ill.

I remember having a conversation not so long ago with my mother, and she asked me, "Do you know the thing I regret most in my life?" She answered herself, "Always being too concerned with what everybody else thinks." She learned this from her very critical mother. You learned it, too, from the fear of making mistakes, or displeasing your parents. As Dr. Borysenko believed, "Mistakes meant I wasn't good enough and people wouldn't like me. I might be ridiculed, rejected, or abandoned."

Having to be perfect is not going to bring you peace of mind; it's going to make you self-critical, anxious, and depressed. Whether or not you like it or understand it, your behavior is largely determined by what others think, not what you would really choose to do. And the basis is fear of rejection and not being loved.

Borysenko described how having to be the perfect child also led to her illness:

> Having to be perfect made it hard for me to take risks and stifled my creativity. It made me competitive, tight-lipped, defensive, and awfully serious about myself. It made for constant comparisons between me and others, during which I always worried about being one up or one down. It made me hypersensitive to criticism, which I heard even where it wasn't intended. I was like a fortress constantly prepared for attack.
>
> Worse still, I was angry much of the time (and nice people shouldn't be angry, right?) Unable to forgive myself or anyone else, I was a prisoner of guilt and resentment. I did my best to hide all this underneath a smile but was ultimately betrayed by my body, which became a breeding ground for stress-related illnesses ranging from high blood

pressure and migraine headaches to a spastic colon and constant respiratory infections.

Borysenko believes that the majority of stress-related disorders are related to an inner feeling of unworthiness developed in childhood.

I suggested earlier that when you had your first symptoms of illness, for you to think about what stress was going on in your life then (or up to 18 months prior to your first symptoms). The unresolved stress could compromise your immune system and contribute to your medical symptoms. In order for the symptoms to be "cured," you would have to resolve the underlying stress. I believe that the stressful situation often can be traced to your childhood and feelings of inadequacy or low self-esteem. You felt forced to live the beliefs and values of your parents, community, and culture, and an artificial and arbitrary ideal which you can never achieve and with which you can never feel comfortable.

Remember when I proposed that we're all looking for peace of mind? And I asked you to think about what it feels like to "walk on egg shells"? You feel ill at ease when you have to worry about and conform to others' ideas about how to be. And who knows, for certain, everything about anything? Mr. or Mrs. Know-it-all? You can't win this one. It is a life of constant stress unless you can become your own person and realize that you'll never have it figured out, never be in complete control, and that it doesn't matter.

It's all made up. And it changes from generation to generation and culture to culture. But your childhood experiences determined your truth. And one of those truths you learned was that you had to conform to feel loved. But things keep changing. As you mature and learn and grow, you realize that your beliefs and values change, too. But deep within, you believe that to change (or not conform) means that you will be unloved, you won't fit in, and you'll be rejected. You're stuck. And you are very resentful. Most of this is taking place in your subconscious mind; you're not aware of this inner conflict consciously. But the dissonance or stress is real, and has real consequences in terms of your health and behavior.

We have to be right. And not only does this complicate relationships, but now we're driven to prove ourselves, to show that we measure up and fit in. But in the process of having to be perfect and constantly trying to fit in and prove our worth, we become quite inflexible. Subconsciously we believe that everything we do has to be done to please our family of origin. But what happens when you find yourself interacting with others who have different families of origin and different beliefs? Something's got to give. You've either got to change, which will create its own stress, or you can remain inflexible, which will disenable you to deal with the inevitable stresses of life. Either way, you lose.

A key to resolving the feelings of inadequacy and resentment is to become more in touch with these feelings. Remember when Dr. Candace Pert's research demonstrated that "stuffing" your feelings, especially feelings of hopelessness and helplessness, would suppress immune function? Subconsciously, a part of you feels quite hopeless and helpless. You want to change and grow, but your childhood conditioning isn't going to cooperate very well. You've got to get in touch with these feelings. To keep them suppressed or repressed will eventually take your health.

How to Reparent Yourself

Earlier I said that your memory is perfect, but that your recall is faulty. You can let your imagination remember events which are contributing to your current symptoms or concerns. If the memory is not too threatening, your defense mechanisms, like suppression, will allow you to remember. This is not a logical process; that is, you don't try to reason what is underlying your current concern, you let your imagination remember.

For example, when I told the story about the little girl who fell in the snow her first day at school, this was her response when we asked her to remember why she feels she can't speak up for herself now. She just closed her eyes and asked herself to become aware of why she was feeling so unsure of herself. She didn't try to figure this out logically; she remained the "passive observer" and simply paid attention to her thoughts, feelings and imagination. And what came to her was this memory of falling in the snow and feeling so embarrassed.

In the therapy of this, it is not enough to just remember the event, you must also bring up the emotion tied to that event. Knowing intellectually what caused your condition is not going to change anything. You've got to release the emotion which is "charging" that memory. Normally people are prone to stuff or suppress their emotions because they feel it is less appropriate socially to cry and to express any sense of vulnerability. So when you practice this exercise, you want to tell yourself to let yourself *feel* the emotion that is related to the memory. Whatever you feel, let the feelings come up for you.

In the same way that you probably empathized with the little girl who fell in the snow when she was laughed at, you must now also empathize with yourself once you remember something and the emotion comes up for you. Allow yourself to remember and re-experience the memory as fully as possible. Hopefully it will be emotionally charged, and you will truly feel the fear, anger, or sadness. Ask yourself, "What did it truly feel like to feel shamed, rejected, abandoned, belittled, ridiculed, abused, silenced, etc.?" Let the feelings come, and, again, empathize with yourself: "This wasn't right. I didn't deserve this. I accept myself. I love myself. I'm learning."

Remember my earlier story about tracking mud into the house after you were told to walk on the sidewalk? Let's say that you had one day to live, and you had your full health and you could do anything you wanted. And on that day, children you loved dearly brought mud into your house. How would you handle those children knowing you had only one day to live? Would you yell at them? Spank them? Chances are you'd be very willing to overlook the mud. You've got one day to live, and you're going to make the most of it, including showing your real love for the children. Maybe you'd even go out and play in the mud with them! You'd have a very different perspective than you would when you're caught up in the frustrations of day-to-day parenting.

As part of the therapy you could also see yourself reparenting you: How would you as an adult have handled you as the child? See yourself with infinite patience and understanding. See yourself as you are now, extending to yourself as a child all the love you so richly deserved and that you so sorely needed. This will transform and modify the earlier belief that you were unworthy and unloved.

Use this same kind of perspective now therapeutically as you sit quietly with your eyes closed and remember when you felt unloved:

1. Firstly, remember the event.
2. Then, let the emotion come. Relive it and feel it.
3. Then empathize with yourself. This felt awful and it wasn't the best way to handle the situation.
4. Forgive the person(s) involved. They did the best they could given their humanness and learned limitations.
5. Then forgive yourself. You made a mistake or didn't live up to some learned ideal. You're human, too! You're learning.
6. Then, reparent yourself. How would your parents or others have acted if they had a fuller perspective? For example, what would have been the most loving response at the time of your falling in the snow or bringing mud into the house? See them now showering you with their love and patience and attention, which you deserve and which they would indeed do if they were truly free to choose how to respond at that time.
7. Then let yourself feel how it would feel to be loved and accepted for who you are. You don't have to be good or right or anything. You are loved no matter what. How would that feel?

Celebrate Your Uniqueness

My mother was born in St. Johns, Newfoundland. My father met her when he was stationed there during World War II. When my mother was 25 years old, single, and still living at home, she was not allowed to go to a party if a Catholic were there. She was raised in a very Protestant family, community, and culture. She was conditioned to believe that it was somehow better to be Protestant than to have another religious belief.

When I was in high school, most of my girlfriends were Jewish. But their parents didn't want them to date me because I wasn't a Jew. I'd have to have a Jewish male friend pick up my girlfriend while I waited in the car on our "double date." When I was younger we lived in a housing project, and there were distinct areas where "the white people" lived and where "the colored people" lived. Having been "brought up" in the 1940's and 50's you can rest assured that I was exposed to limited images and beliefs about the Japanese and African Americans.

All of us have been conditioned to believe in an ideal image of human beings. For some people their learned ideal is that one should be male, white, Protestant, blue-eyed, six feet tall, handsome, masculine, muscular, a doctor or lawyer, in good social-standing, and rich! And women have learned a similar ideal based primarily on their physical appearance.

We have been taught that God is all-knowing and all-loving, and has a unique life plan for each of us. If God wanted us all to be white, blue-eyed, skinny and rich, then why are there so many different kinds of people? Did God make a mistake? If God wanted you to be a certain size, shape, weight, and color, why didn't God make you that way? Should you be some "ideal," which really has been determined by your family, community, and culture? Or should you celebrate your uniqueness? Again, did God make a mistake? Or is there some more Divine, life-plan reason for your uniqueness?

The point of this is that every generation and culture has its own way of determining truth. And this has been passed on to you. On the one hand you have been told that you are loved perfectly, that God loves you unconditionally, whether you're red or yellow, black or white. You've been taught that we are all God's children. As much as you love your children, God loves you more. In the book of Psalms (82:6), God said "You are gods, and all of you are sons of the Most High." Jesus said the same thing in John 10:34. And in John 14:12, Jesus said, "Truly, truly, I say to you, he who believes in Me, the works that I do, he will also; and greater works than these he will do."

On the other hand you have been told and asked to repeat affirmations like, "We are unworthy of you, oh Lord." and "We are like worms groveling in the dust." We are made to believe that we are undeserving of God's love. I have a friend in the clergy who says that you'd think we were born with one foot in hell and the other on a banana peel, and that we're ready to go any moment.

By now you surely understand the power of your thoughts and beliefs. If you could believe that you are loved perfectly and have infinite potential – or you could believe that you are anything but "precious in His sight," and unworthy of God's love, which do you want to believe? Understand, again, that your beliefs have very real consequences. Which belief is more likely to be equated with greater self-esteem and health?

I know that discussing one's religious or spiritual beliefs is a very personal matter. My interest here is not to suggest what you should believe, but to help you understand how your beliefs affect your health and behavior. Actually, about 95% of Americans believe in God. And, along with that belief in God, you believe that God is all-loving. If you truly believe that God loves you, then I ardently recommend that you pray believing that you are loved perfectly. Whether you think of prayer as a form of guided imagery, or believe in the power of prayer for some other more metaphysical reason, use the power of your beliefs to reestablish your self-esteem. Pray, opening yourself to God's infinite love.

Earlier I talked about the therapeutic technique of "reparenting." In the same way that I said that you could now imagine your parents acting in a more loving way regarding your having tracked mud into the house, you can now imagine some spiritual figure reparenting you. For example, how would Jesus have handled the situation?

There's a story in the Bible (John 8) where a woman was accused of adultery. According to Hebrew law, she should be stoned. If Jesus were to go against the law, he too, could have been accused. Jesus knelt and wrote in the sand and said, "Let he who is without sin cast the first stone." One by one the woman's accusers left. When no one stayed to condemn the woman, Jesus said to her, "Neither do I condemn thee; go and sin no more."

Unfortunately we don't usually follow this example. We're usually far more prone to kick ourselves or each other when we're down, when what we really need is to feel loved and supported. We're human and fallible. We're here to learn and experience. And we'll never have it figured out. And maybe that's why spiritually we're taught to love mercy.

10

Who Are You?

When I would ask the question "Who are you?" when I was teaching my program to cancer patients and their families, I'm sure that many of these people questioned its relevance. "What does a philosophical question like that have to do with cancer?" I think it's related to one's peace of mind and being yourself. I've already proposed that when you're able to be yourself and live authentically that you're going to feel more at ease and less stressed. But I believe that knowing who you are can bring you an even deeper sense of peace and joy and health.

If you really were to think about this question "Who are you?" your initial responses are likely to be related to your physical characteristics and learned roles. You're a male or female, a certain size, shape and weight, mother or father, housewife, nurse, teacher, engineer, student, etc. Eventually you'd get around to your mental, emotional, and spiritual characteristics.

I said earlier that in our culture, most women are raised to believe that their primary reason for being and role in life is to marry and raise children. And men's greatest role and sense of self-esteem comes from providing for the family, or their occupation. You learn to identify strongly with these roles. But what happens when the children leave home (the "empty nest" syndrome) or when the male can no longer work or retires? This becomes a potentially very stressful time in your life.

Remember that stress is related to change and adjustment. How well you're able to cope or roll with the punches determines whether or not you'll experience the negative effects of stress. I think that many people don't make a healthy adjustment to life after raising their children or when they retire. Your greatest reason for being has changed dramatically. What now gives you the same sense of self-esteem and meaning?

We grow up with a fairy tale idea of how life should be. We're born, go to school, get a job, work, get married, raise a family, retire, go to Hawaii and live on the beach until we die. I want to focus on the last part. You thought that when the kids were gone and you retired that you'd really kick back and enjoy all of your hard work. The part you left out was that many of us by this time have serious chronic illness. You worked hard and were ready to enjoy the fruits of your labors, and now your health has created another scenario. Many older people joke about spending most of their time going to doctors. Is this what your life was meant to be?

No matter where you are in this fairy tale chain of events, it is imperative that you make time and take time to do more of the things you really want to do. If you keep putting them off, your health will likely disallow you to do those things you always wanted to do. For women, especially, their lives were ones of sacrifice, sacrifice, sacrifice. You learned, and came to believe, that it was more appropriate to always be doing for others rather than taking care of yourself. And you learned to see yourself as "Mother" and "nurturer." And Dad was so busy working and providing for the family that his primary image of himself was "Father" and "provider." This is not who you are. These are learned roles, and only part of the picture.

You Are Not Just Your Physical Body

No doubt you've heard about and thought about yourself as physical, mental, emotional, and spiritual. You are not just your physical body. You are much more. And, so, you are not just Mom or Dad, either. You have learned in a more holistic approach to health that if you ignore the mental, emotional, and spiritual parts of your being, your physical health will suffer. And if you focus on only a certain limited image of yourself, you are likely to create a similar imbalance. And imbalance is not equated with health.

The mental and emotional aspects of who you are clearly affect your health. Your beliefs are potentially as powerful as any medical treatment. And your feelings directly affect how your body resists disease. Any approach to healthcare that would deny or exclude the role of your beliefs and feelings would be incomplete. So, who you are mentally and emotionally is equally as important as who you are physically. Unfortunately, this is not the usual approach to conventional healthcare. The primary focus is on the physical.

When I was Director of Psychological Support Services and teaching my program at Oncology Services' cancer centers, I met literally thousands of patients and family members. It was hard to get to know everyone very well, but there were always those who I worked with more closely and remembered fondly. Months or years later, when I would see their physicians, I would often ask about certain patients. The physician works closely with these people for several weeks, but after time, one really can forget their names. It's difficult to remember the names of so many people. So I would try to help doctors remember by giving additional information such as what they looked like, their occupation and interests, etc. The one thing that usually helped them to remember patients the most was the body-part that was treated for cancer. Oncologists knew their patients most of all as a breast, colon, prostate, lung, or some other part of their body!

This is not meant as a criticism of your physician. This is meant to support my point that healthcare is usually very physically-oriented. When I would go over patients' medical records as part of their care, I would always look to see what was written under "SOCIAL HISTORY." The most common entry was "Unremarkable!" Sometimes there were notations about "smoking" and "alcohol" history, but that was it. There was usually nothing about their beliefs, interests, values, psychological make-up, social support, nutrition, exercise, stress, use of "alternative" treatments, or spirituality. As though these don't matter!

Please understand, again, that physicians are not trained to address the psychosocial and spiritual aspects of people. It would be inappropriate for them to treat you with other than their trained and licensed skills. Unfortunately, most physicians don't realize that these are important, however. There need to be specialists who work with the medical team who have the knowledge and skills to care for other than the physical part of who you are.

None of this is meant to minimize that you are physical and that this is a very important part of who you are. You are a bunch of cells and tissues, organs and systems, muscles and bones that grew and matured into what you see when you look in the mirror. The genes you acquired from your parents and grandparents and throughout your lineage have come together to form your unique physical being. Your physical size, shape, color of your eyes, hair, etc. are all determined by your genes.

Scientifically, you are the chance combination of genes that have been passed on to you by your parents. You are the result (or effect) of your parents (the cause). In this cause and effect relationship, your parents are the result or effect of their parents, or your grandparents. If you follow this back to a logical beginning, who you are physically is related to genetics and can be traced back theoretically to an original gene pool.

What about the Spiritual Part of You?

Philosophers, poets, prophets, and metaphysicians throughout time have attempted to explain the nature, character, and causes of being and knowing, the existence of God, and that which is above or beyond the material world. And while science and medicine are focused on the primacy of one's physical being, most people believe that they are also spiritual beings, even if this can't be measured objectively in a way science or medicine would require.

As I said above, who you are physically is determined by your genes, which theoretically goes all the way back to the origin of the human species. To consider who you are spiritually, if we use this same cause and effect logic, we would have to trace ourselves back to the origin of your spiritual nature and what is beyond or behind the physical. Most people think of this origin as God.

It's hard for a finite mind to consider that there was an Original Cause, God, that had no beginning. Where did this Creator come from? How could God have always existed and had no cause? The wisest minds in history have wrestled with this great question. In this regard Aristotle referred to God as the Uncaused Cause or the Unmoved Mover. However you understand God, and whatever label you choose to give the beginning of creation, you came from this Creator.

Every major religion has attempted to explain the ultimate nature of reality and has advised people how to live. Hinduism, Buddhism, Taoism, Judaism, Christianity, and Islam have all taught that there is an ultimate source of all being, which is omnipresent in all things and that we are one with everything. And each religion has taught the Golden Rule: Do unto others as you would have them do unto you. The ultimate purpose in life is to realize the Eternal Self within, to know of one's union with God, and ways to live in harmony with all of creation. From a spiritual perspective, then, the question, "Who Am I?" could be answered, "One with God."

Jesus said, "I am in My Father, and you in Me, and I in you" (John 14:20). An Islam scripture says:

> . . . Although you may not know it,
> If you love anyone, it is Him you love;
> If you turn your head in any direction,
>   It is toward Him you turn.
> . . . In the light I praised you
>   and never knew it.
> In the dark I slept with you
>   And never knew it.
> I always thought that I was me,
> But no, I was you
>   And never knew it.

We Are One with God

If I were to ask you a very elementary question, "Is God good or bad?" surely you would respond, "Good." We are taught, "God is good; God is great." God is the highest image we could possibly have of ourselves and of anything. If we are one with God, what does this suggest about our basic nature, then, are we good or bad? For you to believe that you are bad when your origin is only great would seem illogical. So how did you come to believe that you are other than good if you are one with God and came from God? The answer is: "learned values."

You learned primarily from your parents that love is conditional. You learned to feel loved and accepted when you were pleasing your parents. And you've transferred this same learning to your belief about God. When you do what God wants, you feel loved. When you break God's commandments, you're to be punished. And this has presented an interesting dilemma. We're informed by our religions that we're one with God and loved perfectly and unconditionally. But we're also told that God is a vengeful, punishing God who would banish us to a burning hell forever. We're depicted as born in sin, unworthy, and made to feel separate from God. How do we reconcile this seeming contradiction?

Historians note regularly that religions often monopolized authority and would use the fear of a punishing God to persecute and deny human freedom. It is one of the interesting ironies that metaphysical systems which were created to help us answer the questions, "Who am I?", "Why am I here?" and "Where am I going?" became so corrupted. Norman Cousins' book, *In God We Trust: The Religious Beliefs and Ideals of the American Founding Fathers*, discusses how most of the founding fathers resisted many of the beliefs of the Bible. They believed that Jesus' moral teachings were sound principles, but that they were likely corrupted and changed throughout history by groups and governments seeking power.

Thomas Jefferson was one of the most outspoken critics of religion. In his book, *The Life and Morals of Jesus*, Jefferson extracted all of the unloving sayings, stories and acts attributed to Jesus. He condensed the New Testament into a rather small book containing only Jesus' loving words and acts, which has come to be known as the *Jefferson Bible*. Jefferson believed that Christianity was "the most sublime and benevolent" philosophy ever created, and yet "the most perverted." He pleaded for people to separate the winnow from the chaff:

> My opinion is that there would never have been an infidel, if there had never been a priest. The artificial structures they have built on the purest of all moral systems, for the purpose of deriving from it pence and power, revolts those who think for themselves, and who read in that system only what is really there.

Does Love Matter?

I'd like to extend the question, "Who are you?" and the spiritual perspective that we are individuations or part of God to a consideration of love. My interest here is to suggest that spirituality and love are significant factors in health and healing.

In 1993, there were two excellent mind-body health videos produced and aired on television. The first was Bill Moyers' *Healing and the Mind*, televised by PBS. The second was *The Heart of Healing*, televised by TBS. Both were documentaries discussing "alternative" approaches to healthcare throughout the world.

Bill Moyers' video begins with an interview in China with Dr. David Eisenberg, a Harvard medical doctor. Dr. Eisenberg headed the study of the use of unconventional medicine in the United States published in the *New England Journal of Medicine* in 1993. He reported that people in 1990 were going to "alternative" practitioners more than their primary care physicians for their health care. This has become the most cited medical journal article in history. Dr. Eisenberg replicated this survey in 1997, and published it in the *Journal of the American Medical Association* in 1998. The survey concluded that alternative medicine use has increased substantially between 1990 and 1997. Bill Moyers' video is an excellent documentary of these alternative medical therapies and how the mind affects the body.

The Heart of Healing video is a similar documentary about mind-body health and of people around the world describing their use of "alternative" therapies, which they believe can heal. In one segment of this video, Roger Pilon, M.D., Director of the Medical Bureau Lourdes, is discussing miracles. Miracles are a controversial subject for science since they imply a suspension of law. The Catholic Church, under very strict criteria, has declared 65 people to have had a miracle. When Dr. Pilon was asked why he believed these people overcame their incurable illnesses, he proposed, "They had faith in someone who loves us."

I was quite taken by this response. The idea of faith and the placebo effect was not new to me at all, but the role of love surprised me coming from a highly respected medical doctor. I remember that I found myself really thinking about this, but I had to keep watching the video.

In the next scene Father Henri Joulia of the Sanctuary of Notre Dame of Lourdes was asked, in a totally separate interview, the same question, "Why did these people have a miracle?" Father Joulia responded, "They had a sense of being loved and cared for." They knew that they were loved unconditionally, "God loves *me*!" "God loves *me*!"

Once more I was taken by the consideration of love as the reason for their cure. When I thought about this more academically I, again, understood how one's belief could make a difference. I knew also of the strong role that social support can play. But I found myself very caught up in the idea that when one felt completely loved that it could affect such dramatic healing. This stayed with me for months.

Then one day in the Spring of 1994 I was watching the Oprah Winfrey Show on television. She was interviewing Maya Angelou, the wonderful poet and orator. I have never heard a better speaker than Maya Angelou, and she always speaks from the depth of her soul.

Oprah was being her very Oprah self, very personable, genuine, and friendly. She asked Maya what it was like to get a phone call from the White House asking her to write and deliver the poem for President Clinton's January, 1993, Inaugural Ceremony. Maya told her, "My knees started to turn to water." When Oprah asked her if she felt any pressure, Maya said, "What allows me to go from darkness into darkness is a profound faith. I am a child of God." (I get chills writing this, remembering the confidence and clarity and peace with which she spoke.)

Maya then remembered and sang a line from a 19th century spiritual song, "I don't believe he brought me this far to leave me." And, again, with great clarity, Maya said, "I know that I'm a child of God," and "I'm up to it" [writing and delivering the poem]. "I come from the Creator like everybody else trailing wisps of glory." She continued, "I gave my energy to God and said if this is what you want done, I will do it."

When Oprah asked Maya if this was one of her proudest moments, Maya replied, "Sometimes people think that the public recognition's the greatest thing that can happen." But Maya proposed, "Some private revelations can be greater." Maya then reflected back to 1953 when a voice and spiritual teacher taught her, "God loves *me*!" Maya thought that this was one of the greatest moments in her life, the knowing that "God loves *me*…and when you *know* it…I can do anything I want to do. I can do it." To this day, whenever Maya repeats to herself "God loves me," she said she is "filled with wonder" knowing that God loves her unconditionally, the "good" and the "bad."

I could never duplicate here in writing about this interview the depth of feeling Maya brought to these words "God loves me." It clearly moved Oprah Winfrey, also. Oprah ended her show with the statement, "The greatest thing you learned which I'm going to take with me is, God loves me." And I cannot express fully enough now how deeply moved I was, too.

A few months earlier I had watched the documentary, *The Heart of Healing*, and heard the medical doctor and priest talk so genuinely about the miracles of Lourdes. The doctor believed the people were cured because they knew someone loved them. The priest responded similarly, and said the exact words Maya Angelou considered her greatest private revelation: "God loves me."

This was a special moment for me, also. It "clicked" for me that, indeed, people could be healed when they knew God loved them. It was a deep realization of who they really are: a part of God. This is who I am! "As it was in the beginning, is now and ever shall be" – I am one with God. Not only am I loved unconditionally by God, but this is who I am.

I wrote earlier about "peace of mind." If there's one thing we're all looking for it's peace of mind. And you get peace of mind when you're being yourself. At the deepest level you are most yourself when you realize your oneness with God!

As I reveal to you this very personal insight of mine, I am deeply respectful of your personal spiritual beliefs. I would not and could not ask you to believe what I believe spiritually. But I feel compelled to report that, historically, this is what every major religion has taught: You are one with God. I believe this message has been greatly distorted by our childhood experiences related to our parents and other authority figures. And historians have documented how religions and governments came to use the fear of God as a way to control people.

I started this chapter of the book by asking, "Who are you?" As I said, most people respond to this question with their physical characteristics and learned roles of mother, father, housewife, nurse, teacher, engineer, student, etc. Eventually you recognize that you are more than just your physical body and learned roles; you are also mental, emotional, and spiritual.

You are most certainly physical. You and physicians and hospitals have addressed the physical part of who you are quite well. You are also mental and emotional. Your beliefs and your feelings play a major role in your health and well-being. And most of you believe that you are also spiritual. If this is who you are, then it makes sense to address the spiritual component of who you are, also.

Joan Borysenko addresses this issue eloquently in her book, *Guilt is the Teacher, Love is the Lesson*:

> When we experience ourselves as this essential center [the core Divinity within each person, who we really are] organized around the Self, rather than as any one of our roles, we can function optimally, unimpeded by fears and desires – as the apostle Paul described it, "in the world, but not of it." Self-realization has also been called enlightenment because it ends the illusion of faulty identification with our ego roles and awakens us to a more basic, enduring identity in which we feel safe, secure, loved, and capable of radiating these qualities to other people. In Self-realization, our personality – our ego – is seen as no more and no less important than the identity we have chosen to accomplish our unique work in the world. It's great to have a personality, all right, but it is no more "us" than the clothes we hang over the back of our chair when we go to bed at night.

Dean Ornish also addresses the role of spirituality and love in his work and research with heart disease. As I said earlier, Dr. Ornish has proven that you can reverse heart disease with a program of nutrition, exercise, and stress management. His research has been published in the world's most respected medical journals.

In his book, *Love and Survival*, Dr. Ornish wrote that when most people think about his research they focus on the diet part. But he believes that as important as diet and exercise are, "that perhaps the most powerful intervention…is the healing power of love and intimacy, and the emotional and spiritual transformation that often result from these." After more than 20 years of research and practice, and reviewing the scientific literature, Dr. Ornish wrote in italics, "*I am not aware of any other factor in medicine – not diet, not smoking, not exercise, not stress, not genetics, not drugs, not surgery – that has a greater impact on our quality of life, incidence of illness, and premature death from all causes*" than the role of love and intimacy.

Dr. Ornish believes that people's "desire for connection and caring" is one of the greatest reasons why people are turning to "alternative" health care approaches. People are willing to pay out of their own pocket to have these needs of being listened to and nurtured and nourished be met. But when Ornish searched the national Library of Medicine database from 1966 to 1997 he found only four articles that mentioned the word love and heart disease. In 1997, when the *Journal of the American Medical Association* reviewed all the known risk factors for coronary heart disease, there was no mention of stress or any psychosocial factor. Ornish found that even a review of the psychology scientific literature failed to have a reference to love.

I have to admit that when I wrote up my research for publication in the *Journal of Alternative Therapies in Health and Medicine*, I consciously chose not to mention the word "love." I reported that "our patients believed that our program helped them the most not due to any specific coping skill they learned, but because they felt listened to, cared for, supported, and a sense of connectedness within the group." I thought that if I used the word "love" the research would sound less scientific and be less well reviewed. I was consciously attempting to report the research accurately, and also to appear scientific. And as Dr. Ornish's review of the literature demonstrated, scientists don't talk about love.

However, there is a substantial and compelling body of research demonstrating the power and role of social support and relationships, which Dr. Ornish cites in his book, *Love and Survival*. Dr. Ornish believes that social and emotional support "relate to a common theme. When you feel loved, nurtured, cared for, supported, and intimate, you are much more likely to be happier and healthier. You have a much lower risk of getting sick, and, if you do, a much greater chance of surviving."

Whatever words or terms we use scientifically to explain the extensively researched role of social support, Dr. Ornish believes it all comes down to, "Do you feel loved and cared for?" This was the response of the Director of the Medical Bureau at Lourdes, explaining why people had a miraculous cure. This was the strongly felt response of the Father at Lourdes and of Maya Angelou. And it is my strongly-held belief that when you feel loved, truly loved, it is intrinsically healing. It is the feeling of resonance deep within you, with who you truly are. And for those of you interested in pursuing this spiritual perspective of who you are, I strongly recommend the books, *Conversations with God*, by Neal Donald Walsh.

Why Suffering?

I'd like to extend this discussion of spirituality and love into a consideration of suffering. One of the questions I've had to help people face regularly in my work is, "Why me?" When I worked at the Rehab hospital, people mostly came in because they had a stroke. I remember telling patients and families that everything would be all right; it was just a matter of time and appropriate treatment. I was so naive at first. After about two months of work there, I began to tell people instead, "Life stinks."

It wasn't unusual for people who had a stroke to have had no major medical history prior to the stroke. People were often "as healthy as a horse" one day and then flat on their backs on a litter the next. How do you make sense of this?

People would tell me that they'd never been sick a day in their lives. They worked on the dairy farm from morning 'til night, never took a vacation, ate right, etc., but here they are in the hospital with up to half of their body paralyzed. This was a huge adjustment. And usually it included questioning their spiritual faith, "How could God let this happen?" And while in my experience people tended to believe that God would never give them more than they could handle, they usually came to a time when their spiritual beliefs were truly challenged.

I mentioned earlier how people diagnosed with major illnesses can feel helpless and hopeless. So can we. Health professionals are highly trained to help people return to health, but it doesn't always go so well, especially with chronic illness. It can be very frustrating and stressful for the healthcare worker when all that we learned and thought would help just doesn't work. So, when I got to the point of saying "Life stinks," it was as much out of my own feeling of helplessness as for the patient and family.

Sometimes I joke that I've already got two strikes against me: (1) I'm male, and (2) I'm trained as a scientist. Males and scientists think that if you know what the problem is, all you have to do is analyze it and solve it. Generally, we're control freaks. And on top of that I was raised by a perfectionist. I had to do it right. I had to fix you.

One evening when I was speaking to a group of parents who had a child die, it became so evident to me that you just don't fix some things. This was the most difficult thing I ever had to do. When you lose a child, it doesn't get any tougher. My experience was that you will almost certainly never get over it. And support by compassionate friends was one thing I learned really could help.

Another really difficult experience for me was if the stroke patient were unable to recover and had to be discharged to a nursing home. Usually families have had a discussion where the parents say to their adult children, "I never want to live to be a burden to you." And before they've finished speaking, the children interrupt and say, "Aw, Mom or Dad, don't be silly. If something goes wrong of course we'll take care of you." And before the children finish explaining why this could never be a burden, the parents add this major caveat, "But whatever you do, don't put us in a nursing home." The unfortunate image of the nursing home is not very attractive.

While I worked at the Rehab hospital I often had to explain to the stroke patient and family that the patient required more care than the family would be able to provide at home. The patient would have to be discharged to a nursing home. Again, I felt so helpless and hopeless.

And let me add here for families who have had to face this situation, "Please be gentle with yourselves." You love your family members, and you really do want to care for them, but sometimes things clearly don't work out the way you planned. And for families who are able to have the person discharged to home, if they need full-time care, this is usually very stressful. Again, please be gentle with yourself. You love the person, but now you're going to have to change your life almost completely, and most of you will resent this. It's normal. Please don't be so tough on yourself when you face such a difficult life challenge.

Perhaps you can see that after having to help others adjust to such major changes and all of the emotional upheaval, I began to ask the question, "Why suffering?" And I found myself asking additional big questions like, "Does life serve a purpose? If it does, then why suffering? And, if there is a God, how could an all-knowing and all-loving God permit suffering?" It didn't make sense.

As I said earlier, I felt very helpless at times in attempting to help people cope with, and make sense of, their illness. This drove me to think very seriously about the question, "Why suffering?" Again, if God is all-knowing and all-loving, how could God let this happen? Is suffering a form of spiritual punishment?

I grew up thinking that this was true to some extent. I was taught that God is vengeful: if I didn't obey His will, I would go to hell and burn for eternity. When I was a young boy I remember hearing that a baby had burned to death in a car crash. I remember asking myself, "What was this baby being punished for?" I found some minimal comfort in being told that, "God works in mysterious ways."

Religion wasn't very appealing to me for most of my life, actually. I was forced to go to Sunday School and church every Sunday. My father made us go. I'm told that I was pretty active as a youngster, and having to sit still and be quiet and listen to teachers or preachers that I usually thought were boring, didn't leave me with a very positive feeling about religion.

I remember when I was a Cub Scout. Scouting was a good time. I usually had fun, even though the cub pack was under the auspices of our church. And I could be with a lot of my friends.

One day we were told that we could invite someone whom was not currently in our pack to come to one of our meetings. My best friend then was Barry, so I made sure to ask him to come to our next group. He was all for it, and we were both excited about going.

Barry and I played little league baseball together. I think we wore our baseball hats almost everywhere we went. One day when we were riding the bus past his church, St. Stephens, he told me that I had to tip my hat. Barry was Catholic, and he said you had to tip your hat whenever you went by the church. That was fine by me, and I tipped by hat. I went to the Methodist church down the street, and I realized that we had different beliefs like holy water, catechism, confession, and not eating meat on Friday. But tipping my hat was a new one.

But what really got me was when Barry told me that he couldn't go to my Cub Scout meeting. My Cub Scout pack met in my church, and when he asked his mother if he could go, he was told that a Catholic couldn't go into a Protestant church! This was another, in a long procession of rules and beliefs, that just didn't make sense and that began to drive me away from religion. When I went off to college, and my dad died, that was the end of my religious practice.

Between age 18 and 32, I was mostly of a mind that life didn't serve any purpose, and that when you died, that was it. And my experience in college seemed to support my turning from religion. I was trained as an engineer at first. Chemistry, calculus, and the emphasis on research to determine if something were valid didn't support a role for religion. Even when I started to study psychology, it was all based on science.

Initially, when I met Ken McCaulley in 1977, I didn't appreciate or understand his interest in the spiritual. But it was as though it was time for my life to take a very different direction. Ken had a way of demystifying a lot of what seemed like arcane religious doctrine, and I slowly warmed to the idea that, indeed, life did serve a purpose, and it seemed to be related to learning to love.

The point of relating my early experience with religion is to help you understand my dilemma later in trying to make sense of suffering. I really wanted to help people with strokes who were coming into the rehab hospital. I didn't like feeling helpless and not in control. So I was driven to try to make sense of suffering.

Suffering seems to force us to question, "Why?" and give meaning to our experience. As Joan Borysenko says in her book, *Fire in the Soul*, "More than any other question, 'Why me?' puts us face to face with what we really believe." Earlier in this chapter I proposed that spirituality and love are significant factors in health and healing. I'd now like to consider them as a way to make sense of suffering.

Does Life Serve a Purpose? – The Role of Love and Compassion

The idea that life served the purpose of learning to love was not new to me. I was taught that in Sunday school. But it was blurred and buried under so many other religious beliefs that eventually I became estranged to religion as I just related. But now I found myself trying to find the potential truth and meaning taught by various enlightened seers, prophets, and mystics.

In the New Testament (Matthew 22:36-40) when Jesus was asked,

> "Teacher, which is the greatest commandment in the law?" Jesus replied: "Love the Lord your God with all your heart and with all your soul and with all your mind. This is the first and greatest commandment. And the second is like it: love your neighbor as yourself. All the laws and prophets hang on these two commandments."

This very pithy response certainly seemed to focus on the importance of love. And, as I noted earlier, the Golden Rule, "Do unto others as you would have them do unto you," is the dominant and common advice given by all the major religions regarding how to live.

I also was aware of the research by Dr. Raymond Moody. In his book, *Life After Life*, he described a common scenario for people who have had a near death experience. People who are clinically dead and then return to life often report an experience of being separate from their bodies and traveling through a "tunnel" before coming into the presence of an overwhelming light. This light is experienced as the most intense feeling of love and acceptance. People tend to interpret this light as the presence of God or some spiritual being related to their earthly religious experience. As part of their life review, people are asked by this Supreme Being of Light two basic questions: "Have you learned to love?" and "Are you satisfied with what you've learned?" To learn to love and to gain knowledge appeared to be the purpose for human existence according to Dr. Moody and his research with near death experiences.

As I thought more about the possibility that life served the purpose of learning to love, I found myself asking the question: When we got to the end of our physical life, how would we know whether or not we had learned to love? Would we add up the number of times we hugged or kissed someone? Would we have to have a certain number of good deeds? I asked these questions in earnest, and I found that I really wasn't sure what it meant to love.

In my scientific training I was taught that in order to measure something you had to define it first. And in order to do that, sometimes you had to give it an "operational" definition. What objective evidence was there to measure whether or not something happened? If we're trying to measure or observe love, what behaviors would define and indicate that someone was demonstrating loving behavior?

Again I reflected on my Christian religious training and remembered when the prophet Micah (6:8) told what the Lord required: "To act justly and to love mercy and to walk humbly with your God." The Apostle Paul talked about the importance of faith, hope, and charity. I thought about Jesus and the qualities and character of his person. I also remembered my Boy Scout training and that one was to be thrifty, brave, reverent, etc. I thought that these would be examples of loving behavior; that is, if one were just or fair, merciful, humble, charitable, and reverent – these would be demonstrations of love.

I thought of other qualities or traits that similarly would demonstrate love: compassion, kindness, caring, listening, sensitivity, support, tenderness, patience, sincerity, loyalty, friendship, sympathy, respect, courage etc. Then it occurred to me that these were the very qualities or behaviors that we would admire most, especially at a time of crisis. I thought about patients and families who had strokes or great pain and upset, and how the experience of suffering and distress could teach us the real value of love. It is when we are feeling most travailed that we truly learn to appreciate loving acts.

If life serves the purpose of learning to love, times of suffering may actually be blessings in disguise! This doesn't mean that suffering is necessary or that it is the only or best way to learn to love. Just as I said in earlier chapters of this book: stress usually isn't stress unless you think it is. Criticism isn't criticism unless you think it is. And suffering isn't suffering unless you think it is. But the reality is that you're likely to perceive stressful times with normal human fears and anxieties and not see them as unique opportunities for learning and personal growth.

Remember, in raising your children, how much you loved them? You'd like to have wrung their necks a few times, but you loved them dearly. You wanted them to grow up to be happy, healthy and responsible. And sometimes you realized that they were going to have to learn some things the hard way. It wasn't your preference. You loved them, and would never have wished them harm or upset. But you knew that there were some lessons in life that they had to learn.

Perhaps we could use this same scenario in thinking about our life purpose of learning to love. In the end, what's most important is that we learn. God wouldn't ever wish us harm or that we learn the hard way. But if the purpose of life is to learn to love, is it unreasonable to think that there might be some built-in system to help make sure that we do what we came to do?

Human existence has been referred to by metaphysicians as "a veil of tears." It seems to be a "given" that life is going to have its turmoil. However, if life is about learning to love, which I believe is best exemplified by demonstrating compassion, then human existence with all of its seeming tragedy and suffering, may be just what the doctor ordered.

The Four Noble Truths of Buddhism deal with the inevitable fact of suffering. Life is suffering. A fundamental practice for Buddhists is to pray thanking their illness, crisis, or suffering for aiding their spiritual growth. In his wonderful book, *A Path With Heart,* Jack Kornfield talks about his training and experience as a Buddhist monk. One chapter is titled, "Turning Straw Into Gold."

> Like the young maiden in the fairy tale "Rumpelstiltskin" who is locked in a room full of straw, we often do not realize that the straw all around us is gold in disguise. The basic principle of spiritual life is that our problems become the very place to discover wisdom and love.

In her book, *Minding the Body, Mending the Mind,* Joan Borysenko, proposes similarly that stress is an opportunity for learning and growth:

> Shakespeare said, "When the sea was calm all boats alike showed mastership in floating." Only in a storm are they obliged to cope. Storms and struggles, chaos and tragedy have always been looked upon as the teachers of valuable, if unwelcome, lessons. In the struggle to survive a stressful situation, a new way of being often emerges that is much more satisfying than the old. Every religion and the great myths and fables of all cultures discuss change and growth through the archetypes of death and rebirth. Easter and Passover, symbolic of death and resurrection, are also metaphors for escape from our past conditioning and outmoded concepts – and rebirth into freedom. The phoenix

that arises from its ashes and the seed that dies to give birth to the flower are all variations on the theme of life as a continuous process of growth.

In his book, *Man's Search for Meaning*, Viktor Frankl talks about his experience as a prisoner in a concentration camp. His experience with extreme suffering and indignities led him to develop a form of psychotherapy where he believed many neuroses were the result of the failure to find meaning and responsibility in the distressing experiences of life. His philosophy states: "...the central theme of existentialism: to live is to suffer, to survive is to find meaning in the suffering."

Stephanie Matthews Simonton has written a great book, *The Healing Family*, for families facing illness. She has worked extensively with cancer patients and families dealing with the stress of serious illness. She has found that as people search to give meaning to their illness, they begin to discover and believe that they can have some control over their disease and lives. They are no longer victims of something beyond their control. I'd like to quote a paragraph from her book to summarize the consideration of the question, "Why me?" and how serious illness or crises can be transformed into richer and more fulfilling life experiences as we begin to give meaning to and reprioritize our lives:

> It would be pollyannaish to suggest that cancer is a positive experience; of course, it is not. But those who truly come to terms with it *use* it in positive ways, to grow and change toward better lives. Often they realize that they have given their lives over to making it in the world – making money, earning some kind of external success that they believe will validate them as worthwhile people. But they haven't spent time with their children. They haven't laughed and talked and shared the little and big things that have meaning for them. Until the diagnosis, every member of the family got up in the morning and rushed out to school or the office, never taking time to see what a pretty day it was. One patient told me that her youngest son used to frequently go outside in the morning and come back with a flower for her. She always accepted it with thanks, but until cancer showed her she was mortal, she never realized how loving and sensitive that little boy was.

11

Intuition and Creativity

Intuition by definition is "knowledge based on insight or spiritual perception rather than on reasoning." Intuition is like the "Aha" effect. It feels right. You just instantaneously know what's true.

This is obviously counter to reason and science, methods we have come to use, respect, and rely on especially in our formal education. Can you imagine being in college and basing your answer to a test question on other than objective data, fact, reason, or research? It seems so illogical.

And isn't that part of the questionable image of intuition? It's entirely subjective; it's like a hunch and very much "feeling-based."

In this culture we allow that women can be "intuitive," but males, as a rule, treat this as a feminine trait to be tolerated, but not often respected. Men, of course, are not intuitive. They have "gut" feelings. I say this with a sense of humor, but, also, to begin to make the point that we in fact use intuition all of the time, but are prone to believe that reason is a more preferred and accurate method in determining truth.

How Do We Determine Truth?

How do we know what's true? My opinion is that most of us rely on our direct experience. We were there. We saw it and heard it. We've lived it, so, we know from our experience what's true.

While I would not have you discount your life experience, I think that most of you understand that one's experience is, in fact, quite subjective. This is how "fish stories" get told. When you first catch the fish, it's a certain length. But when you recount the experience, the size of the fish has a way of changing, and usually becoming larger.

Our senses are actually very selective. When we experience something, we only are aware of and recall certain parts of that experience. Your truth, or what you perceive, will be affected by your conditioned, subjective filters.

For example, depending on one's age, experience, gender, ethnic background, education, etc., if a person were to describe someone, chances are he or she would focus on and talk about that person differently than another person would. Which is more true? Both are valid, but your subjective perceptions would describe different parts of the person. Both are only part of the picture, and based on what's important or relevant to you.

So, the idea that any one person has or knows the whole truth about something is inherently flawed. What you believe to be true is colored by innate and conditioned or learned factors. Remember, it's not that this is wrong; it's just that an individual's experience and what he or she believes is true is necessarily biased.

But what if a group of people saw and heard the same thing, and all agreed about what they experienced, would this be a better way to determine the truth? This is how the jury system is intended to work. A jury of our peers is seated to evaluate and agree on what's true. I trust that most of you understand that while this is a good system, it also has inherent flaws. Remember the O. J. Simpson trials? When my friend and mentor, Ken McCaulley, was teaching psychology many years ago, another teacher came into his room one day and asked him to help make this point in his class.

This other teacher was having difficulty explaining the subjectivity of experience, and, more specifically, how this is true also in the way juries evaluate the evidence and truth of a matter. So Ken and this teacher decided to make up a brief script. Ken was to go into the other classroom at a designated time and say, "When you tell Dr. Gregg something about me, tell him the truth." That's all he would say.

Then he would hit this teacher three times on the left shoulder with what looked like a wooden rod. In fact, they took a mailing tube and stuffed it with rags so that it wouldn't sound hollow, and covered this tube with wood-looking contact paper. It is important to know also that Ken was five feet nine inches tall, weighed 180 pounds, wore glasses, and was wearing a light gray suit.

As arranged, Ken walked into the other classroom where about 30 people were seated for class. He walked up to their teacher and said, "When you tell Dr. Gregg something about me, tell him the truth." He hit the instructor three times on the left shoulder with the mailing tube, then headed for the door to leave the room.

A number of students jumped from their seats to go after Ken. From their point of view Ken had just assaulted their teacher, and they were not going to let him get away. Their instructor anticipated this, and immediately intervened and told them to take their seats. They were all now going to file a police report and really get this guy.

The students responded to this plea from their teacher and his request that they now write two paragraphs. In the first paragraph they were to describe everything which took place. And in the second, they were to describe the assailant. They were going to get the police after him.

The students took this assignment well, but what they reported will likely surprise you. Approximately 30 students sitting only a short distance from this event reported in relative agreement what they saw and heard.

In fact, Ken said, "When you tell Dr. Gregg something about me, tell him the truth." However, the students reported in one way or another that Ken "threatened the teacher with his life." They all said that Ken hit their teacher 10 or more times on the head. No one said that he actually hit him on the left shoulder. Everyone claimed that Ken was six feet or taller, and that he weighed over 200 pounds. No one reported that he was wearing glasses. And all said that he was wearing a dark-colored suit (most said "black"). How could 30 people sitting so close to this incident report it so differently than what actually took place?

In this case, Ken, as the assailant, was envisioned as the bad guy. He hit their teacher, with whom the students identified. And we all know that bad guys wear black. They, of course, don't wear glasses. And they are necessarily the bigger, bully-acting type, who pick on helpless victims.

If ever you want to confirm the accuracy of such an occurrence, I recommend that you video and audio tape the event. This will give you the objective record and evidence. But, again, how did these people not only distort the truth, but manage to agree on what happened? The answer is that you tend to see what you expect to see, and you tend to hear what you expect to hear.

This is demonstrated in what are called "prejudice cards." A trained person holds up a picture of something for a brief period of time, then asks the person viewing the picture to say what he or she just saw.

For example, let's say that this is a school setting in a predominantly caucasian neighborhood. The teacher holds up a picture of a white man stabbing a black man. What will most students report they just saw in this picture? Most will report that a black man was stabbing a white man. Exactly the opposite. How could this be? Again, you tend to see what you expect to see. And the really scary part about it is that this means you. *You* tend to see what you expect to see. And *you* tend to hear what you expect to hear.

I trust that you can appreciate, then, that even when a group of people agree on what's true, while this often can give greater confidence about "the facts," there remains a subjective element which needs to be acknowledged and understood.

The reality that numbers of people and their collective experience and agreement can't always be an accurate way to determine truth allows me to reinforce another point. In earlier chapters I talked about the need to be tolerant of individual differences as part of stress management. The folly and arrogance of criticism is that no one can ever know everything about anything. So, for yet another reason, I encourage you to be appropriately cautious when you might insist on the truth of something. The probability is that your perception of the truth is only part of the picture and biased by any other number of factors including what you expect to be true.

If anything, it seems that I may be trying to make a case for science. In science researchers attempt to control for contaminating factors such as individual biases and subjectivity. In science everything must be objectively measured. But in this approach, as I've discussed before, if it's not objectively measurable, then science tends to propose that it's not valid or true.

Understand that science is a method. And it, too, has its inherent biases regarding how to determine truth. And, unfortunately, because science has questioned the very existence of subjective phenomena such as the mind and mental events, research often is not even conducted to attempt to measure what is apparent common sense such as the will to live.

Again, this is not to suggest that you shouldn't trust your individual or collective experience or the scientific method to determine what's true. Just understand that none of these approaches are foolproof. And if we can accept that there is no sure way to know what's true, exercising one's intuition as yet another factor in helping us to address our concerns and to determine the truth may not seem so far-fetched. And this would seem to be what using your head *and* your heart is all about.

Intuition Is a Fact of Life

A few years ago I read an article in the newspaper where it was reported that the Vatican was now accepting Galileo back into the church. You may remember historically when Galileo was excommunicated by the Catholic Church for determining that the earth was not the center of the universe. Now the Vatican was releasing a statement saying that it recognized that there is a role for science, but that, of course, the primary way to determine truth is still divine revelation.

What an interesting dilemma this presents. Our formal education, medicine, insurance reimbursement, and so much of what we do relies so heavily on science and research. And yet our spiritual training says that through prayer and meditation we can receive insight into all of life's concerns. "Call to me and I will answer you, and will tell you great and hidden things which you have not known." (Jeremiah 33:3.) "Ask, and it will be given you; seek, and you will find; knock, and it will be opened to you." (Luke 11:9.)

Most people use prayer for insight and guidance. When people are facing difficult decisions, it is common for them to "pray on it." Whatever their religious beliefs, people look to their God or related spiritual figures for support and direction. Many in the Catholic Church pray to saints for help. Millions of people have prayed to Saint Jude, the Saint of the Impossible, when they were seriously ill, and "know" that their prayers were heard and answered.

But can you imagine your physician basing your diagnosis and treatment on some form of spiritual guidance? I've asked this question regularly in my classes. And most people are very clear that they would find it quite incredulous that their doctor would base their treatment on anything other than science. It's interesting, again, though, that all religions throughout history have used non-logical, subjective, and intuitive means to base their decisions.

In the Christian Bible and the story of the birth of Jesus, many were exuberant at the coming of what they believed to be the Son of God. Of course others, like King Herod, were not pleased, and ordered that the baby be found and killed. Then one night an angel appeared in a vision to Joseph and said that he should move the baby Jesus to Egypt for safety. And according to this biblical story, Joseph and Mary acted accordingly.

If you really stop to think about it, this is about as major a decision as anyone would ever have to make. The life or death of Jesus, when and where He should be moved, was based on a "vision." Yet two paragraphs earlier I noted that most people would have scoffed at having their medical treatment based on such a vision. How do we reconcile this?

We could argue that these were special times and special people, and that the use of dreams and visions was somehow more appropriate then. In fact, the Bible is full of examples of people, who Christians revere greatly, being given spiritual insight through their dreams. But when we examine the historical evidence, we find that people have been given divine guidance throughout history.

The fact is that prayer is an important part of the daily life of about 75% of Americans. About 60% report that faith is the most important influence in their lives. Yet faith by definition is "the conviction that a thing unproved by evidence is true."

Currently, approximately two-thirds of Americans report having experienced extra sensory perception (ESP). Nearly one-half of American adults believe that they have been in contact with someone who has died, usually a dead spouse or sibling. About one-half of Americans believe that their pet dogs respond to their thoughts. And even the U.S. Central Intelligence Agency (CIA) admitted publicly in 1995 to conducting more than 20 years of research with intuition for intelligence collection. Dr. Harold Puthoff, who did much of this research at Stanford Research Institute, concluded that "the integrated results appear to provide unequivocal evidence of a human capacity to access events remote in space and time, however falteringly, by some cognitive process not yet understood."

Intuition is certainly well-recognized in artistic expression. In fact in a study of artistic people, it was reported that they often tended to remember and use their dreams as a source of insight and inspiration.

The highly acclaimed singer and songwriter, Billy Joel, said that all of the music he has composed came from his dreams. Many of the greatest composers, including Mozart and Beethoven, have dreamed the symphonies they wrote.

One day I was listening to a radio interview with the jazz pianist, Keith Jarrett. The interviewer was being quite complimentary about a new record album Keith had just released. When this interviewer made some especially positive critique about one of the songs he had written, Keith said, "I didn't write it; I just heard it and wrote it down."

The novelist, William Styron, who wrote *Sophie's Choice*, said that he received the insight for the outline and story for this book in a dream. Robert Louis Stevenson was similarly inspired by a dream to write *Dr. Jekyll and Mr Hyde*, as was Samuel Taylor Coleridge to write *Kubla Khan*. Socrates was instructed in a dream how to put *Aesop's Fables* into verse. Shakespeare and so many of the most gifted writers in history have credited their dreams and times of reverie for much of what they wrote.

It is even somewhat common for writers to have the experience of having to reread what they wrote, for at times they were unaware of what they had just written. It was as though they didn't actually write the material, and that some other seemingly supernatural force had taken over their handwriting.

William Blake claimed that his major prophetic poem, "Jerusalem," came to him entirely from his "spiritual perception." He said that he wrote:

> ...from immediate dictation, twelve or sometimes twenty or thirty lines at a time without premeditation and even against my will; the time it has taken in writing was thus rendered non-existent. And an immense poem exists which seems to be the labor of a long life all produced without labor or study.

Pitirim Sorokin founded the departments of sociology at the University of Minnesota and at Harvard University. In his best-selling book, *The Crisis of Our Age*, he states that "there is hardly any doubt that intuition is the real source of knowledge, different from the role of the senses and reason." His survey of the literature found that philosophers including Plato, Aristotle, Plotinus, St. Augustine, Descartes, Thomas Hobbs, Henri Bergson, Baruch Spinoza, Carl Jung, and Alfred North Whitehead all agreed that intuition is the basis of truth.

Many inventors, including scientists, also claim that their ideas came from dreams. Albert Einstein said that he received his theory of relativity from his dreams (and that he had to study for years to make sense of this information). Kekule's concept of the structure of the benzene ring came during a dream. Elias Howe's idea for putting the eye of the sewing machine needle near the point was a result of having a dream where a tribe of savages carried spears in which the heads of the spears had eye-shaped holes.

Many other acclaimed geniuses including Leonardo da Vinci have used their dreams and intuition to create their inventions. Even Descartes prayed for a method to determine the truth, and received a vision of analytic geometry. A novel anecdote told about Thomas Edison is that whenever he was having difficulty with one of his inventions, he would take a 15 or 20 minute nap and consult with his board of directors.

My Personal Experience with Intuition

I remember being exposed to using dreams for insight back in the early 1970's. I thought this was pretty strange stuff then. But in 1977 I was experiencing a great deal of stress related to owning a clothing store, and my friend, Ken McCaulley, said that I needed a hobby to help relieve this stress.

Interestingly, I didn't really have a hobby then, and I couldn't think of anything that I'd really like to do as a positive diversion. So Ken suggested that I ask my dreams. Even though this was quite new to me, I decided to take it seriously since my business-related stress was really quite great.

That first night I had a dream that I was gardening. I had never gardened before, or even thought of gardening. But I decided to act on my dream, and asked my landlord if I could use a space behind the house for my garden.

For the first time in my life I found that I could be late to work. I was always very compulsive and punctual, but now I found that I could become so involved in tending my garden that I lost track of time. I loved it. And to this day, my favorite hobby is gardening. When my wife, Shelly, and I moved to California, our greatest interest was to find a place and piece of land where we could garden more year-round.

Because of my successful experience with this dream, I actually began to keep a dream journal. I found that within one month I was recalling four or five dreams every night and taking about an hour the next morning to record them.

At some point in my paying attention to my dreams, I realized that I would also awaken with a line from a song running through my mind. And I forget exactly how this happened, but I soon realized that this line from the song was giving me intuitive information. It could be something as simple as hearing a song about rain, which was telling me that it would rain that day.

But the time that really got my attention was one morning when I awoke with a song, and I couldn't figure out what it meant. Several hours later that day when I started my car, the radio came on playing that song. I thought, "What a unique coincidence." I really didn't give it much more thought, but the next day made me realize that this was almost certainly no coincidence.

That next morning I awoke humming two songs, which was unusual. And I hadn't heard either of them in a long time. I was disappointed because I couldn't see any intuitive meaning for either of them. Many hours later I again was driving in my car, and the first two songs that were played on the radio were the two I had awakened hearing.

I knew enough about mathematics, probabilities and permutations that the odds of my hearing three songs back-to-back that I heard in my mind many hours before was not likely coincidence. It may not sound like much, but I remember how meaningful this was to me then.

I now looked forward to hearing these early-morning songs. And before long I found that I would get lines from songs throughout the day. It was as though part of my psyche was talking to me through pieces of songs. This led me to seriously study, practice, and develop my intuition. And as you might imagine, Ken McCaulley was my greatest supporter and teacher.

At some point Ken revealed to me that he had been "psychic" all of his life, and had gone to a psychiatrist for treatment because he and his family thought that he was "crazy." For example, Ken could hear the telephone ring and know who it was before anyone answered the phone.

Fortunately for Ken, although many years later, he was treated by a psychiatrist who was more understanding of his extra sensory perception. With this psychiatrist's support and guidance, Ken literally began to read one or two books daily about intuition and parapsychology.

Many years later Ken went on to develop and teach courses in parapsychology. But now Ken and I began to sit daily to practice and develop our intuition. And at some point Ken began to go into a trance state and speak a truth and wisdom that was far beyond his current knowledge and intellect. I valued these sessions so highly that I audio-recorded each one and have kept them to this day. (I have about seven years of these tapes which I hope to transcribe and put into a book in the near future.)

Needless to say I had a great deal of experience in working with Ken to help me understand and respect the use of intuition as another way to know what's true. But I want to mention some other experiences that I hope you will find helpful in supporting the use of intuition as a natural complement to the use of reason and logic.

As I began to share with others my experience and interest in intuition, I came to hear many similar stories where people "just knew" something. One woman was on vacation and her sister had no way to get in touch with her to tell her that their mother had become gravely ill. The vacationing sister reported, however, that she "knew" that she had to return home, even though she didn't know why. She arrived home in time to see her mother before she died. The sisters were certain that some type of intuitive process was at work.

Mothers often can sense that something's wrong with their children without any objective evidence. And even when I've asked clergy how they know God has answered their prayers, the most common response was, "I just know." Of course, it's just this kind of answer that will drive most scientists crazy. How can you "just know"?

I remember when a friend asked me if I knew who Depak Chopra was. She had never heard of him, but had had a dream where she was interviewing for a job and told that if she knew Depak Chopra she could have the job. She remembers spelling out the name very clearly in her dream. I was glad then to share with her a book of his, and told her that I had just been thinking of buying a series of his audio cassettes. This woman went on, "coincidentally," to study and practice alternative forms of healing. She feels certain that she was guided by this dream to this type of work.

When my wife bought two new dressers for our bedroom, and I began to transfer my clothes to the new dresser, I remarked that I was glad to have four smaller drawers that were just the right size for my socks, because now I could separate colors. I often found it difficult to tell black from blue in a not well-lit bedroom. My wife then proceeded to retrieve her dream journal, and read word-for-word what I had just said from a dream that she had had months before. Every detail was in her dream journal: me, what I said, the dresser and socks!

My wife has a nephew who has a young son. One day when they were looking at photographs, the nephew asked his son if he knew who the people in the photographs were. The young son had never seen his grandfather (he died before he was born), so the nephew was surprised when his son regularly identified him in pictures. When the nephew asked his son how he knew that this was his grandfather, the son replied, "He comes to play with me every day!"

Brian Weiss' book, *Many Lives, Many Masters*, gives some insight and explanation as to how this might happen. Dr. Weiss is a psychiatrist who in 1980 was treating a woman for recurring nightmares and anxiety attacks, and, when more conventional methods of therapy were ineffective, tried hypnosis.

Under hypnosis the woman recalled many "past-life" memories, which appeared to be directly linked to her symptoms, and led to her cure. While this, in itself, is interesting, what was more astounding was that while this woman was in a trance state during her hypnosis she began to speak a spiritual wisdom that clearly was not coming from herself. This spiritual "Master" who was "channeling" this wisdom offered messages on such topics as:

> ...life after death; our choosing when we are born and
> when we will die; the sure and unerring guidance of the
> Masters; lifetimes measured in lessons learned and tasks
> fulfilled, not in years; charity, hope, faith, love; doing
> without expectation of return...

Dr. Weiss had no training or preparation for this kind of experience. He claims still to have no scientific explanation for what happened. He graduated Phi Beta Kappa, magna cum laude, from Columbia University, received his medical degree from Yale University, was nationally recognized for his research in biological psychiatry, and became Chief of Psychiatry at the University of Miami. He was aware of some of the research in parapsychology, but it all seemed very farfetched to him.

But the story doesn't stop here. This "Master" wisdom, which spoke through his patient, now also began to give Dr. Weiss very meaningful, relevant facts about himself and his family. The "Master" said that he was actually here for Dr. Weiss, primarily, not the patient, who was the vehicle for this information. Dr. Weiss was given very detailed knowledge specifically about his father and son, both who were deceased. These facts were not known by anyone, let alone his patient. Dr. Weiss' life would never be the same again. Despite being trained in the scientific method of observation and validation, he now "knew" that intuition could reveal truths that mainstream science could not explain.

My wife had read Brian Weiss' book, and I especially remembered her telling me that the information revealed was intended primarily for Dr. Weiss, not just insights that led to his patient's cure. The reason I mention this particular experience is that only weeks after my wife shared this story with me, I had a very similar experience.

I had been conducting workshops on "How to Develop Your Intuition," and a woman asked me if I would work with her personally. During one of our first sessions, while in a trance state, her "inner guide" (a process I'll explain in detail in Chapter 12) revealed to me that she was there to help me! We received much information intuitively that helped my friend, but her intuition claimed to be there, primarily, for me. It was then that I remembered my wife telling me about Brian Weiss' experience, and I went home to read *Many Lives, Many Masters* with a greatly renewed interest.

Actually I had had years of experience of talking with what Ken McCaulley and I called "mentors," when he would go into a trance state daily for most of the years we worked together. As I said earlier, from 1978 through 1985, I had lengthy conversations with these "mentors" and, also, those who were referred to as "Master Teachers." In the first chapter of this book I mentioned that meeting Ken McCaulley had changed my life dramatically. And this is one of the greatest reasons: being exposed to this daily source of wisdom. I had a million questions. And as truly skeptical as I was initially, these "mentors" and "Masters" gave me facts and information that were consistently and clearly proof to me of their reality and the validity of intuition.

This experience with Ken McCaulley's unique intuitive ability (and my own developing intuition) actually led to a very lonely experience for me in graduate school. I now knew that intuition was a normal part of human intelligence, but in graduate school everything had to be supported with scientific research. So for the five years it took for me to earn my master's and doctorate degrees, I had to keep my special knowledge and experience to myself for fear that revealing my interest in intuition would keep me from receiving my Ph.D.

Unfortunately, Ken's health began to deteriorate in 1985 due to a series of strokes. His poorer health also disallowed his ability to "channel" information intuitively. So when I met this woman in 1996 to help her develop her intuition, I was thrilled to have the experience again of communicating in this way with a spiritual wisdom.

My interest in intuition continued following Ken's health decline, but in 1987 I began my work as a staff psychologist in a rehab hospital. And in 1988 I became Director of Psychological Support Services for the physician management group where I developed and taught my program, "Taking Control of Your Health," to their cancer centers. These positions kept me in a very scientific environment where I continued to be reluctant to share my very personal and strong interest in intuition. I was becoming aware, however, that intuitive approaches were being used in medical settings, such as when I interned with Carl Simonton at his cancer center. (I'll talk much more in depth about the uses of intuition in medicine in Chapter 12.)

So, again, when I had the experience with this woman in 1996 helping her develop her intuition, I was elated. But in 1998 I was given another true gift.

From time to time my wife and I had thought about taking a cruise, but for various reasons we never did. But then we heard that in January, 1998, there was an "Intuition" conference headed by Larry Dossey, Joan Borysenko, Raymond Moody, Dannion Brinkley, and others, which was being held on a cruise to the Caribbean Islands. We couldn't resist, and signed up for the cruise.

I was very familiar with Larry Dossey and Joan Borysenko. I had read all of their books and attended a number of their workshops and presentations. And while I had read Raymond Moody's and Dannion Brinkley's books, I had never seen either of them in person. So it was a treat to hear more about their work and experience with near-death experiences.

Dr. Moody has been a true pioneer in this work, and his books and research have contributed greatly to the search for answers about some of life's mysteries, including extra sensory perception. His first book documenting the experience of people who were clinically dead and revived, *Life after Life*, has sold more than 14 million copies world-wide. Interestingly, this book was published in 1975, the year Dannion Brinkley had his first near-death experience.

In 1975 Dannion was struck by lightning, and almost instantaneously found himself "engulfed by peace and tranquility." For a moment, at first, he experienced great pain as the electricity of the lightning coursed through his body. But then he realized that he was not in his physical body, and that he was viewing his body below him on the bed, apparently dead.

When the ambulance arrived, medical technicians attempted to save him, but declared him "gone." Dannion now heard "the sound of chimes," and a "tunnel" began to surround him. He realized that he was moving at a high rate of speed through this "darkness," but could see a light in the distance which grew brighter and brighter until he was "standing in a paradise of brilliant light." He soon felt "a deep sense of love" as a "Being of Light" approached him. Then this Being of Light "engulfed" him, and he began to re-experience his whole life. You can read about Dannion's remarkable experience in his best-selling book, *Saved By the Light*.

The introduction to this book was written by Raymond Moody, who states, "Dannion Brinkley's near-death experience stands as one of the most remarkable I have heard." Although Moody has investigated more than a 1000 near-death experiences, he is especially impressed with how Dannion "was allowed a glimpse of the future."

As part of Dannion's experience in this "spiritual realm," 13 Beings of Light shared with him 117 revelations about the future, 95 of which have come true as reported in his 1994 book. Moody also reports in the introduction that when he first interviewed Dannion, he was certain that these revelations were "nonsense, the ravings of a man fried by lightning":

> For instance, he told me that the breakdown of the Soviet Union would occur in 1989 and would be marked by food riots. He even told of a great war in the deserts of the Middle East that would be fought when a small country was invaded by a large one. According to the Beings of Light, there would be a clashing of two armies, one of which would be destroyed. This war would take place in 1990, Dannion insisted. The war he was talking about was, of course, the Gulf War.
>
> As I have already said, I considered his predictions to be pure nonsense. Over the years I have just nodded and written down what he has said. For a long time I thought that his brain was somewhat scrambled by the incident, and I was

willing to give him a considerable amount of latitude. After all, I reasoned, who wouldn't be a little strange after being struck by lightning?

Later it was I who acted like a person struck by lightning when I realized that the events he had told me about were coming true! How could this be? I wondered. How could a near-death experience lead to the capacity to see into the future? I didn't know the answer.

I have been a close friend of Dannion since we first talked in 1976. In those intervening years another revelation has made me feel as if I have been struck by lightning. Dannion Brinkley appears to be able to read minds!

He has done this many times with me – simply looked me right in the eyes and told me what was going on in the most personal aspects of my life. More important, I have seen him apparently read the minds of total strangers, telling them what they received in the mail that very day, who telephoned them, or how they felt about their spouses, children, even themselves.

He doesn't do this in the form of vague proclamations. Rather, he is incredibly specific. He once came into a college classroom where I was teaching and knew details of the personal lives of every student in the room! He was so accurate and specific in his readings that all the class members were gasping and some were openly weeping at his revelations. I must point out here that he had never spoken to a single one of the students before entering the room. They were all strangers.

I have seen him "read the minds" of perfect strangers so many times that it has become almost commonplace in my life. In fact, I have come to cherish that moment of recognition when a person's skepticism is replaced by awe, then wonder, at the realization that his most private thoughts are being read like an open book.

Dannion had a second near-death experience 14 years later, where he received yet more spiritual insights, and was encouraged to use his psychic gifts to help the dying. Indeed, Dannion has gone on to develop a hospice program called Compassion In Action.

While we thoroughly enjoyed hearing and talking with these recognized authorities about their experience and knowledge about intuition, another special treat was meeting Patti Aubrey-Carpenter, a Spiritualist Minister from Cassadega, Florida. She was also a presenter for the conference. Patti's session largely involved her giving "messages" to people in the audience.

My wife, Shelly, and I arrived a little late for this session, but we had no sooner gotten seated, when Patti asked me, "May I come to you (could she give me a message publicly that she was receiving intuitively)?" I couldn't have been more receptive.

She then proceeded to "read me like a book." My wife was especially impressed by how much Patti seemed to know about me when we had never met before, and there was no way that she could have known other than intuitively what she was now saying. The part that really got my attention was when she said that I would be writing this book and that "It will revolutionize medicine!"

Immediately following her presentation, Shelly and I scheduled private "readings" with her. During these private sessions, which we audio-taped, Patti gave us very detailed and meaningful information about ourselves. Among many other things, Shelly was told that she had very powerful healing abilities, which she would develop and practice, and that she was very intuitive. In fact, my wife is a massage therapist and therapeutic touch practitioner.

When we returned home from this cruise, we discussed any number of things, but I was especially interested in talking about Shelly's "reading" from Patti, and if she would be interested in developing her intuition. I had worked with her several times before using receptive imagery to help her gain insight into some personal issues, but I was curious if she would be willing to experiment with the intuitive abilities that Patti had described in her private session. I was somewhat surprised when Shelly said that she had been hoping that I would ask.

Then came the gift. Shelly immediately tapped into a spiritual wisdom that we now call "John." Not only was I blessed to have Shelly for my wife and lifetime partner, but now we could share her unique intuitive ability to guide us though our personal and professional lives.

Because of my deep respect for this wisdom, I have tape-recorded all of these conversations with "John" (which at some point we may also share in a book). John often reminds me that I have my own intuition, and that I should continue to develop it, and that I have no need to rely on Shelly or him. The fact is that we all have this ability, which we can develop and use.

You can learn to discern the truth for yourself. The key is discernment. In time, with practice, you can become quite accurate at knowing what is right for you. It will *feel* right. And even if what felt right at the time turns out to be less than completely true, my opinion is that it was the right thing for you to do then. It was what you were open to and ready for at that time. For those of you who may be interested in developing your intuition, a guided imagery script is in the Appendix of this book.

Again, while I'm promoting intuition as a way to determine truth, especially about what you should do regarding your health, remember to consider the judgment of trained medical experts. But there is ample evidence historically for the use of intuition in medicine. And I think you may be surprised at the number of examples and evidence for the effective use of intuition in healthcare today, which I present in the next chapter.

12

Uses of Intuition in Medicine

Dr. Jeanne Achterberg reported in her book, *Imagery in Healing: Shamanism and Modern Medicine*, that "dreams and visions are universally the most common method of inquiry into the cause and cure of disease." Their use reached its peak during the Grecian era when Asclepius "became the patron, the demigod, and the chief representative of healing for centuries." More than 200 temples were built throughout Greece, Italy, and Turkey to honor Asclepius and his healing "mode of gentleness and concern, love, and dignity." Achterberg noted that patients' dreams and visions were used as primary healing tools:

> To begin with, the Hippocratic Oath, the ethical code of honor still taken by every practicing physician today, is a dedication to the mythical founding family of medicine, whose contribution was a method for healing with imagination. It begins: "I swear by Apollo the Physician, by Asclepius, by Hygeia and Panacea and by all the Gods and Goddesses, making them my witnesses, that I will fulfill according to my ability and judgment this oath and this covenant."

Hippocrates, the "Father of Medicine," was trained in the Asclepian tradition. Many other Greek physicians including Galen continued this practice of medicine where "the patients' imagery or dream content was believed to offer clinically important diagnostic information."

Dr. Achterberg reported that the Middle Ages also had its effect on the practice of medicine. Religious and folk traditions came to dominate methods of healing at that time. From the sixth to the 14th centuries, healing was often the province of "wise women," or "witches" as they came to be called by many.

These women possessed unique abilities to prophesy and intuit patients' diagnoses and treatments. They came to be respected as truly learned and wise by many physicians of their time: "Paracelsus, the Renaissance giant of a physician and founder of modern chemistry, credited his understanding of the laws and practices of health to his conversations with the wise women." But Achterberg concluded that while practically everyone, it seemed, believed in the magic of these wise women, practicing anything supernatural was declared heresy by the church and usually punished severely. According to the priesthood, one's religious faith was the only cure. Literally millions of women came to be tortured and killed, accused of practicing medicine outside the auspices of the church.

Over time many of the Asclepian medical traditions were adopted by the church, but the reason for healing would now be attributed to saints. The dream therapy of Ascelpius was commonly practiced, but the patron saints of healing, Saint Cosmas and Damian, now became the dream messengers of cures. According to Dr. Achterberg:

> Thus, the methods of the shamans and the wise women – healing in nonordinary reality and invoking visions of spirit guides – has been a part of Christianity since its inception. Only the names have been changed.

Of course these women healers also came to be castigated because of the advent of science. Intuition is the antithesis of the scientific method. And when the Cartesian belief of separation of mind and body became dominant, any holistic approach incorporating mind, body, and spirit was simply unacceptable.

It is truly remarkable, given the dominant role of the scientific method to determine current medical practice, that intuition has made a significant comeback in recent years. I'd like now to mention a few of the major uses and evidences of the effective practice of intuition in medicine today.

Your Inner Guide or Advisor

At the start of this book I mentioned my internships and work with Dr. Carl Simonton at the Simonton Cancer Center. He co-authored a book, *Getting Well Again*, with Stephanie Matthews-Simonton about their psychosocial approach to cancer treatment. The 15th chapter of this book is titled, *"Finding Your Inner Guide to Health."* Here they detail how "the unconscious mind communicates with the conscious self through feelings, dreams, and intuitions."

Through what they call the "Inner Guide process," patients are advised firstly to practice mental relaxation. Once feeling comfortable and relaxed, they are then asked to imagine a "living creature–a person (whom you do not know) or a friendly animal…If this person or creature makes you feel warm, comfortable, and safe, you know it is an Inner Guide."

Patients are then instructed to engage the person or creature in a conversation and to discuss their problems. People commonly then receive information and advice about their feelings, motivations, and behavior. "The guide can tell you when you are making yourself sick and suggest what you can do to help yourself get well." The Simontons reported:

> …patients are often more responsive to insights achieved in consultation with their Inner Guides than they are to the observations of a group leader or a therapist. Because the Inner Guide is an aspect of their own personalities, relying on such a guide is a healthy step toward taking responsibility for their physical and psychological health.

I explained in Chapter 4 that guided imagery is essentially mental rehearsal. You imagine what you want to happen, and because your brain doesn't know the difference between fact and fantasy (perception is reality), your brain processes this imagined event as it would an actual experience. Thus, belief can become biology.

The use of intuitive imagery is different from guided imagery and is sometimes called receptive imagery. Instead of imagining what you want, you allow for a creative flow of images, feelings or thoughts to come into your awareness. It is quite spontaneous. You become the passive observer. It's a very creative experience, and usually enjoyable and very meaningful. It's an adventure where you never quite know what's going to appear to respond to your inquiry about some problem or ailment.

I have used and worked with this approach for more than 20 years. I first learned about it when I took Ken McCaulley's classes in 1977. It indeed appears that intuition is a natural part of one's intelligence and psyche. Your unconscious mind or psyche appears to be a fundamental balancing mechanism constantly striving to bring to your awareness areas that are of priority and need your conscious attention.

Your subconscious mind, or the part of you that has access to your spiritual nature, appears to have a full knowledge of everything about you. This includes knowing why you are sick and what you can do to get well.

To become good at making this contact with your inner self requires practice. But my consistent experience is that you can begin to make this contact and get insights immediately. More than anything, your success will be predicated on your openness and your intention. If you sincerely mean to communicate with your inner awareness, you can develop a very meaningful and accurate ability to understand your condition and circumstances.

In developing this intuitive ability, however, I would advise you to consider it as a very valuable tool, but not to devalue other tools you have available as well, including logic and reason. Remember the adage: to use your head and your heart. Your head or intellect is very good at reason and judgment. Your heart can give you an even greater knowledge related to the world of feelings and issues underlying physical symptoms.

I could cite many examples of how I have used this intuitive approach, but I'll detail just one. It was one of the most dramatic experiences I've had for a number of reasons.

While I was teaching my program in a hospital in Pennsylvania, I met a man, Bob, diagnosed with lung cancer, and his wife, Marie. They came to a number of my series of classes, and he responded quite well, doing better than his original prognosis. However, after time, he presented with additional symptoms, and his wife phoned me asking for advice. Among other things, I recommended that they ask themselves intuitively what to do.

They phoned later that week to say that Bob, after practicing the Inner Guide technique, had been talking with an image of a headless male figure who called himself "Tom." Apparently Tom was giving Bob some helpful insights regarding his condition. We were all pleased, and Bob began to do well for another extended time period.

Then one day I got a rather desperate phone call from Marie saying that Bob had been hospitalized and could I come to see him. When I got to the hospital I realized that Bob's condition was very serious, and he was expected to die.

Fortunately Bob was quite alert, and I asked him if I could speak with Tom, Bob's "inner guide." We were able to make contact with Tom, but we didn't get any particular information that I thought would help. However, as we were ending this session, and Bob began to change his focus from an inner awareness to his outer environment, he sat straight up in bed and said, "I know what it is!"

Bob then tearfully revealed something that he had held secretly inside for years. With Marie also present in the hospital room, Bob now told Marie that earlier during their marriage he had planned to have an affair. He didn't actually go through with it, but he had gone so far as to rent the motel room and planned to meet another woman there for an affair. Bob said with great remorse, "I just had to get this off my chest."

Interestingly, Marie confided that she knew about it, but had chosen not to say anything. Bob was feeling awful, but now somewhat relieved. I explained that I thought it would be a good idea for them to talk about this, and I excused myself saying that I would phone later.

I knew that this emotional release, especially because of the way it happened, was going to make a difference in Bob's physical health. It is fairly common in hypnosis for the subject to gain valuable insight while coming out of the altered state of consciousness. And I knew that when Bob was able to express his deeply suppressed feelings, especially with his very supportive and loving wife, whom he thought he had wronged, he was going to feel much better.

I phoned the next day, and to my pleasant surprise, Bob had been released from the hospital. Understand that from a medical perspective this simply couldn't have happened. Bob really was only days away from death. But now he was at home feeling much better.

I ran into one of Bob's physicians the following Monday at another hospital, and I said that I had talked with Bob over the weekend and that he was at home doing pretty well. The doctor looked at me with the strangest expression and said, "He's dead."

I asked the doctor when he had died because it seemed so unlikely to me. He said that he had seen Bob Friday, and that there was no way Bob lived through the weekend. I then explained that I had worked with Bob on Friday and that he was discharged to home on Saturday. Again I said that I had talked with him on the phone only yesterday.

This doctor was not pleased with me. He was certain that Bob was dead, and he had a secretary phone the hospital to confirm Bob's status. The hospital, in fact, confirmed that he had been discharged.

The doctor was quite confused. I told him that I was sure, actually, that Bob would do okay. I forget exactly what this physician said in response, but he was very upset with me and actually bet me that Bob would still soon die.

I know this sounds awful, to talk so candidly about what really happened, but I agreed to take his bet. Please forgive me, but I hoped to make a point. We agreed to bet 100 dollars, but now the doctor wanted 30 days. Bob should be dead, or soon die, but I had to bet that he would live at least 30 more days! I took the bet. I knew that I had really gone out on a limb, and in front of several other hospital staff who couldn't quite believe what we were doing.

God, forgive me.

I maintained contact with Bob and Marie, but most certainly did not tell them about our bet. Bob continued to do well. In fact, at one point, he went on a fishing trip with some of his buddies. When the 30 days expired I wasn't quite sure how I would approach Bob's doctor. But I didn't need to worry. On the 30th day the doctor came to me with a 100-dollar bill, and had one of the radiation therapists photograph him handing me the money. (I've kept the photo to this day.)

I was very relieved and pleased for several reasons. I told Bob's doctor that I would be glad to explain why I thought Bob had done so well, and the doctor seemed to accept that it could have made a difference. It certainly helped to solidify my role in patient care. And that was the point in taking the bet. I wanted to show that a psychosocial approach could make a difference.

I then explained to Bob and Marie about the bet, and gave them the 100 dollars. Actually, Bob didn't live much longer, but the weekend before he died he went on another fishing trip with his buddies. I'm certain that Bob's psychological make-up affected his symptoms and his recovery. And I am also certain that his personal emotional work affected the quality of his life and death.

Another example of this intuitive approach in medicine today is the work of Dr. Martin Rossman, the author of the foreword to this book. Dr. Rossman is a general practice physician in Mill Valley, California, and is a Clinical Associate at the University of California Medical Center in San Francisco. He is also the co-founder and co-director of the Academy for Guided Imagery, and is author of the book *Healing Yourself: A Step-By-Step Program for Better Health Through Imagery* published in 1987 and revised in 2000. Dr. Rossman's book is the one I have used and recommended most in my clinical practice of using imagination and intuition as primary healing techniques. It is full of excellent imagery exercises and documentation of the effectiveness of this approach.

Dr. Rossman's approach starts with progressive relaxation. Once relaxed, he asks you to open communication between your conscious and unconscious mind in order to "become aware of unconscious patterns, needs, and potentials for change." He believes that healing is an unconscious process and that you can invite an image of your symptom or problem to come into your conscious awareness, which can reveal information regarding the healing or resolution of the symptom or problem:

> By using receptive imagery to explore your emotional reactions to your medical circumstance, you may emerge with a clearer sense of how best to treat an illness or live well in spite of it. You may also better understand how your life-style choices may be affecting your health. If your illness is fulfilling some emotional need, coming to terms with that need may ease your physical symptoms.

Dr. Rossman's co-director of the Academy for Guided Imagery is Dr. David Bresler, a health psychologist and board-certified acupuncturist who has authored more than 100 publications, including the books *Free Yourself from Pain* and *Mind, Body, and Health: Toward an Integral Medicine.* He is also founder and former director of the UCLA Pain Control Unit.

Dr. Bresler used guided and receptive imagery as an integral part of pain management in the UCLA program. He would tell his patients to imagine a favorite place that's beautiful, peaceful, serene, and secure where they felt rested, relaxed, comfortable, and energized. Once they found their favorite place, he would tell them to allow a friendly creature like Bambi the deer or Chuckie the chipmunk to come and be with them there. This friendly creature could act as their inner advisor, giving advice about any problem, including how to control their pain.

Dr. Bresler reports great success with this technique in helping people manage and sometimes eliminate their chronic pain. You can simply ask your pain to take some form or image, and ask it what you can do to make the pain go away.

Dr. Andrew Weil is a graduate of Harvard Medical School and Director of the Program in Integrative Medicine at the University of Arizona. He is the author of a number of best-selling books, including *Spontaneous Healing* and *Eight Weeks to Optimum Health*. In *Spontaneous Healing*, he talks about his personal and professional experience with what he calls "interactive guided imagery."

Dr. Weil's wife, Sabine, has had a history of back trouble with pregnancy. While pregnant, in 1991, they had the help of a therapist to ask Sabine to mentally relax, and then to put her attention on the part of her back that hurt. When Sabine said that all she could see was "black," the therapist instructed her to ask the "blackness" if it had anything to say to her. With some surprise, Sabine said that "it's really angry at me for not taking care of it."

The therapist then directed Sabine to ask what her back wants, and it said to put warm towels on it. When Sabine agreed to do that, she said that her back pain began to subside. And when Sabine asked it to go away entirely, the pain stopped. This was her fourth pregnancy, and she had always had back pain the last two months of pregnancy. Yet her back pain now did not return.

Three weeks before Sabine's due date, the baby was in a posterior position. Her last baby had been posterior, which caused a long, painful labor. Sabine now enlisted the help of a hypnotherapist who encouraged her to talk with the baby, asking the baby to turn around to help the delivery. Within 20 minutes the baby turned around. The baby was delivered right on her due date, and labor lasted only two hours.

Shortly after Sabine's experience, Dr. Weil developed a skin infection which produced several painful red lesions on his leg. Eventually this spread further on his leg and to his arm and face. Dr. Weil was about to make an appointment with a physician when his wife encouraged him to call the therapist who had helped her with her back pain. Dr. Weil objected initially saying that this was a bacterial infection and needed a medical intervention.

Dr. Weil said that he called the therapist "more for Sabine's sake than mine," and over the phone they conducted a session where Dr. Weil was instructed to talk to the lesion. He then saw "a mass of swirling, trapped, angry red energy which instructed him what it needed to heal" (basically, rest and hot peppers to stimulate his circulation). Within 24 hours, he observed that all of the sites of infection were clearly healing.

The experience with his wife's back pain and pregnancy, and his own with the bacterial infection left him "convinced that no body problem is beyond the reach of mental intervention, especially since mind/body techniques are very time– and cost-effective and are unlikely to cause harm." Dr. Weil's professional experience with guided imagery and visualization therapies has led him to conclude "that no disease process is beyond the reach of these therapies."

It may seem quite odd that you could talk to your pain, infection, tumor, or any other symptom and actually have a conversation with it. The fact is that no one knows for sure whether or not you're actually talking to your symptom, your subconscious mind or psyche, a spiritual all-knowing part of you, or anything else. But it certainly appears that you have an intuitive part of you that does know what you need to do to balance and heal. The evidence is becoming quite compelling.

Even the former medical expert for the "Today Show," Dr. Art Ulene, has written a book, *Feeling Fine*, and describes a technique similar to Dr. David Bresler's. He advises people to develop a "creative advisor," which he says is a symbol for your inner self and the right hemisphere of the brain which uses intuitive functioning. Dr. Ulene claims that he has his own personal creature, a rabbit named Corky, to help him solve his personal problems.

Dr. Bernie Siegel describes his use of an inner guide in his very popular book, *Love, Medicine and Miracles*. Bernie's guide is a bearded, longhaired young man named George, who wears an immaculate flowing white gown and a skullcap. Bernie explains George as a "meditatively released insight from my unconscious," and that he has become an "invaluable companion ever since his first appearance." Bernie confides that George has given him frequent and consistent advice about medicine and healthcare which has highly influenced his medical practice and beliefs.

Dr. Gerry Jampolsky is founder of the Center for Attitudinal Healing and the author of best-selling books, which include *Love is Letting Go of Fear* and *Out of Darkness Into the Light: A Journey of Inner Healing*. In the latter book, Dr. Jampolsky talks very openly about the power of learning to listen to his inner teacher. He has taught this approach to millions of people through his lectures and books, but in *Out of Darkness Into the Light* he talks about his personal journey to find peace of mind by consulting what he believes is a spiritual part of himself. This inner guidance instructed him to start his educational Center for Attitudinal Healing based on the spiritual principles of *A Course in Miracles*.

Dr. Elmer Green and his wife, Alyce, are the Directors of the Voluntary

Controls Program, Research Department of the Menninger Foundation. They talk very openly about their personal and professional use of meditation for insight in their book, *Beyond Biofeedback*. Dr. Larry LeShan is an avid practitioner of meditation, and has used it personally and also extensively with cancer patients to help them listen to their inner voice for guidance in their healing. Dr. Joan Borysenko discusses her personal and professional experience with meditation in her best-selling book, *Minding the Body, Mending the Mind*. She states that meditation "releases the inner physician by quieting the mind so that the body's own inner wisdom can be heard." She has used meditation extensively for insight with her patients as co-founder and co-director of the Mind/Body Clinic, New England Deaconess Hospital, Harvard Medical School.

While there are many more psychologists and physicians using intuitive approaches in their practice, I want to focus on just one more as an example of the exemplary work being done regarding this inner advisor technique.

Earlier in this book I mentioned the research of Dr. Dean Ornish. He demonstrated that you can reverse heart disease through a program of nutrition, physical exercise, and stress management. The stress management component included many techniques such as yoga, relaxation and visualization. Dr. Ornish claims that these "are powerful tools not only for 'stress management' but also for helping us learn to open our hearts to our feelings and to inner peace."

One of the guided imagery exercises he asks his patients to use is to visualize an image of their heart, then to see their heart beating regularly, pumping a healthy amount of blood with each beat. They are also encouraged to see the arteries in their heart dilating and allowing more blood flow, new blood vessels growing and supplying oxygen and other nutrients to their heart, and the blood flowing smoothly and unobstructed. He explains that visualization can be used in this "directed way...using images that may influence directly what is happening in the body." But he also believes that imagery can be used "in a more receptive mode – that is, to help us become more consciously aware of previously hidden information that can have a powerful influence on our health and well-being."

In his book, *Dr. Dean Ornish's Program For Reversing Heart Disease*, Dr. Ornish reports that his patients:

> ...often have a significant dissociation between their feelings and experiences or between their thoughts and feelings. In other words, their feelings are often walled off – not only from other people but even from themselves. If you ask them what they are *feeling*, usually they will tell you what they are thinking...

Therefore, a fundamental part of the healing process in

our program was to create a place in our group support
sessions that felt safe enough to allow our participants to re-
experience and, in a sense, re-own and re-integrate those
feelings that they had quite literally disowned by walling
them out of their experience.

Using imagery, we can often begin a dialogue with
these inner walls, as extraordinary as that might seem.

When Dr. Ornish has asked his patients to visualize their hearts, a
frequent image is one of a wall or fortress around the heart. He believes that
this is a symbol of how people have protected their hearts from pain:

> ...we figuratively protect the heart by building walls
> (emotional defenses) around it.
>
> In this metaphor, eventually we have a well-fortified
> fortress around our heart. But it's a double-edged sword, for
> *the same wall that protects us can also isolate us*. This
> isolation, in turn, can lead to chronic stress and, in some
> cases, physical heart disease.
>
> At one stage of our development, these walls may have
> been protective, even necessary for our emotional survival.
> But *what begins as protective can itself become destructive
> if the walls always remain up*.

In an earlier chapter I discussed how we learn to feel rejected and
unloved in childhood. We learn to disconnect from these painful feelings
through any number of addictions or behaviors attempting desperately to
please others and hide our pain of feeling rejected and unloved. Dr. Ornish
believes that in order to avoid the rejection and pain, we unconsciously build
figurative walls to protect ourselves, to keep others at a distance, to avoid
having to deal with our vulnerability and issues of intimacy. You also wall
off parts of yourself like the expression of feelings that you view as
threatening. Dr. Ornish is convinced that through receptive imagery, you can
begin a dialogue with yourself, and intuitively gain insights and information
on how to heal:

> In order for us to risk letting down these fortress walls
> and lowering the drawbridge, then we need to see that
> there's a reason for doing it. When we understand that these
> walls can create pain and illness, then that pain, whether
> physical, emotional, or spiritual, can be a catalyst for
> allowing the healing process to begin. But even then it may
> not be enough, because it's so scary to open up. That fortress

almost develops a will of its own, where it really believes that it's protecting us even when it's part of the problem. The wall may not believe that its job may not always be necessary.

This is not always a conscious choice. We may not even be aware of this process until we begin doing the imagery exercise. Our pain or illness can get our attention so we can begin looking at those parts of our lives that are making us suffer or become sick...

If we put up walls to protect the scared child that we may have within ourselves – this child that feels unworthy, not quite good enough or attractive enough to be loved for who we are rather than for what we do – then it's really hard to begin that process of opening up. The wall tells us, "You're going to make a fool of yourself if you show that part of yourself to other people. And they will reject you. So I will protect you from that."...

Instead, if we can learn to recognize and even to have a dialogue with both the barriers we've erected and our heart that is hiding inside, we can begin to reintegrate ourselves. This leads not only to greater intimacy between us and other people, but also a more fundamental kind of intimacy with the various aspects of ourselves that we may have walled off or disowned.

Dr. Ornish instructs his patients that one way to gain access to unconscious information is through the "inner teacher or inner advisor" visualization. Like the other practitioners I've mentioned, he claims that once you put yourself in a relaxed, meditative state, you can become aware of an image of your inner teacher which "is simply a representation of your inner self." The image may be a person, animal or inanimate object, but you will recognize it "because of its compassion, love, and wisdom."

Dr. Ornish reports that other images may come into your awareness, such as a wall, fence, or barrier. This image may have its own voice, different from the inner teacher's:

Introduce yourself to this wall or barrier and ask its function. In most cases, the wall's purpose is to keep something out or to keep something in. Usually it is to keep out perceived danger or threat and to keep in feelings that are believed to be dangerous or threatening.

Thank the wall for protecting you – for at some point in your life it *was* protective and perhaps even necessary to your emotional survival. After you have thanked the wall, listen for its reply, if any. Sometimes the wall will acknowledge you – saying "Well, it's about time!" or "Thank you" or in some completely different way. Or not at all.

Ask the wall when it first appeared. What was happening in your life at that time? When did the wall become necessary, and why? Listen for the reply, if any. (The reply may come in words, images, sounds or symbols.)

Then ask the wall if it would be willing to open a little, to part, to become transparent, or in some other way to allow you to see what is on the other side. Explain to the wall that it can come back immediately if you find that experiencing what is on the other side of the wall is too painful. At this point, the wall either will begin to open or it will remain closed. Or it may become even bigger!

If the wall is willing to begin opening, pay attention to what is on the other side and what feelings and images may be contained there. This, in turn, may generate a whole new series of questions and information. Continue this process only for as long as you feel comfortable.

In most cases, what is on the other side of the wall is described as light, love, joy, release, and other happy images, and it becomes clear to you (and even to the wall) that it is no longer needed at this stage of your life. Sometimes, though, the images are painful or frightening. Usually, though, the experience is healing. If the images behind the wall are really too painful for you to experience, then the wall is not likely to open.

Sometimes there are walls within walls, like layers of an onion. If you find other walls, begin this same process again. The new wall may have the same voice as the previous wall, or it may have its own voice.

Once you have gotten past the walls (assuming that you even had any walls to begin with), listen to the information from your inner teacher. In my experience, the wise figure generally does not volunteer very much information; it waits until you ask, as it might in real life. If you ask specific questions, then you are likely to receive specific answers. Each answer, in turn, may lead to another question. If you are uncertain of the meaning of an answer, then ask your inner teacher to clarify it for you.

Sometimes your inner teacher may even refer you to

other teachers or resources, whether inner or in the real world. (Sometimes even inner teachers are specialists!) If your inner teacher refers you to a second inner guide, then your inner teacher will provide you with whatever information you need to find the second one.

When you are ready to end your session, ask your inner teacher to tell you the best way for you to reestablish contact with it in the future. It will tell you.

Dr. Ornish's extensive research and experience have convinced him that meditation and receptive visualization can give us insights that can literally and figuratively open our hearts and affect emotional and physical healing.

A Scientific Explanation of Intuition

One way to explain scientifically how intuition could work is based on physics, including the laws of sympathetic resonance and harmonic induction. A practical way to explain these laws would be with the example of tuning a piano.

In tuning a piano, the tuner strikes a tuning fork and adjusts the string of each piano key so that it is the same frequency as the tuning fork. Now imagine that there were a room full of tuning forks, all freely suspended (that is, none of them were lying against another surface–they 're all hanging from the ceiling separately). When the tuner strikes a tuning fork, it will vibrate and hum. But if one of the other freely suspended tuning forks is the same frequency, it will also vibrate and hum. Literally, when you strike the tuning fork, its movement sends out a frequency which will cause another tuning fork to vibrate if it is the same frequency. It sounds a little Californian, but when they're on the same wavelength, they literally communicate with one another. So, when a mother and a child, or best friends, are in rapport (on the same wavelength), it could explain how they can sense and respond to each other.

Let me remind you that everything that exists is a form of energy. Thought is also a form of energy, which has its own unique frequency or vibratory rate. Remember, for example, that thought has to be an energy of some kind in order to explain the placebo effect. Clearly, when one believes something is true, an energy is projected through the body which can literally affect physical structure and function.

This thought energy also is projected outside of the body. For example, in research conducted by William Braud and Marilyn Schlitz, people were placed in separate, isolated rooms. One person would send a thought to the other attempting to influence their state of tension or relaxation, which was recorded on a polygraph. They concluded that psychophysiological activity could be significantly affected by another person's thoughts.

Since energy can change form but not be destroyed, once a thought takes place, it is and remains an energy indefinitely. For example, sound travels at a certain frequency or rate of speed. If one were to travel in a space ship at faster than the rate of sound, you could actually catch up to an earlier radio broadcast and hear it "live" at some point in space.

So, every thought which has ever been thought still exists as a frequency. And anything which vibrates at the same frequency could be sensed (transmitted and received). Thus, when Carl Jung talked about a "collective unconscious," he could have been explaining that every thought that has ever been thought remains as an energy. And whenever another person later in history is thinking about the same thing, or wanting information about something, these thoughts, being on the same frequency, could be sensed or communicated with one another.

In theory, then, one could get information about any subject which has ever been thought about, simply by desiring that information. I need to add a major caveat here to explain, however, what also affects the ability to sense or intuit information.

One time I heard a physician describe how he had worked with a boy for a substance abuse problem. They made good progress, and over time they lost contact with one another, but the physician said that he wondered occasionally how the boy was doing. Then years later, as he was driving his car, the doctor said that he saw the boy "by his old haunts." He was especially interested in speaking to the boy, but this didn't appear to be the right time.

Then, two weeks after seeing the boy, the doctor ran into the boy's mother, and said that he had just seen her son and wanted to know how he was. The mother said that her son had died one month ago, but added that the boy had really liked working with him, and would have liked to have seen him and thanked him before he died. Very interestingly, the doctor had seen the boy two weeks earlier, but he had died one month ago!

I was familiar with this possibility, especially from reading Dr. Elizabeth Kubler Ross's books. She reported many incidents of "seeing" someone who was dead, whom she had worked with while alive, during her research with death and dying.

During a later conversation with the physician who told this story, another doctor overheard us and discussed how he had seen a number of his dead patients. When a third doctor heard us talking, he interjected, skeptically, "I hope I never see any of my dead patients!" And I said, "you never will."

The reason I said this is because the doctor was on a different wavelength. If you're trying to tune your radio to station number 93.7, but you're on station 94.5, you're only going to hear that frequency to which you are tuned.

So, another way to explain why some people are not intuitive, is because they're not open to it; they're on a different wavelength. And appreciate that scientists would be especially prone to not be intuitive if their strong belief is that only objective, measurable research can determine truth. Both the reliance on logic or reason and the being closed to the possibility of intuition, would disallow the solely rational person to sense or receive this type of insight.

One's openness and intention are very important in the experience of intuition. Research in the field of creativity suggests that openness and a playful mind are essential. Creative insight usually does not come when one is at the desk trying to figure things out logically. It comes after an incubation period, when you're driving home from work, playing golf, or taking a shower.

Also, just because you receive the insight, doesn't mean you'll understand it. For example, do you think that the laws or lawful relationships for the invention of the light bulb only came about with the birth of Thomas Edison? Or did these laws always exist, and it took someone as unique as Edison to tap into this insightfully and make sense of it? Albert Einstein said that he got his theory of relativity from his dreams, but had to study for years to understand and explain it. So, a working knowledge of that subject matter must also exist for someone to exercise intuition effectively.

A Personal Experiment

I'd like to suggest an experiment where you can test for yourself the ability to communicate mentally with another person. Ken McCaulley taught me this approach many years ago.

Choose someone with whom you have an especially good rapport. Then imagine that you are making a phone call to that person. Firstly identify yourself, and then call out to this person. Again, all of this is done mentally; this is not an actual phone call. The best time to do this is when it is strongly on your mind (the message you want to send), and when your receiver is passive, such as when they are sleeping. Their distance from you (the next room or thousands of miles away) doesn't matter.

Then your first thought-message is to say, "I love you." This is to establish the rapport. Even if you're mad at this person you can still say, "I love you," with the idea that you genuinely want what's best for this person, even if you're upset with him or her. Then say whatever you'd like to say, but also end your message with, "I love you no matter what you do (whether or not you respond to my message the way I'd like you to)."

For example, let's say that a mother has a son who goes to elementary school, and every day when he comes home from school he automatically sits down in front of the T.V. to play a computer game. The mother's experiment can be to see if she can talk mentally to this child to get him to change that behavior.

So, the mother ideally would talk to her son mentally when she was highly motivated to get through to him, and when he were asleep or resting. She would identify herself ("This is Mom") and call out his name ("I'd like to talk with you, son.") She would then say, "I love you," and that she would like him to help her demonstrate whether or not he can hear her mentally.

The experiment would be that mom would ask the son, when he comes home from school one day next week, to firstly go to her, give her a hug, then go play the computer game. This behavior would be quite out of the ordinary, and she's asking for a specific behavior to demonstrate he's heard her. I recommend that you send the same message daily for a week to give it time to be "heard." I find that this works especially well with young children, who generally seem to be more open and receptive to one's loving thoughts. This includes even the suggestion to newborns about sleeping-in in the mornings, and giving Mom and Dad a break.

As I noted earlier, we use intuition daily, whether or not we realize it. Your thoughts are sensed. You can now, hopefully, test this for yourself, and begin to use it quite purposefully.

13

Creating a Personal Health Plan

When I taught this final class in my six-week series, "Taking Control of Your Health," it gave me a good opportunity to summarize and bring together the key aspects of the program. It was intended to help people identify more concretely and specifically what was most important in their lives. I then would encourage them to make a greater effort to do more of the things which gave their lives meaning and joy.

I found that if people listed the things which made their lives richer and fuller, it usually contrasted greatly with how they actually spent their time. So I would ask why it was that they spent so little time doing those things that meant the most to them: "Why aren't you doing more of what you'd really like to do?" That you would need permission, in some sense, to justify doing more of what gives your life greater joy and meaning seems a little crazy.

When people are asked to reflect back on their lives, and what they would do more of, and what they would do less of, they consistently say that they would play more and work less. It's not too late. So, this is the time to begin to identify, prioritize, and act on how you truly want to spend the time you have left on this earth.

In my counseling training at the University of Akron, I often found that students chose a field of study, and then hoped that it would suit them. They had it backwards. You need to start with who you are. In the counseling center we regularly would talk with these students and help them discover more about who they were, and then help to identify a career that suited their unique make-up.

It's interesting to note here Dr. Carl Simonton's very clear position and summary of his cancer center program: A major factor in the development of cancer is trying to be who we are not. A major factor in the cure of cancer is opening to who we are.

Treat this chapter as a kind of workbook where you begin to identify who you are. Then use this information as a prescription for conducting your life, and as an important part of taking control of your health.

Interests

For the final class, I would ask people initially to list their interests. We were going to identify what brought us greater joy and meaning. The common sense is that when you're busy doing what you like to do, you tend to forget your aches and pains. But this was really the first step in determining who they were. It's when you are able to be yourself that you have the greatest peace of mind.

People commonly listed things such as gardening, hiking, traveling, going out to dinner, sewing or knitting, painting, singing, reading, sports, cooking, shopping, and sex. It was fun to watch them as they talked about their interests; many did so with great passion. And that's the ideal: that you would indeed live your life with greater passion. Please take the time now to list your interests and passions, the things that give you a greater enthusiasm for life and will to live.

Needs

The next step in determining who you are, and what matters most to you, is to list your needs. This one is especially important. Remember how I said early in this book that if you don't get your needs met appropriately, you'll get them met inappropriately? If you get a cold or the flu, you often say that you need to rest. The implication is that had you rested, you might not have gotten sick. What are your needs?

I usually took extra time with this one. I often started by reminding people about their needs related to their self-esteem or sense of self-worth. I've proposed that in childhood we learn to a great extent that we're "no good," unloved and only okay when we're pleasing others. Yet, your real happiness comes when you are able to be yourself.

When you're feeling good about yourself is also when you love others best. Remember my story about deer hunting? After getting the buck, our deer hunter felt better. But he or she also was now nicer to live with. This is like the idea, "You can't love someone else until you love yourself." It's when you feel good about yourself that you feel lighter, more spontaneous, more giving, and more loving. So, do you have a need to feel loved? Respected? Listened to? Understood? Cared for? Time for yourself? How do you feel good about yourself?

I said this earlier, but I want to repeat it here so that you'll remember to take this into account in considering your needs about self-esteem. My assessment of most of the women who came to the cancer centers for treatment where I worked was that they were nurturers, and their greatest sense of self-esteem came from getting married and raising their family. Men's greatest sense of self-worth came from being the provider for the family. Their work or occupation was primary. But what happens when the children leave home and Dad retires or can no longer work? How do you still feel important and needed when your greatest sense of who you are will have changed dramatically? We all have lots of needs. You may have a need to laugh, a need for order or neatness, a need for honesty, a need to have fun, and so forth. The logic is that if you like to laugh, then make more time to do things or be with people who make you laugh. If you have a need for honesty, do what you can to avoid people who you know you can't trust or who lie.

Honor your uniqueness; this is who you are. And in loving others, hopefully you're supportive of their unique ways of doing things, too. You need to get your needs met, but also respect another's way of doing things, even if they're very different from yours. Please take the time now to think about and list your needs.

Values

The next step is to determine your values. What is it that you find most important, precious, significant, and desirable in your life?

In all the years that I've done this exercise where people have listed their interests, needs, and values, the big three are your spiritual beliefs, family, and friends. If you could take your whole list and then prioritize what is absolutely the most meaningful, it is almost always headed by these three values.

Some of you may have already thought of these when you considered your interests and needs. It doesn't matter where you list what matters most to you, whether you think of it as an interest, need or value. The important thing is that you recognize what makes your life worth living.

And now you need to act. Now that you've identified who you are and what gives you the greatest joy and meaning, make a daily effort to live your interests and values, and to meet you needs.

However, you're likely to find that this wonderful and thoughtful list can become lengthy. You may find yourself looking at the list and thinking, "There's no way I can do all of this." People often have very busy schedules, and you may think I've just asked you to make it busier. Remember, if you don't get your needs met appropriately, you'll get them met inappropriately. If you're running around always doing for others, and not taking care of yourself, you genuinely risk your own health. The key is balance. My suggestion is that you pick *one* thing from your list every day, and do it (Doctor's Orders!)

Keep your list handy. Post it on the refrigerator door or somewhere

where you can remember to ask yourself, "Have I been taking my medicine?" Having fun is very good medicine. Being yourself is what will bring you the greatest peace of mind. And this is what health and quality of life are all about.

Also, listing your interests, needs, and values is not an exercise you complete in one sitting. This is something, hopefully, that you will update regularly. Your interests, needs and values will change. Hopefully, you are constantly changing, learning, and growing.

Feelings

The next step is to become more aware of your feelings. Your feelings are an essential part of who you are; they're what make you human.

Unfortunately, we've been conditioned to believe that some feelings or emotions are more appropriate than others. As I said earlier, males were taught that big boys don't cry. And women were taught to always act like ladies, and to suppress their anger.

Research suggests that when you express your feelings, rather than suppressing them, it tends to enhance immune function. Stuffing your feelings tends to suppress your body's ability to resist disease.

So, in this class I ask people to think about a significant feeling or emotion that they had at some time of crisis in their lives. For example, what was the outstanding feeling you had when you or someone you love was first diagnosed with cancer? Most people say they felt fear, overwhelmed, hopeless, helpless, depressed and confused.

It's interesting to realize that generally we think that we always should be positive, keep a stiff upper lip, and not be depressed or anxious. That's just not reality. It's not human. And it's not healthy.

I found that it's been very helpful in class to have people publicly state these so-called negative feelings they've had. Seldom do they mention more so-called positive ones at a time of crisis. People have, and need to express, a whole range of emotions. It's healthy to bring more joy and hope into our lives, but it's essential that we honor and express those emotions at times when we truly do have other feelings like sadness, fear, anger, and depression.

Writing Your Own Prescription

I sometimes called this final class "Writing Your Own Prescription." Dr. Carl Simonton believed that you could divide life's activities into six categories: social support, nutrition, play, life purpose, imagery or meditation, and exercise. This was his way of asking patients and families at his cancer center to identify what was most important in their lives. He found that developing this personal health plan was a good way to guide people in the direction they chose to go, with "desire' being the primary force to direct them. Of course this was primarily intended to help them identify who they are.

Social Support

Research has demonstrated consistently that when people have good social support that they are healthier and live longer. Loneliness and isolation can be devastating. But it isn't the number of social interactions you have, it's the quality of those contacts or friendships that really counts. Even if you have just one good friend who you can truly be yourself with, this is very healthy. You need to be able to express your feelings and to feel at ease. And that's what friends are for.

So, I want you to list people and groups who you can be with who are truly supportive of you. This may include family, friends, church or support groups, or any person or place where you feel nurtured, at ease, and most yourself. The prescription is that you now have to spend more time with these people on a regular basis.

Nutrition

This one just makes sense. Nutrition is simply an essential part of being healthy. What do you want to eat to get well or stay well? It is important that you list what you "want" to do, not what you think you "should" do. In fact, this whole exercise is meant to help re-prioritize your life to do more of what you want to do, and less of what you've been conditioned to believe you should do. You need to be yourself.

There's a fine line, however, with nutrition. I encourage you to consider the research that eating more vegetarian, less saturated fats, more high fiber, less calories, and less food is in your interest. This doesn't mean that you give up eating everything you like. As I said before, I think that taking the fun out of eating is the greatest reason why people don't stay on diets. Even if you take "baby steps" in this direction (for example, eating a more vegetarian diet), this is a start. Please now list the foods you would like to eat to take more control of your health.

Play

This prescription is very much related to what you would have listed under your "Interests," or what brings you joy. I have found that this is where people have the most difficulty: taking time to do things just for fun.

We've come to believe that work is to be valued, and that play is so much idleness. This is a huge mistake. As I mentioned before, all work and no play not only makes Jack a dull boy, it will take his health.

Rather than re-listing everything you already noted under your interests, I want you to think about things you can do to feel silly. Silly is good. Feeling silly is a good example of "letting your hair down" and being yourself.

Young children are great at this. They usually could care less about what others think; they're out to have fun. It wouldn't occur to them that they're being silly; they're being themselves.

So, your prescription is to do more things where you can be more child-like. Playing with young children is a good example, especially if you know you're not being watched by another adult. Children have a wonderful way of engaging us to be more playful and to quit acting our age.

Dressing up for Halloween is another example. Take time, make time, to do things that make you feel lighter. You definitely don't need to be so serious all of the time. Remember to take your "lighten up" pill 1X daily.

Life Purpose

Unlike having fun, this one is more serious and sobering. This is where I'd like you to think about a spiritual side of life. Does life serve a purpose? What is a moral code that resonates with how you understand who you are? What is your very personal relationship with God? Do you even believe in God? What are your beliefs about your connection or place in the universe?

If you believe that life does serve a purpose, that we are not just a species evolving a la Darwin, then it makes sense that you make an effort to live in accord with that purpose. The tradition of religions and related philosophical systems, is that life serves the purpose of learning. According to the "near-death experience" literature, life serves the primary purpose of learning to love and developing compassion. What do you believe?

Your prescription is to create a greater harmony between what you believe spiritually and how you conduct your life. The Golden Rule: Treat others the way you would like to be treated, is the consistent admonition of all spiritual systems. And, indeed, if the spiritual belief that "you reap what you sow" is a reality, this is a pretty good prescription to take and keep filled.

Imagery and Meditation

This prescription takes into account any mental relaxation approach that you would like to practice as part of your health care, such as meditation. It is also where you would list what you want to do regarding the use of guided imagery, self-hypnosis or the use of affirmations. These approaches allow you to harness the power of your beliefs and the placebo effect. And this is also where you can list whatever you'd like to do to practice and develop your intuition.

Meditation is an ages-old practice that is intended primarily to experience inner peace and happiness. It is a process of narrowing your attention, quieting your mind, and is a very effective stress management technique. It is especially good at helping to shut down the very self-critical, perfectionistic part of you. And it is an excellent tool to help discover who you truly are.

Receptive imagery or interactive imagery, such as the inner advisor technique, is certainly another prescription that I would hope that you write for yourself. Your ability to connect with your subconscious mind, a spiritual part of you, or however you understand this creative process, may be the most effective tool you have to guide you in any aspect of your life. This is something you really could do 1X daily that will almost certainly improve the quality and length of your life.

Exercise

Exercise, like nutrition, just makes sense. These two, along with stress management, are the major components of any wellness program. Your body is designed for you to be physically active. Aerobic exercise is ideal, but one half-hour of daily activities such as work around the house, walking, and swimming will double your odds against having a heart attack or heart disease.

Exercise can also affect your mood and reduce depression. It also burns off calories, helps to metabolize "stress" hormones, lowers blood pressure, and increases blood flow, oxygen and energy levels. It simply makes you feel better about yourself.

But remember not to take the fun out of your exercise. Go for a walk in a garden or in the woods. Walk with a friend or your dog. Play with your children or grandchildren. It's fun.

Your prescription is: *GO FISHING!* 1X daily.

Afterword

I have taught the PROBE course or "Taking Control of Your Health" classes for more than 20 years. I thought that it would be relatively easy to sit down to write this book because it really is what I've lectured about and studied for so long. I have to confess that writing *Doctor's Orders: Go Fishing*, however, has been quite a struggle for me. My wife reminds me occasionally, "You teach what you need to learn the most."

Writing this book has further reinforced for me just how difficult it can be for people to live their lives according to what they know they could or should do to help themselves. I am convinced of the value of the content of this book, in its insights and suggestions for improving health. I have seen them work time and again, especially in my work with cancer. But I feel compelled to remind you that this is a lot easier said than done. Be gentle with yourself and with others as you consider the recommendations offered here.

When I lecture I commonly end by saying that I don't want you to believe anything (or everything) I've said, because we all have our own truth, understanding, and awareness. What is right for me or anyone else may not have the same meaning or work as well for you. In the process of learning, we are constantly discarding some of our beliefs and opening ourselves to new possibilities. Honor where you are now.

This book states where I am at the present time in my understanding. I most certainly didn't always believe everything in this book. In fact, much of what I now believe I was pretty uncomfortable or out of touch with earlier in my life.

One of the things I am as certain as I can be about now is the role of what has often been referred to as "tender loving care" or TLC. Throughout my writing of this book I have been reminded intuitively that nothing heals like love and tenderness. This was Dean Ornish's conclusion after many years of practice and research with heart disease. It was my conclusion in my practice and research with cancer. But I'm restating it here because I feel compelled to share with you from another perspective what truly is the most important factor in our health or healing. I "know" intuitively, and in my experience, that feeling listened to, cared for, and a genuine connection with someone creates or allows for a flow of energy that is as potentially curative or healing as anything else you can do.

Thought is an energy. The placebo effect would not work if this were not so. You have the ability to send healing thought-energy through your body and to others. The research and experience with imagery techniques and prayer confirm this.

Love is an energy. When love is expressed, it puts us most in harmony with our sense of oneness, which is who we are. As I reported earlier in this book, the one core belief of all major religious and philosophical systems is that we are one with everything. I do not think it is spurious or coincidental that this has been the single common thread running through metaphysics in recorded history.

The second most consistent spiritual thread is the moral code of conduct that we should treat others the way that we would like to be treated. In fact, this is often called "The Golden Rule." I believe that there is real wisdom and healing in this message.

You reap what you sow. This is supported by the laws of harmonic inductance and sympathetic resonance in physics. A very practical reason, then, for doing unto others the way that you would have them do unto you, is because whatever you are thinking, feeling, saying, or doing is constantly broadcasting waves of energy. And whatever is in harmony with (on the same frequency as) this energy will be attracted to you, or you to it. Thus, the rationale for love.

This does not mean, however, that if you are consistently living love, that you will always have perfect health. It just increases your odds. And this is the best anyone can do.

No healthcare approach offers a guarantee that you will be well. But I believe that any form of medicine that does not incorporate love or a spiritual component is incomplete and, therefore, potentially less effective. I noted earlier that Dr. Ornish concluded in his book, *Love and Survival*, that people's "desire for love and caring" is one of the greatest reasons why they are turning to "alternative" medical care.

The most cited medical journal article in history is the survey which appeared in 1993 in the *New England Journal of Medicine*, titled "Unconventional Medicine in the United States" by Dr. David Eisenberg. It reported that people are seeking alternative therapies more frequently than their visits to primary care physicians. A follow-up survey published in the *Journal of the American Medical Association* in 1998 concluded that visits to alternative medical practitioners have increased almost 50% since the original survey.

There is sound reason for this phenomenon. The role of TLC and the nurse–patient and doctor–patient relationship has begun to disappear. The promotion of reassurance, caring, communication and connection are generally discouraged in corporate healthcare as not being cost- or time-efficient.

There simply must be more time spent between any healer and patient. The real business of medicine is not which therapy works best, but what is best for the individual. Any approach that does not honor the core of humanity in treatment is severely limited.

Human factors and relationships are the greatest factors in healing. Whether we call it love or social support, connecting with someone emotionally and spiritually is the essence of life and health. I strongly encourage you to draw on your own experience to understand the wisdom of these statements.

Additionally, because the power of thought or beliefs is so great, I urge you to consider and use imagery techniques as part of your regular health care. Dr. Jeanne Achterberg reports that the strongest database in the literature for cancer care is in the use of mind-body approaches such as guided imagery, hypnosis, and meditation. Dr. Marty Rossman states that imagery is the "Rosetta Stone" of mind-body therapies. The surveys reported earlier by Dr. David Eisenberg note that imagery techniques are the most widely used complementary and alternative therapies. There is good reason for this – they work.

People have used prayer successfully to heal throughout history. Prayer is a form of guided imagery. I am often asked by families and friends what they can do to help someone diagnosed with cancer. My second most common suggestion is that they pray for that person. I am convinced that prayer is an energy, like any thought, which can be sensed by others and affect their healing. And because prayer contains the element of compassion, it transmits the most harmonious energy of all, one that resonates with our sense of oneness.

Along with the use of imagery, I encourage you to develop your intuition. This is my most common recommendation when I'm asked what people can do to help themselves or others. You have the ability to tap into a wisdom within yourself that knows what is right and best for you. Please take time to honor, respect, and develop this unique gift.

Lastly, when I lecture I always say in closing that I welcome any questions and comments. And, so, I want to end this book by sincerely asking for any feedback you might have about anything I've written. You can contact me on my web site at www.jps.net/dsshrock or write me at P.O. Box 250, Penn Valley, California 95946.

But, whatever you do: GO FISHING!

Appendix

Guided Imagery Scripts

This appendix includes the six guided imagery scripts that I used as part of my "Taking Control of Your Health" program. Each script or mental exercise reinforces the information presented in the six classes that comprised this program.

The first guided imagery exercise was the one I used as part of the research with cancer patients. It is intended to be used specifically as a tool for dealing with cancer.

Of course this first exercise can also be used by anyone as a relaxation exercise and as mental rehearsal seeing your immune system working properly. You can simply modify the script to read "foreign substances" instead of "cancer," and substitute "medications or another therapy" for "chemotherapy and radiation."

Ideally, you would record these exercises on an audio tape recorder in your own voice, leaving appropriate pauses and time to imagine the suggestions offered in the scripts. These guided imagery exercises also have been recorded in my own voice and are available for purchase on cassette tape. Send $12.00, plus $3.50 for shipping and handling ($15.50 total – payable to "First Publishers") to "Taking Control of Your Health," c/o First Publishers Group, 220 Reese Road, State College, PA 16801.

Class #1 – Guided Imagery Script
©2000 Dean Shrock, Ph.D.

Make yourself comfortable. Close your eyes. Take several deep breaths inhaling fully and deeply. As you breathe in, repeat the word "relax," and feel yourself becoming more relaxed with each breath. Allow your body to feel so relaxed that it is very much like a floating feeling. As you relax, your blood circulates more freely and easily throughout your body, and you can feel your body becoming warmer and your limbs becoming heavier as you relax, breathing slowly and easily.

As you proceed through this mental experience, you will always be able to hear my voice and follow my instructions. The following statements are for your well-being. Your acceptance of these statements, plus your desire to make them a part of your physical and mental functioning, makes it so.

I know that my thoughts have very real effects regarding my health: If I'm happy or sad, feeling relaxed or tense, these feelings or thoughts can cause real changes in my blood pressure, heart and pulse rates, oxygen consumption, release of numbers of hormones in my blood stream, and so on. While our thoughts, beliefs, attitudes, moods, feelings, and emotions are not physical in a normal sense, they must be an energy of some form if they are able to bring about these physical changes in our bodies. Indeed, Dr. Jacobsen, in his progressive relaxation technique, and others have shown that by imagining ourselves relaxed, we can measure real physical changes in our body showing that we are more physically relaxed. Dr. Jacobsen further demonstrated that if you lift a 10 pound weight with your arm, you can measure the neuromuscular response necessary to lift that weight on an EMG graph. He similarly showed that if you imagine lifting the weight, but don't even move your arm, the readout on the EMG is nearly identical to when you actually lift the weight. It's as though the mind or brain does not distinguish between fantasy and reality; the body responds to the dominant pattern or image that the brain is processing, which can further explain the well-known placebo effect.

The placebo or expectation effect is yet another clear demonstration of the real effects our thoughts and mental processes can have on our physical bodies. Some medications, for example, are referred to as "sugar pills" or placebos; they have no active substance that could account for a health change. But if you expect to feel better because of having taken this medication/placebo, approximately 1/3 of the time you will improve, not because of the medication or treatment, but because of your belief or expectation that you will get well.

So you can see that your beliefs can be a powerful tool in helping you get well. Thereby it makes sense that we use our thoughts and beliefs to reinforce the body's natural healing processes.

When the immune system is working properly, no virus or foreign substance can exist very long. Your immune system works very well to identify, destroy and eliminate these substances all the time. The fact is that we all have cancerous cells in our bodies many times throughout our lives, but when your immune system is working properly, the cancerous cells are identified, destroyed, and eliminated quite normally and easily from our bodies. So at this time, I want you to imagine/visualize your immune system functioning in a very healthy, normal, and balanced manner. See your brain as a control tower and that you are now sending out the message that your immune system identifies any foreign substance including cancerous cells in your body. Cancer cells are easy to identify because of their angular shape and irregular motion. Take your time and imagine your immune system as a kind of perfect radar system sending out its radar and identifying any of these confused and deformed cancer cells. Once you've identified where these cells are or might be, now imagine your immune system mobilizing itself to destroy the cancer cells. It is important also to know that cancer cells are in fact much weaker and far fewer in number than your white blood cells in your immune system. See your cancer cells literally or symbolically as something weak and small relative to your vigilant, powerful white blood cells. Take your time and see the white blood cells literally or symbolically totally surrounding and destroying the cancer cells. See your immune system functioning in a perfectly normal, healthy, and balanced manner. Now also see your radiation treatments, and any other treatment you may be undergoing, such as chemotherapy, also doing its job properly. Take your time and see the radiation as a powerful ally that goes right to the cancer cells and destroys those cells, while leaving the surrounding cells and tissues normal and healthy.

See and feel your body becoming stronger as the cancer cells are destroyed and eliminated normally through your urine and stool. Just as your radiation treatments and chemotherapy can aid your immune system in destroying and eliminating cancer cells, so can your thoughts and beliefs assist this normal process.

Again imagine yourself calm and relaxed, breathing in slowly and easily, and the blood circulating freely and easily throughout your body, carrying the oxygen and nutrients your body needs to be healthy. Feel yourself relaxed and calm and comfortable. Your body feels warmer. Your arms and legs feel heavier. Feel energy returning to your body as the natural healing processes are being remobilized. You are now more hopeful and positive about your treatments and your body's ability to restore greater health. Your renewed optimism brings a smile to your face, and a greater feeling of self-confidence and satisfaction. And anytime you smile or see anyone else smile it reinforces this renewed enthusiasm for life you now have, and strengthens the pattern and expectation of improved health and control over your life.

Your outlook is now more hopeful and positive as you also begin to refocus your energy and thoughts on doing more of what you really like to do. I want you to think about your interests, needs, and values. What really matters to you? Think about some of the things you do; are they compatible with a lifestyle that is energizing and satisfying? Remember the power of your thoughts and how they can affect the body. Are your thoughts, beliefs, attitudes, and emotions uplifting and fulfilling?

Consider again your real interests, needs, and values. And as you think of these things that give you enjoyment and inspire you, you give energy to enriching yourself and your health. And while you reflect on these things that you find fulfilling and rewarding, remember to approach them with patience and gentleness. Remember that your body responds better to relaxation than tension. Go about your life with a renewed sense of pride, honoring your strengths and any current limitations. But gently yet firmly resolve to make the best of any given moment and situation. Accept yourself for what you are, but plant the seed and pattern of what you want to be in your mind as a pattern for the brain to process and your body to respond to. Gently. With love. Patience. Caring. Hope. And a renewed enthusiasm for life.

Slowly, begin to open your eyes, adjusting gradualiy to the light, becoming more aware of your environment...Feeling relaxed and comfortable...And your body functioning in a perfectly healthy, normal, and balanced manner.

Class #2 – Guided Imagery Script
© 2000 Dean Shrock, Ph.D.

Make yourself comfortable. Close your eyes. As you proceed through this mental experience, you will always be able to hear my voice and follow my instructions. Now let your imagination go, and imagine that you are going on an all-expenses-paid vacation to anywhere in the world, which for you would be the ideal place to relax. Most people imagine being in a warmer climate and near water. You can draw on your actual experience, or just imagine what it would be like to be there. Also, you can go with anyone you like, as many people as you would choose to be with (and remember, all-expenses-paid,) or you can be by yourself.

You don't have to worry about how you would get there (plane, boat, train, car), just imagine you are now getting off the plane or out of the car. You step out into glorious sunshine, robin-egg blue skies, maybe a puffy white cloud or two; everything is picture-post-card perfect.

Imagine you are now going to wherever you are staying, and, again, everything feels just right: clean, comfortable, and everything else that appeals to your sense of feeling at ease. This is your time to enjoy yourself and just relax. Now imagine you are changing into whatever clothes would best suit your going out by the water. Remember, you can imagine yourself on a porch, patio, beach, or riverbank. Feel free to follow my voice and suggestions, or to go off on your own to enjoy any thought, feeling, or image that appeals to your sense of enjoyment and relaxation for your vacation.

As you walk toward (or look toward) the water, look around you and be aware of all of the natural beauty of plants, flowers, and trees. What plant life would you find most appealing? Take your time and enjoy this natural beauty.

Then find a spot near the water where you can sit down and be perfectly relaxed. Because this is your imagination, you can have anything you want to sit on: a blanket, bench, lounge chair, or even a down-filled recliner! Take your time and imagine yourself very comfortably seated in your chair. Then look around you again and observe more of your surroundings: the sand, grass, seashells, driftwood, and plant life.

Remember, you can be alone or with anyone you like. Are there others by your beach or lake or stream? If there are, what are they doing? Resting, walking, fishing, boating, playing? Take your time and let yourself enjoy how relaxed and at ease they seem to be.

Now put your attention on the water. What color is it? Blue, green, clear? I'd like you to now pick a wave, or notice the movement of the water. It has a very rhythmic and undulating movement which is very tranquil and relaxing. Take your time and watch your wave roll toward the beach or down stream.

Notice the reflection of the sun in the water. It is quite bright. And because of the motion of the water, it causes the reflection of the sunlight to sparkle and dance. If you'll look more closely, you'll see there are lots of other colors reflected in the water. As your wave hits the shore or bank, it splashes and has a rather musical quality, which is also very serene and relaxing.

Remember: with your imagination you can make this scene perfect for *you*. What temperature would be ideal for you? Is there a breeze? Can you see or hear birds or any other sounds? Are there any smells or scents that appeal to you?

Now put your attention on the sun and how warm and pleasant the sun feels on your skin. Feel the sun on your toes and feet and just how good it feels to be totally relaxed and on vacation. This is your time truly just to relax and feel good. Now feel the sun on your legs: your calves, knees, and thighs. As the warmth of the sun is absorbed by your body and transferred to your muscular system, it literally causes your muscle fibers to lengthen and relax. In fact, a physical definition of relaxation is a lengthening of muscle fibers. This is why you can feel yourself becoming more relaxed and drowsy while sitting in the sun.

Now feel the pleasant warmth of the sun on your chest and arms and shoulders. Feel your chest and shoulders rise gently as you breathe slowly and deeply. Feel the air fill your lungs, and as you breathe out, you release any sense of stress or tension.

Now feel the sun on your neck and face and scalp. Feel the muscles in your neck, jaw, chin, cheeks, eyes, temples, and brow relax deeply as you focus attention on them. Feel the sun bathing your scalp, radiating its relaxing warmth throughout your head, and completely through your body.

And anytime you think of water in any way, it causes you to become instantly relaxed and calm. Everything about your body now functions and continues to function in a perfectly healthy, normal and balanced manner.

Slowly begin to open your eyes, adjusting gradually to the light of the room. You become more aware and more alert, only feeling good.

Class #3 – Guided Imagery Script

Make yourself comfortable. Close your eyes. As you proceed through this mental experience, you will always be able to hear my voice and follow my instructions. Let your imagination go. Imagine you're designing your fantasy personal relaxation room. It can be any size or shape, and large enough to have anything you want.

The center of the relaxation room is a tub or spa. Normally tubs are made of porcelain or fiberglass. Your tub is made of anything you want. Let your imagination go. It could be made of mother of pearl, for example, or glass with an aquarium that surrounds you. Imagine the most luxuriating, relaxing room and features you can dream up.

What would the fixtures or faucet of your tub look like? It could even be a natural spring or waterfall. What would the surface around your tub be made of? Plush carpet? Hand-painted, imported tile? Redwood?

You can have any selection of plants and flowers surrounding your tub and room. You can have a skylight so that these plants or flowers can be growing live. Or you can have an assortment of cut flowers in elegant vases. What flowers would you have? Roses? Lilacs? Tulips? Take your time and imagine their colors, beauty, and fragrance.

One wall of your relaxation room is for knickknacks, things you've collected that have extra special meaning for you. A table or shelves has photographs of special people and memories. What photographs would you have? Take your time. Another cabinet or set of shelves has true knickknacks full of meaningful memories: things from throughout your life that you remember fondly. Take your time and enjoy these favorite things. Another cabinet or shelves hold a collection of something very special, such as fine china, or antiques of any kind. Let your imagination go. If you could have a collection of something very special, what would you have?

The second wall is a large picture window. You can look out, but no one can see in. If you could have any view that would be the most beautiful and relaxing scene you could imagine, one that you could view while you soaked and relaxed in your tub what would it be? Majestic mountains? Fields of wild flowers? An ocean view? Take your time and enjoy this special natural beauty.

A third wall has the most advanced, high-quality stereo system ever built. And it's playing your favorite music. What music would you like to hear? Take your time and imagine just how good it would sound, and how good you would feel lying back, listening, so relaxed.

The fourth wall has a selection of some of the finest art in the world. If you could borrow any of the world's masterpieces, what art or sculpture would you enjoy viewing? Take your time.

If you have a pet animal and would like to have your pet or pets in your relaxation room, you can imagine them near.

In case you're hungry or thirsty, there's a catered tray of any food or drink you love. Imagine this tray full of your favorite food. And if you like, you can reach out and eat or drink to your heart's content.

Now that you've built and decorated your relaxation room, I want you to imagine you're going to get into your tub. Seat yourself comfortably and safely on the edge of your tub so that your feet are in the tub. Now reach over and turn on the water so that it begins to fill the tub. Make sure the water is the perfect temperature you want. And remember that this is not ordinary water; it's water imported from Lourdes, France, a natural hot springs, or other water with special healing properties.

Imagine this warm, soothing water swirling gently over and around your toes and feet, and how good it feels. Also, there's a selection of bath oils and scents you can add to your water that is comfortably within your reach. If you'd like to put some in the water, you can do that now.

Now the water filling your tub is gently swirling around your ankles and the calves of your legs. Imagine just how good that feels – as though someone is gently massaging your calves.

Now imagine you are going to seat yourself safely and comfortably in your tub. Feel yourself reclined in your tub so that you feel truly comfortable and relaxed.

Now the water in your tub is covering your legs and hips. Imagine this warm, soothing water swirling gently around your legs and hips. And remember, as the warmth of the water is transferred to your muscular system, it automatically causes your muscle fibers to lengthen, and you automatically become more relaxed.

Feel how good that feels now as this warm soothing water swirls gently around your abdomen and lower back. As it rises gently up your rib cage and farther up your back, you may find yourself becoming drowsy as your muscle fibers lengthen, and you become deeply relaxed. Every organ and system in your body now functions more efficiently, and everything about your body now functions and continues to function in a perfectly healthy, normal and balanced manner.

Now imagine the water covers your arms and hands and chest, and as it just covers your shoulders, the water automatically shuts off. Imagine yourself slumped and reclined so peacefully as your body relaxes completely. And anytime you see water, hear water, or think of water in any way, it causes you to become instantly relaxed and calm.

Slowly begin to open your eyes, adjusting gradually to the light in the room. You become more aware and more alert, adjusting comfortably to your environment. Eyes open, fully aware, fully alert and only feeling good.

Class #4 – Guided Imagery Script
© 2000 Dean Shrock, Ph.D.

Make yourself comfortable. Close your eyes. As you proceed through this mental experience, you will always be able to hear my voice and follow my instructions. As you begin this mental exercise, you can pay attention to whatever you're thinking, feeling, or doing. You may be thinking about making yourself comfortable where you're sitting, or you may be thinking you're not comfortable, and maybe not at all relaxed at this time. You may be wondering about your health, even quite concerned. Know that it's okay to be thinking what you're thinking and feeling what you're feeling. Validate yourself for where you are now. You may think you're not in control of some things in your life. Maybe you're not. Remember: Who knows everything about anything? A way of regaining control is in being yourself, by paying attention to whatever is going on in your conscious awareness. By being fully present in or with your experience, you can learn to trust yourself and take control.

Other things and people have conditioned you to think a certain way, feel a certain way, and behave a certain way. Do you remember how you were told as a child, "You're only okay 'If' " – if you're perfect, if you behave, if you clean your plate? Big boys don't cry? And little girls must always be lady-like? All of these thoughts and beliefs have conditioned you to have less self-esteem or less sense of self-worth than is healthy or appropriate. All the "shoulds" and "have-tos" and "musts" that you've been taught, are somebody else's ideas of how to be. Remember: Peace of mind comes from being yourself, where you don't have to think about how you should be.

You can take your control back if you want to. Take your time now, and imagine anyone who ever told you how to be, and see yourself giving him or her that idea back. Thank them for their very well-meaning intentions, but now you choose to be yourself.

You see, everyone else has been conditioned to be a certain way, also. They were conditioned by family, community, and cultural beliefs that made them believe what they believe. With your intelligence and reason, you now can begin to feel more at ease with just who you are: *your* thoughts and *your* feelings. Remember: Who knows the exact right way to do everything or anything? To be no one but yourself is really very hard when everyone else is trying to tell you how to be. Remember the story of the father and son loading the donkey to go to market? And every villager had a different way to do it? Which one was right? In the end, we decided, the only thing that makes sense is that you decide for yourself. For you to have true peace of mind, you must live your own truth.

So, right now, you can think what you're thinking, feel what you're feeling, even not pay attention to my voice. Just feel free to pay attention to whatever comes into your awareness.

What you may find interesting to think about is that something within you knows who you are. Sometimes we call it your subconscious or unconscious mind. You can think, feel, act or not think, not feel, and not act all at the same time, and your subconscious understands any and all of the mixed thoughts and feelings you've ever had. There's no wrong way to do this; only a right way – your way.

Your subconscious knows who you really are and remembers times when you felt at ease and felt good about yourself. You don't have to do the work. Just let your subconscious do it. You can just sit there and observe some moment that your subconscious will bring to your awareness when you felt more yourself, this peace of mind.

Just let any thoughts, feelings, or images come that your subconscious remembers – and then let yourself feel how good that felt – to be yourself – that peace of mind. Take your time now and remember an occasion when you really felt peace of mind. And from now on, anytime you hear the words "should," "have to," or "must," it triggers these deep feelings of peace of mind, and you can now be yourself.

Now you can let your subconscious mind remember a time when you felt funniest, a time when you laughed hard. You laughed so hard you almost fell over. It was that funny. And you laughed that hard. And it felt so good. Just let your subconscious mind remember. Your subconscious mind knows how you felt then. Your body remembers, and your body can respond in an automatic, subconscious way to bring you more joy now. Let yourself feel now how good that felt to feel funny, light-hearted, and carefree. Take your time. And from now on, anytime you hear the words "should," "have to," or "must," it triggers these deep feelings of laughter and joy.

Now you can let your subconscious mind remember a time when you felt confident – when you knew, and you knew that you knew. You felt totally self-assured. Just let your subconscious mind bring this memory of self-confidence to you. Let yourself feel how good that felt – full of trust, self-reliance, and hope. Take your time. And from now on anytime you hear the words "should," "have to," or "must," it triggers these deep feelings of confidence and self-assurance.

Now you can let your subconscious mind remember a time when you felt proud, really proud of something you did. You felt a deep sense of self-esteem and personal satisfaction. You can let your subconscious mind bring this awareness of pride to you. And then let that feeling of accomplishment radiate through you – how good it felt to do something by yourself that pleased you. It pleased you so much you didn't really need anyone else's congratulations or acknowledgment. But oftentimes these moments are shared by and with others, and if you would like to remember how others felt about your success, how others were pleased and excited too, let yourself now feel those feelings. Maybe they even wanted to boast and brag about you a bit. Take your time. And from now on, anytime you hear the words "should," "have to," or "must," it triggers these deep feelings of pride and fulfillment.

Now you can let your subconscious mind remember a time when you felt physically your best. You felt healthy, whole, and vigorous. Your subconscious mind remembers when you felt your healthiest. It knows how you were when you were your healthiest. Your body remembers, and your body can respond in an automatic, subconscious way to produce this healthy condition, like a plant that knows how to grow all by itself, as long as there aren't any blocks to its natural growth and change. You don't have to know consciously how to do this; your subconscious knows. Your subconscious knows you and what you do well. It knows your experiences of confidence and competence. It knows what brings you joy and health. It knows you as much more than any symptoms you might have. You can allow these feelings of health to come into your awareness which can begin to transform thoughts and feelings that might block your natural health and growth. Take your time, and now let these feelings of wholeness, vigor, confidence, and competence fill your heart and mind: who you really are. And from now on, anytime you hear the words "should," "have to," or "must," it triggers these feelings of health and vigor.

Now you can let your subconscious mind recall a time when you felt loved. Truly loved. Perfectly loved. A deep feeling of someone loves me. For who I am. I felt loved – with all my faults and shortcomings intact. With all my unique thoughts and feelings and behaviors, someone loved me. Maybe you remember a parent who loved you, or a romantic relationship, or your personal understanding of your connection to God as part of your spiritual beliefs. Let your subconscious mind remember. Your subconscious mind knows when you felt loved and how that feels. It knows you have great worth and great self-esteem. It knows that lots of things have happened to block this awareness of who you really are. Let it remember. Let those feelings of love radiate through you, all those feelings of encouragement and support. You can open your heart and remember the love of a parent, spouse, or God. Your subconscious mind remembers. It knows who you are. Take your time, and now see that love filling your heart and mind, flowing through your body and energizing you.

It has always been okay to be you. Whatever that is. Spiritually, most people believe God has a plan for everyone, a unique plan. Celebrate your uniqueness. Follow your bliss.

And from now on, any time you hear the words "should," "have to," or "must," it triggers these deep feelings of love, encouragement, and support.

You can begin to slowly open your eyes, adjusting gradually to the light. Becoming more aware and more alert. Or you can ignore my voice and continue to pay attention to any thoughts, feelings or images.

Class #5 – Guided Imagery Script
© 2000 Dean Shrock, Ph.D.

Make yourself comfortable. Close your eyes. As you proceed through this mental experience, you will always be able to hear my voice and follow my instructions. In the last mental exercise we talked about how your subconscious knows everything about you. It knows what it's like for you to feel healthy. And it knows what made you healthy. If you could access that subconscious and ask it what you need to do to be healthy, it presumably could tell you. Indeed many health professionals today call this approach an inner advisor or inner guide technique.

There is an inner advisor, your subconscious, that knows who you are: your needs, interests, values, and everything about you. Through a form of focused attention, sometimes called meditation, you can become aware of this information about yourself. In the last mental exercise your subconscious mind remembered times when you felt peace of mind, funny, confident, proud, healthy, and loved. Your subconscious mind or inner guide can similarly remember any of your experiences, including any blocks (things that have happened to block the natural functioning of your body in a very healthy, normal, and balanced manner).

Remember, as best we understand the function of the immune system, whenever it is functioning properly, it automatically identifies and neutralizes or controls foreign substances, including cancer cells. Also remember: Everyone probably has cancer cells in the body all the time. So, when the body is functioning properly, it should automatically identify and control the cancer cells in your body. Your subconscious mind presumably knows how this automatic process works, and might know, then, what would be blocking your immune system or any other part of your body from you enjoying perfect health.

A state of relaxation seems to facilitate the ability to access your subconscious mind or inner advisor. If you would like to meet your inner advisor, you might find it helpful to think of yourself on vacation, relaxed near water, or in your relaxation room soaking in a tub as you did in an earlier mental relaxation exercise. Take your time now and imagine yourself relaxed in this way.

Once you feel relaxed, you can let your subconscious mind take the form of an inner guide and let it come into your awareness. What is especially interesting about this approach, is that your subconscious mind or inner guide can take a great variety of forms. It may appear as a person (sometimes someone deceased), a spiritual figure, an object (perhaps a sunflower), an animal (owl, fox, bear), or just a shape, color, or feeling.

Imagine yourself relaxed, and invite your inner guide to join you. Be the passive or curious observer, and simply pay attention to any thoughts, feelings or images. *Remember: This is not something you do, but instead, that you let happen. Sit quietly and now let your inner guide appear.*

Whenever you become aware of your inner advisor, you may want to thank your advisor for coming to meet you. Know that this advisor is only compassionate, kind, caring and loving. If any other images or feelings come into your awareness, you may want to question whether or not this is your true inner advisor. Feel free now to ask this advisor why it is there, and why it has chosen to appear in this form or in this way. Please continue to take your time, and be the passive, curious observer as you meet and talk with your advisor.

Remember: Your subconscious mind or inner guide knows all about you. It knows what brings you peace of mind and joy. It knows your strengths and weaknesses. It knows your deepest thoughts and feelings – and loves you unconditionally. It knows that you have great worth, and as surely as a parent loves a child, would offer its assistance to any sincere request for help. If there is any area of concern you have at this time, you can ask your inner guide now for assistance. Take your time and remember to be the grateful, passive observer as you meet your guide. Feel free now to ask about your concern.

If you have not made contact with your inner guide in some meaningful way at this time, you can now ask to meet this guide at another time, or for it to make its presence known in some other apparent way. If you have been able to access your inner guide, and would like to thank the guide for appearing and its assistance, please feel free to do this now. You may also want to make arrangements for meeting again.

You are able to access this inner wisdom through any of the many forms of meditation, through your dreams, or some other creative process. You are able to develop this sense of intuition that now can be used along with your reason, intellect, and science to help you gain insight into your self. And from now on, anytime you hear a telephone ring it triggers and develops this creative, feeling, intuitive part of you.

If you choose, you can begin to open your eyes, adjusting slowly to the light, becoming more aware and more alert. Or you can fall off to sleep and awaken with information you may now ask of your dreams. Remember, when you awaken, your first thought is: What was the dream? Record it in some way; you can take time later to interpret it.

Class #6 – Guided Imagery Script
© 2000 Dean Shrock, Ph.D.

Make yourself comfortable. Close your eyes. As you proceed through this mental experience, you will always be able to hear my voice and follow my instructions. By now it is becoming more apparent that psychological factors like "a strong will to live," your beliefs and attitudes, a sense of joy and enthusiasm, stress and peace of mind can all contribute to your health or the disease process. As the saying goes, "When you're busy doing what you like to do, you tend to forget your aches and pains."

It seems prudent, then, to identify what is most important in our lives as part of a personal health plan. This is just a first step in determining who you are. It's when you are able to be yourself that you have the greatest peace of mind.

What are your interests? Think about what brings you the greatest joy and meaning. What brings you feelings of passion? People commonly list things such as gardening, hiking, traveling, cooking or going out to eat. Take your time, and now imagine yourself doing these things that bring you joy and meaning. See and feel yourself living your life more fully and richly.

Another step in determining who you are, and what matters most to you, is to consider your needs. Remember: If you don't get your needs met appropriately, you'll get them met inappropriately. If you get a cold or the flu, you often say that you need to rest. The implication is that had you rested, you might not have gotten sick.

What are your needs? Do you have a need for self-worth, to feel respected, listened to, cared for, and loved? How do you feel good about yourself? Take your time and now imagine yourself getting your needs met appropriately, especially your needs related to feeling loved and cared for.

Another step in discovering who you are is to determine your values. What is it that you value most in life? If you could make a list of all of the things that truly give your life the greatest meaning, and then prioritize them – your spiritual beliefs, family, and friends usually top this list. Take your time and now see yourself taking appropriate time for your spiritual beliefs, family and friends.

The three major components in any wellness program are nutrition, physical exercise, and stress management. Please take your time and now see yourself following your personal health plan as it relates to eating and exercising. What foods would you like to eat to be healthier? See yourself now eating and enjoying these foods. What physical activities and exercise would you like to include in your personal health plan? See yourself now exercising with ease and enjoyment. See yourself being active and having fun.

What mental relaxation exercises would you like to include in your health plan? See yourself now sitting in a focused state of attention practicing guided imagery or meditation. Feel yourself becoming relaxed as you open yourself to a deep sense of inner peace.

You can also see yourself practicing the inner advisor technique. Take your time and now see yourself opening to and receiving spiritual guidance or insight from you subconscious mind.

Dr. Joseph Campbell, one of the world's greatest scholars on the wisdom of myths and parables, often exhorted people to follow an ages-old dictate of the heart, "Follow your bliss." Doctor's orders: See yourself now going fishing one time daily.

Remember, in creating this health plan or prescription for yourself, to be gentle with yourself and with others when you find you are not following your plan perfectly. Change is difficult. The goal is to be more yourself – to think, to feel, and to act in a way that has meaning for you and that brings you joy. And from now on, any time you think about health or healthcare it triggers and encourages you to follow your personal health plan that has meaning for you.

Slowly begin to open your eyes, adjusting gradually to the light in the room. Becoming more aware and more alert. Remaining perfectly relaxed and comfortable. And everything about your body now functions and continues to function in a perfectly healthy, normal, and balanced manner.

Index

A

Achterberg, Jeanne, 41, 65, 159, 160, 185
Ader, Robert, 28
Affirmation(s), 45, 54, 125, 180
Alternative Medicine, 5, 11, 26, 27, 40,
  59, 92,108, 129, 132, 135, 151, 184,
  185, 209
Angelou, Maya, 133
Anxiety, 52, 63, 82, 98, 151
Attitude(s), 27, 45, 60, 74, 189, 191, 207
Autogenic Training, 41, 45, 52, 62

B

Balance, 19, 22, 47, 60, 62, 96, 99, 102,
  166, 177
Belief(s), 8, 18, 25, 26, 27, 28, 29, 30, 31,
  32, 35, 36, 37, 39, 40, 41, 50, 51, 55,
  56, 57, 59, 60, 64, 65, 66, 89, 90, 97,
  99, 101, 102, 105, 118, 122, 124, 125,
  126, 128, 129, 131, 132, 134, 136, 138,
  139, 146, 160, 161, 166, 173, 177, 180,
  189, 190, 191, 199, 201, 207
Benson, Herbert 29, 45
Biofeedback, 9, 31, 34, 59, 61, 62, 63, 64,
  65, 66, 167
Bohm, David, 62, 63
Borysenko, Joan, 121, 122, 134, 139, 141,
  153, 167
Braud, William, 58 171
Bresler, David, 164, 165
Brinkley, Dannion, 104, 153, 154, 155

C

Campbell, Joseph, 23, 208
Cancer, 7, 9, 10, 11, 12, 13, 17, 18, 21,
  22, 26, 27, 30, 31, 32, 33, 36, 37, 39,
  42, 43, 45, 55, 56, 65, 66, 71, 72, 73,
  74, 75, 76, 90, 95, 96, 97, 98, 99, 100,
  101, 105, 127, 128, 142, 153, 160, 162,
  167, 175, 178, 187, 190, 203
Caregiver, 21
Carlson, Richard, 81

Compassion

Compassion, 105, 139, 140, 141, 155,
  169, 180
Connectedness, 49, 115, 135
Cousins, Norman, 18, 31, 65, 131
Creativity, 119, 121, 143, 173
Criticism, 17, 86, 87, 88, 91, 93, 94, 121,
  129, 140, 145

D

Depression, 31, 52, 60, 76, 82, 98, 119,
  120, 178, 181
Dossey, Larry, 18, 29, 30, 57, 83, 97, 153
Dream(s), 8, 62, 102, 147, 148, 149, 151,
  159, 160, 173, 195, 204, 205

E

Eadie, Betty, 104
Eisenberg, David, 132, 184, 185
Eliot, Robert, 82, 83
Emotion, 13, 27, 28, 48, 51, 58, 61, 113,
  123, 124, 178, 189, 191
Endocrine System, 39, 79, 84
Enthusiasm, 10, 16, 19, 37, 69, 176, 191,
  207
Exercise, 17, 18, 46, 52, 53, 56, 62, 65,
  72, 73, 76, 77, 95, 99, 117, 123, 129,
  135, 167, 169, 173, 177, 178, 179, 181,
  187, 199, 203, 207, 208
Expectation(s), 25, 31, 35, 37, 40, 43, 50,
  55, 59, 60, 65, 152, 189, 191
Extra Sensory Perception, 147, 150, 154

F

Faith, 29, 30, 34, 38, 39, 51, 102, 105,
  132, 133, 136, 140, 147, 152, 160
False hope, 12, 31
Family, 19, 21, 22, 32, 33, 36, 42, 74, 82,
  88, 89, 95, 105, 106, 107, 117, 122,
  124, 125, 127, 128, 136, 137, 140, 142,
  150, 152, 159, 177, 178, 179, 199, 207
Fawzy, Fawzy, 12, 13

Feelings, 11, 13, 15, 18, 21, 27, 29, 45, 46, 47, 48, 60, 62, 66, 90, 98, 99, 106, 112, 115, 119, 122, 123, 128, 134, 143, 160, 161, 162, 163, 167, 168, 169, 170, 178, 179, 189, 199, 200, 201, 202, 204, 207
Fishing, 16, 18, 49, 56, 80, 81, 86, 108, 118, 163, 164, 194, 208
Frankl, Victor, 34, 142
Fun, 21, 22, 23, 74, 77, 88, 111, 112, 138, 176, 177, 178, 179, 180, 181, 208

G

God, 5, 21, 29, 54, 57, 58, 82, 85, 93, 97, 98, 102-105, 116, 118, 120, 125, 126, 129-134, 136-141, 146, 147, 151, 159, 163, 180, 201, 202
Gray, John, 21
Green, Alyce, 34, 61, 62, 65, 66, 166
Green, Elmer, 34, 35, 61, 62, 65, 66, 166
Guided Imagery, 8, 9, 36, 37, 41, 42, 44, 46, 49, 51, 52, 53, 54, 55, 56, 57, 59, 60, 61, 62, 63, 64, 65, 66, 126, 161, 164, 165, 166, 167, 180, 187, 189, 193, 195, 199, 203, 207, 208

H

Health, 3-6, 10-13, 17-19, 21, 22, 26-29, 38, 39, 41-43, 45, 46, 49, 53, 54, 60, 62, 65, 68, 69, 71-77, 83, 85, 95-100, 102, 107, 111, 112, 114, 117, 122-124, 126-129, 132, 134-136, 139, 140, 153, 157, 160-162, 164-167, 175-180, 183-185, 187, 189-191, 194, 196, 199, 201, 203, 207, 208
Helpless, 18, 28, 32, 83, 84, 106, 123, 136, 137, 139, 145, 178
Helplessness, 13, 18, 60, 66, 82, 106, 123, 136
Holistic, 27, 128, 160
Hope, 9, 12, 17, 18, 21, 22, 31, 33, 38, 39, 64, 66, 85, 89, 94, 119, 120, 140, 150, 152, 172, 178, 181, 191, 200
Hopeful, 28, 191
Hopeless, 18, 28, 32, 83, 84, 123, 136, 137, 178
Hopelessness, 11, 13, 18, 31, 60, 82, 123
Hypnosis, 35, 36, 41, 45, 54, 61, 62, 120, 151, 163

I

Imagery, 8, 9, 36, 37, 41, 42, 44, 46, 49, 51, 52, 53, 54, 55, 56, 57, 59, 60, 61, 62, 63, 64, 65, 66, 126, 156, 159, 161, 164, 165, 166, 167, 168, 169, 178, 180, 181, 187, 189, 193, 195, 199, 203, 207, 208
Imagination, 35, 41, 49, 50, 53, 60, 123, 159, 164, 193, 194, 195
Immune function, 10, 12, 13, 28, 76, 96, 98, 123, 178
Immune system, 9, 18, 27, 28, 31, 39, 42, 43, 56, 61, 96, 98, 99, 122, 178, 187, 190, 203
Inner Advisor, 165, 167, 169, 181, 203, 204, 208
Inner Guide, 160, 161, 162
Insecurity(ies), 48, 89, 94, 112, 119
Intention, 47, 51, 56, 114, 161, 173, 199
Interests, 19, 103, 129, 176, 177, 178, 179, 180, 191, 203, 207
Intuition, 143, 146, 147, 148, 149, 150, 152, 153, 155, 156, 157, 159, 160, 161, 164, 171, 173, 174, 181, 204

J

Jacobsen, Edmond, 43
Jampolsky, Gerry, 166
Joy, 10, 16, 18, 19, 21, 22, 38, 46, 49, 74, 86, 117, 127, 170, 175, 176, 177, 178, 179, 200, 201, 204, 207, 208

K

Kabat-Zinn, Jon, 47, 48
Klopfer, Bruno, 37, 39
Kornfield, Jack, 141

L

Lerner, Michael, 26, 75, 76
LeShan, Larry, 11, 12, 167
Lichtenstein, Paul, 95
Listen, 89, 94, 105, 106, 114, 115, 138, 166, 167, 170
Listened to, 21, 105, 106, 135, 176, 207
Listening, 49, 140, 148, 196

Love, 11, 16, 20, 22, 49, 88, 93, 94, 100,
103, 104, 105, 106, 107, 113, 115, 119,
120, 121, 123, 124, 125, 126, 130, 131,
132, 134, 135, 136, 137, 138, 139, 140,
141, 152, 154, 159, 166, 169, 170, 173,
174, 176, 178, 180, 191, 196, 202

M

McCaulley, Ken, 7, 8, 13, 107, 108, 138,
144, 145, 149, 150, 152, 153, 161, 173
Meaning, 16, 18, 19, 22, 27, 34, 45, 49,
51, 53, 56, 61, 66, 82, 83, 86, 88, 91,
96, 113, 127, 139, 142, 150, 170, 175,
176, 177, 195, 207, 208
Meditation, 8, 41, 45, 46, 47, 48, 49, 53,
61, 62, 63, 146, 167, 171, 178, 180,
181, 203, 204, 208
Mental, 6, 11, 12, 15, 27-29, 39, 41, 42,
44, 45, 49, 50, 53, 56, 59-61, 64, 68,
98, 127, 128, 134, 141, 146, 160, 161,
165-167, 173, 174, 180, 187, 189, 193,
195, 199, 203, 207, 208
Mind, 3, 4, 8, 10, 11, 13, 16-18, 20, 25-
28, 30, 33-35, 39, 41, 44, 46-49, 54,
55, 64, 65, 68, 81, 86, 87, 98, 99, 100,
104, 106, 107, 112, 113, 118, 121, 122,
127, 130, 132, 134, 138, 139, 141, 146,
149, 150, 160, 161, 164, 166, 167, 173,
176, 178, 181, 185, 189, 191, 199, 200-
204, 207, 208
Mind-body, 39
Mindfulness, 45, 47, 48, 49, 75
Moody, Raymond, 104, 139, 153, 154
Moyers, Bill, 26, 47, 132

N

Near-Death Experience(s), 153, 154, 155,
180
Needs, 19, 20, 21, 22, 32, 71, 75, 92, 104,
112, 135, 145, 164, 176, 177, 178, 190,
191, 203, 207
Nhat Hanh, Thich, 49
Norris, Patricia, 31, 66
Nutrition, 7, 17, 18, 71, 72, 73, 74, 75, 95,
99, 129, 135, 167, 178, 179, 181, 207

O

Oneness, 134, 183, 185
Ornish, Dean, 46, 71-73, 135, 167-171,
183, 184

P

Passion, 16, 49, 176, 207
Payer, Lynn, 26
Peace of Mind, 49, 86, 87, 99, 100, 107,
118, 121, 122, 127, 134, 166, 176, 178,
199, 200, 203, 204, 207
Pelletier, Kenneth 27, 33
Pendergrass, Eugene, 98
Pert, Candace, 28, 98, 123
Placebo, 25, 28, 36, 39, 40, 49, 57, 60,
132, 171, 180, 189
Pray, 29, 57, 66, 93, 94, 96, 97, 103, 126,
141, 146
Prayer, 29, 30, 41, 45, 47, 54, 57, 63, 82,
94, 102, 126, 146, 147
Pribram, Karl, 62, 63
Progressive Relaxation, 41, 43, 44, 45,
52, 53, 54, 57, 164, 189
Psychological, 3, 6, 10, 12, 13, 29, 43, 62,
71, 73, 74, 76, 85, 88, 98, 128, 129,
153, 161, 164, 207
Psychology, 7, 8, 9, 41, 42, 51, 88, 92, 97,
135, 138, 144
Psychoneuroimmunology, 13, 28, 98
Psychosocial, 10, 11, 12, 13, 18, 26, 33,
129, 135, 160, 164
Psychosomatic, 28, 29, 34, 62, 98
Puthoff, Harold, 147

Q

Quality of Life, 10, 12, 75, 135, 178

R

Receptive Imagery, 156, 161, 164, 168,
181
Relaxation, 9, 41, 42, 43, 44, 45, 47, 49,
52, 53, 54, 57, 58, 62, 63, 65, 80, 160,
164, 167, 171, 180, 187, 189, 191, 193,
194, 195, 196, 203, 208

Religion, 130, 131, 134, 138, 139, 141
Religious, 29, 30, 34, 45, 57, 125, 126,
    131, 138, 139, 140, 146, 159, 160
Reparent(ing), 123, 124, 126
Rossi, Ernest, 39
Rossman, Martin, 4, 164, 185

S

Schlitz, Marilyn, 171
Self-esteem, 19, 83, 111, 112, 114, 118,
    119, 122, 126, 127, 176, 177, 199, 201,
    202
Self-hypnosis, 8, 9, 180
Selye, Hans, 79, 80, 84, 95, 107
Shaman, 96
Shamanism, 41, 96, 159
Siegel, Bernie, 11, 12, 166
Simonton, Carl, 3, 5, 9-13, 26, 153, 160,
    175, 178
Simonton, Stephanie Matthews, 11, 142,
    160
Social Support, 33, 129, 132, 135, 136,
    178, 179
Sorokin, Pitirim, 148
Spiegel, David, 12, 13
Spiritual(ity), 8, 26, 27, 29, 34, 35, 46, 97,
    98, 102, 103, 104, 105, 126-156, 161,
    166, 168, 177, 180, 181, 201, 204, 207,
    208
Spontaneous Remission, 30, 97
Stress, 17, 18, 46, 47, 48, 59, 61, 63, 65,
    72, 73, 77, 79-85, 92, 95, 96, 98, 99,
    107, 111, 114, 122, 127, 129, 135, 140,
    141, 142, 145, 149, 167, 168, 181, 194,
    207
Stress Management, 17, 18, 46, 72, 73,
    79, 81, 82, 95, 96, 99, 135, 145, 167,
    181, 207
Subconscious, 20, 54, 112, 122, 161, 166,
    181, 200, 201, 203, 204, 208

Suffering, 30, 36, 82, 103, 136, 137, 139,
    140, 141, 142
Suinn, Richard, 43, 51, 52
Support, 9, 10, 15, 33, 74, 75, 80, 99, 107,
    115, 128, 129, 132, 135, 136, 137, 138,
    140, 147, 150, 153, 168, 178, 179, 202
Systematic Desensitization, 52

T

Thoughts, 15, 27, 35, 37, 44, 45, 48, 50,
    60, 63, 66, 112, 123, 125, 147, 155,
    161, 167, 172, 174, 189, 190, 191, 199,
    200, 201, 202, 204
Truth, 8, 87, 100, 101, 108, 122, 125,
    139, 143-146, 148, 149, 150, 156,
    157, 173, 183, 200

V

Values, 19, 83, 90, 96, 117, 118, 119,
    120, 122, 129, 131, 177, 178, 191, 203,
    207
Visualization, 35, 46, 63, 166, 167, 169,
    171

W

Walsch, Neal Donald, 136
Weil, Andrew, 73, 165, 166
Weiss, Brian, 151, 152
Wellness, 9, 18, 27, 62, 181, 207
Will to live, 11, 16, 17, 18, 19, 31, 32, 33,
    51, 97, 146, 176, 207
Winfrey, Oprah, 133
Winter, Bud, 44, 51

Y

Yoga, 34, 45, 46, 48, 62, 65, 76, 167